The Gallo-Roman Muse

The
Gallo-Roman Muse

Aspects of Roman literary tradition in
sixteenth-century France

DOROTHY GABE COLEMAN

CAMBRIDGE UNIVERSITY PRESS

CAMBRIDGE

LONDON · NEW YORK · MELBOURNE

Published by the Syndics of the Cambridge University Press
The Pitt Building, Trumpington Street, Cambridge CB2 1RP
Bentley House, 200 Euston Road, London NW1 2DB
32 East 57th Street, New York, NY 10022, USA
296 Beaconsfield Parade, Middle Park, Melbourne 3206, Australia

First published 1979

Printed in Great Britain at the
University Press, Cambridge

Library of Congress Cataloging in Publication Data
Coleman, Dorothy Gabe.
The Gallo-Roman muse.

Bibliography: p.
1. French literature – 16th century – History and
criticism. 2. French literature – Roman influences.
3. Latin literature – History and criticism. 4. Rome
in literature. I. Title.
PQ239.C64   840'.9'003   79-71
ISBN 0 521 22254 0

For Bob

Contents

Abbreviations

BHR   Bibliothèque d'Humanisme et Renaissance (Geneva, Droz)

BN   Bibliothèque Nationale, Paris

Cotgrave   *A Dictionarie of the French and English Tongues*, London, 1611

NOTE

Classical authors are in general quoted from modern editions but where the quotation is Montaigne's the text of the 'exemplaire de Bordeaux' is retained, even when it is at variance with modern editions.

Acknowledgements

My first debt is to Mr Raymond Griffiths of Ystalyfera Grammar School who taught me at an early age how to appreciate Roman poetry. Second, constant discussion on poetry with Odette de Mourgues has sharpened my views and she has read and criticised this book at an earlier stage with infinite judgement and tact. Where there is still some dissension between us may I say that I am probably wrong and she probably right. Third, my husband, whose knowledge of Classical literature is deep, has always been an encouragement and stimulus to me even though we disagree on some of the topics in this book. And finally Michael Black who, as always, put my arguments in a finer shape and my style in a more intelligible harmony.

I

Introduction

The present study makes no pretence of covering the whole sixteenth century. It does no more than offer a light which will clarify some things, give hints as to what can be further examined and suggest the importance of Roman studies in French Renaissance literature. This may seem to ignore the indigenous French tradition and the verbal gymnastics of the *grands rhétoriqueurs*. I may seem to be taking a biased view of the sixteenth century and deliberately missing out intermediaries like the Provençal poets or the contributors to *Le Jardin de Plaisance*. But I have come to see the Roman tradition as the catalyst which definitively transforms French literature. Superficially, the time dimension is vast; there is an enormous leap from Classical Rome to Renaissance France. But as we shall see, it is only superficially so.

Three topics I have completely omitted in this work – reluctantly, since they would affect the shape of the argument – Neo-Latin literature, Greek literature and the classical influences mediated through Italian literature. To include them in this study would have doubled its length and obscured the issues.

My use of the term 'Roman tradition' embraces three distinct periods in Roman literature: the late Republic, notably Lucretius, Catullus and Cicero; the Augustan age, which includes Vergil, Horace, Propertius, Tibullus and Ovid; and the Empire, which is represented by Martial, Quintilian, Juvenal, Lucan and Tacitus. As it seems a general law among all literatures that verse develops before prose, I devote the first half

of this book to Scève and the Pléiade and the second half to
Montaigne.

I shall be examining two main aspects: rhetorical theory
and bilingualism. We often accept somewhat casually that
the sixteenth century was bilingual without getting close to the
questions that this raises. Bilingualist research is hard on the
heels of Beckett but has missed Montaigne, whose *langue
maternelle* was Latin and not French. We talk rather glibly of
the rhetorical tradition in the sixteenth century, but do we know
what kind of rhetoric we are talking about? Do we even know
what rhetoric is about? Perhaps it is wrong to identify classical
rhetoric with the sterile idiom of verses composed by eighteenth-
century Neo-Latinists as academic exercises or literary *divertissements*. I believe that we must study in far greater depth the
tradition which comes to be ingrafted on French literature in
the Renaissance. We must start by opening our minds to Roman
literature and by recognising that the handbooks of rhetoric by
Cicero and Quintilian are really only the theory. It is important
first of all to see the practice.

2

Roman writers and the sixteenth century: a re-evaluation

The raw materials of poetry have changed but little in two millenia. Of course fashions change and languages change. But the poetry of the human condition remains the same: it is written by human beings about human beings, for human beings to read. This is the first thing to understand when we are talking of Roman writers in sixteenth-century France. Poetry is not prosaic discourse. Theoreticians are not poets. Cicero is not Catullus nor is Sébillet Ronsard.

We shall have no clue as to what the Roman tradition really meant in the sixteenth century unless we have taken account of the tradition of creative literature in Rome. A recent international conference held at King's College, Cambridge, on 'Classical Influences on European Culture from 1500 to 1700' serves to show in what direction scholarship is going.[1] There are several points at which we are brought to an awareness that everything is yet to be done, and brought to the importance of looking into the exact contexts of Latin works which influenced the vernacular literature. For example many sixteenth-century writers used both their mother tongue and Latin: Calvin is an obvious example, for he wrote first in Latin and subsequently 'translated' his work into French. Or Bodin, who 'translated' his *De la république* (1576) ten years later into Latin. Was there a conception that certain themes and certain semi-philosophical attitudes belonged to the Latin language rather than to French? What was the audience envisaged for the two languages? The problem of readership is vital, and research into the motivation

---

[1] *Classical Influences in European Culture. A.D. 1500–1700*, edited by R. R. Bolgar (Cambridge, 1976).

of writers using the vernacular and Latin is needed. Or consider the starting point of Mrs Mann Phillips's paper on 'From the "Ciceronianus" to Montaigne' (Bolgar, *Classical Influences*, pp. 191–7) which is that 'more investigation is needed on the relationship between discussions on Latin style...and French style'. She takes as one example Erasmus's anti-Ciceronian argument on style and Montaigne's equally anti-Ciceronian views of how to write: the two are joined in that the influence of Latin 'from being purely external and decorative, had become internal and structural – a way of thinking rather than a process of ornamentation'. This is very suggestive for all sixteenth-century writers, *because* the century was a bilingual one – just as Rome had been during the late Republic and in the Empire. In the index there is an entry for 'research opportunities', among which are: a study of Latin/vernacular bilingualism and the character of Renaissance commentaries on classical authors. And Dr Bolgar in his introduction to the different papers stresses that 'The relationship between the classical and modern cultures was much more subtle than the simple concept of one borrowing from the other immediately conveys' (*Classical Influences*, pp. 10–11).

Research into the role of Rome is helped by two recent books which deal with the Latin poetic tradition. They are Kenneth Quinn's *Latin Explorations. Critical Studies in Roman Literature* (London, 1963) and Gordon Williams's *Tradition and Originality in Roman Poetry* (Oxford, 1968).[1] Several points stand out from these studies which reorientate our view of the role that Rome played in the French Renaissance. The two authors are mainly concerned with poets such as Vergil, Horace, Propertius, Tibullus and Ovid, who created, in the first century B.C., a rich poetic tradition. It becomes evident when interpreting Roman poetry that though the theoreticians of poetry talked in rhetorical terms, the poets were influenced more by what their predecessors wrote than what the theorists said about them.

The *O.E.D.* defines rhetoric as 'the art of using language so as to persuade or influence others; the body of rules to be

---

[1] A shortened and simplified version of which appeared later in a paperback, *The Nature of Roman poetry* (Oxford, 1970).

observed by a speaker or writer in order that he may express himself with eloquence'. Secondly it may mean 'a treatise on or "body" of rhetoric'. In other words, rhetorical training implied that one could as an apprentice learn the elements of oratory or writing. But this did not mean that one was automatically going to be a great poet. The rhetorical education implicit in Cicero and Quintilian is of course one that *all* Romans who were at all educated had experienced. It follows that rhetoric is not in itself an appropriate critical tool by which to evaluate these poets. The distinction between rhetoricians and poets is crucial, and it is not admitted by some French Renaissance scholars. For example Grahame Castor in his *Pléiade Poetics. A Study in Sixteenth-Century Thought and Terminology* (Cambridge, 1964) says: 'I have already pointed out that classical antiquity did not make any clear distinction between rhetoric and poetry, and that this tendency persisted throughout the Middle Ages and well on into the Renaissance' (p. 99). Or Donald Stone in his *French Humanist Tragedy* (Manchester, 1974): 'We have been slow to recognise the pervasive influence of rhetoric in sixteenth-century France despite the fact that writers of the day did little to hide its importance...' (p. 29). And he follows this statement by showing how Cicero and Quintilian recommend recipes for oratorical excellence in their rhetorical treatises. But Castor and Stone beg the question: were sixteenth-century poets influenced more by Roman theorists than they were by Roman practitioners of poetry? The art of rhetoric or communication was so intensely and so systematic-ally studied in antiquity that rhetoric was bound to be copied by the sixteenth-century French writer. If, however, Du Bellay and Ronsard wanted to create poetry that was the equal of Greek and Roman poetry, then the first thing they would do was to study the poets and not the theoreticians of rhetoric. Gordon Williams puts the point about Cicero's poetic merits very honestly in *The nature of Roman poetry* (Oxford, 1970), p. 9:

> ...a number of factors conditioned his serious, old-fashioned view of poetry: he was a good verbal technician but had little real poetic instinct; his inclinations were to literary seriousness

and thematic grandeur, and his political ambitions in a milieu dominated by the Republican nobility made him conformist and traditional.

Cicero's poems are excruciatingly dull. He was no poet. And Quintilian never had any pretensions in that line. Furthermore, what of Aristotle in the minds of Roman poets? Professor C. O. Brink in his *Horace on Poetry. Prolegomena to the Literary Epistles* (Cambridge, 1963) states that the Classical scholars of the nineteenth and twentieth century 'took it for granted that Aristotle was the determining person in Horace's criticism' (p. 19). But goes on to say later that he does not know of 'evidence of any first-hand knowledge of Aristotle's *Poetics* in Horace's time' (p. 140). If we turn to Castor's book, *Pléiade Poetics*, we find Aristotle and Horace presented very differently: the first as a genius, the second as a second-rate man. Horace is not even named by Castor among the first-rate Greek and Roman poets who influenced sixteenth-century France, being included presumably under the phrase 'together with many others of lesser note' (p. 8). But a little later Castor says, 'In the sixteenth century, however, apologists of poetry began to use the argument contained in Aristotle's *Poetics*; previously his theories had been generally known only in the watered-down versions presented by Horace and other late popularisers' (p. 11). The true positions of Horace and Aristotle will be suggested later, under the re-orientating distinction between practice and theory, but it suffices to say here that the comment is rather misleading. If one were to 'class' Aristotle, he would merit an alpha plus for intellectual acumen but gamma minus for imagination. And imagination is the first quality we think of in reading poetry.

The range and frequency of sixteenth-century imitations of models from Greek and Roman literature causes at first sheer bewilderment in the mind of a twentieth-century reader. He may well apply the label, 'slavish imitator', to any poet and feel that he has solved the problem, but he will not have understood it. The same process is used by those classical scholars who decry at times the slavish imitation of Roman poets 'copying' their Greek models: Vergil 'copying' Theocritus or Homer, Catullus 'copying' Sappho or Callimachus, and

Horace 'copying' Alcaeus or Pindar. Indeed, the very way a Classical scholar edits an edition – by accumulating sources, references and allusions to writers from Greek literature – invites this conclusion. But the scholars too are dominated by the same Romantic critical canon – that what issues from the mind of genius has nothing to do with any previous writer. Sem Dresden in his essay, 'La notion d'imitation dans la littérature de la Renaissance'[1] says with a sigh of anguish, 'Je constate, tout d'abord, que l'imitation se produira inévitablement dans un univers livresque. Elle aura lieu en passant d'une œuvre écrite à une autre œuvre qui lui ressemble et qui n'est pas la même.' The famous *univers livresque* of the Pléiade is only a fault if looked at through the parochial spectacles of a post-Romantic scholar. For the whole of the Graeco-Roman poetic universe was *livresque*, and we misunderstand a literary culture if we denigrate it for having recourse to previous features in the tradition. The tradition that poetry induces poetry is brought out well by David Jones in his *Epoch and Artist* (London, 1959):

> The artist, no matter of what sort or what his medium, must be moved by the nature of whatever art he practices...The artist is not, necessarily, a person vastly more aware than his friends and relations of nature (or of anything), but rather he is the person most aware of the nature of an art. The inception or renewal or deepening of some artistic vitality comes to the artist via some other artist or some pre-existing art-form, not via nature (p. 29).

We must examine the Roman tradition not merely because it gives an historical perspective on the French Renaissance but also because it embodies this specific aesthetic canon. As Eliot said in 'Tradition and the Individual Talent', in *Selected Essays* (London, 1953),

> No poet, no artist of any art, has his complete meaning alone. His significance, his appreciation is the appreciation of his relation to the dead poets and artists. You cannot value him alone; you must set him, for contrast and comparison among the dead. I mean this as a principle of aesthetic, not merely historical, criticism (p. 15).

[1] In *Invention et imitation. Études sur la littérature du seizième siècle*, by H. Naïs, S. Dresden, M. A. Screech (The Hague and Brussels, 1968), p. 29.

Every great poet reads poetry. Roman poets read Greek poets. French Renaissance poets read Greek and Roman poets. The creative re-adaptation of models is part of the conscious allusive process that any great poet uses. For he deliberately wants in his poem the echoes of a legend or the rich associations of mythology, and his return to previous poets means that he is carrying forward to his successors the constant ebb and flow of tradition and civilisation. The *poeta doctus* of the first century B.C. read extensively among the older Greek epic, tragic and lyric poets and also in the works of the Alexandrians. This extensive reading was followed by translation; but as Gordon Williams says this was not enough: 'The simplest form of relationship which a Roman poet could establish with his Greek predecessors was sheer translation. But a real poet would be dissatisfied with such simplicity.'[1] It was precisely on the point of translation that Du Bellay advised that: 'Celuy donques qui voudra faire œuvre digne de prix en son vulgaire, laisse ce labeur de traduyre.'[2]

Professor Williams considers in some detail in his longer book how imitation may vary between a very close parallel with the original model and a very wide range of freer proximity. He takes as his example Vergil, who used both Greek poetry and earlier Roman poetry in this way; an allusion, a reference, a simile here or a comparison there – all indicating that Vergil was using the technique of literary allusiveness. Another example, this time from a generation earlier, is provided by Catullus, who in 'translating' Sappho in poem 51 shows how deeply allusiveness was engrained in his poetry. And then there comes 'a more remote form of the relationship... the composing of a Latin poem so that although there is no question of translation yet the reader must recall some piece of Greek writing if he is to grasp the full complexity of the Latin poem.'[3] This remoter relationship implies that the poet is trying to make a pact with his reader: the reader will have to work in order to catch the nuances in the poem. And this is difficult: in

---

[1] *The Nature of Roman Poetry* (Oxford, 1970), p. 55.
[2] *Deffence et Illustration de la Langue françoise*, ed. H. Chamard (Paris, 1961), pp. 41–2.
[3] See in particular chapter 3, 'The blending of Greek and Roman' in the book *Tradition and Originality in Roman Poetry* (Oxford, 1968).

appreciating Roman poetry the reader needs to recognise the Greek models; so too in reading Ronsard he has to detect Greek and Roman poets who act as models in the poetry.

The reader has to read and re-read the classical poets before he can fully appreciate Renaissance poets. Obviously, critical editions give us references to Horace or Pindar in Du Bellay or Ronsard. But the mere reference is only the first step towards understanding what Ronsard or any other poet was about. We have to go further and read the relevant poem of Horace or Pindar and then come back to the poem of Du Bellay or Ronsard. This process of 'creative borrowing' is a technique that any great poet – not only Roman, not only French sixteenth-century writers – uses. Thus Dresden envisages an entirely modern and too limited situation when he says (Naïs, Dresden and Screech, *Invention et Imitation*, p. 28):

> Dans un seul sonnet, une ligne sera empruntée à Virgile, un autre passage rappellera Horace etc...ce n'est pas nous qui aurons découvert cette imitation, c'est l'éditeur. Une conclusion paraît s'imposer: les grandes éditions, celles dont à bon droit nous nous servons tous et toujours, nous font parler trop facilement d'imitations.

He envisages exclusively an unsophisticated reader relying entirely on a critical edition. But not every reader need be so helpless. If he were, then an essential ingredient in that excitement which every serious reader of poetry properly feels, namely the combination of echoes of other poems in the poem that he is actually reading, would be lost to him.[1]

In this re-orientation of attitude towards the Roman poets, Quinn and Williams are at one in emphasising that Horace's 'Epistula ad Pisones', or the *Ars poetica* as it is more generally known, is really a poetic art seen through the practice of poetry as composed by Horace himself. It is miles away from the scientific compendium that the non-poetic temperament of an

---

[1] Robert Griffin in his *Coronation of the poet. Joachim du Bellay's debt to the Trivium* (Los Angeles, 1969, p. 21) puts his finger on the true evaluation of poetry, imitation and rhetoric as seen by sixteenth-century writers when he says: 'Renaissance distinctions hold rather between good and bad grammar, logic, rhetoric and poetry. Whenever such a separation exists in Renaissance discussions, it is found on a theoretical, not a functional level.'

Aristotle would and did produce. The overt didactic form of the
Ars poetica is belied by the way Horace's rules and ideas are
introduced in an autobiographical context. Often, however, his
statements were taken up by subsequent centuries, and in
particular by the Middle Ages, torn from that context and read
as if they were commonplace generalisations. For instance,
Horace tells the Pisones (in rather a delightful conversational
manner) of something he has found very difficult in his own
practice,

> Brevis esse laboro
> Obscurus fio..
>
> (lines 25–6)

Horace is pointing to one of his faults – if it can be called a fault
– namely the desire to be brief and dense without being
unintelligible. This is a difficulty inherent in all writers concerned with 'translating' intellectual and emotional thoughts,
inner thoughts, in to a public form. And it is the same kind of
difficulty we have to grapple with in talking about Mallarmé
or Valéry, Scève or Ronsard, Montaigne or La Fontaine. The
'Epistula ad Pisones' offers the reader the chance of eavesdropping on a poet–critic's reflections. This is what sixteenth-
century poets saw in him, and what demonstrates how deeply
he had entered French sensibility.

Modern scholars of the French Renaissance (and generally
perhaps scholars of pre-Romantic Europe) have over-
emphasised rhetoric – the tools of the writer's trade – and have
turned to Cicero and Quintilian as *the* writers in whom we study
rhetoric, and have underestimated the importance of the poets
of Rome and the way they had penetrated French sensibility.
In every field of literature – poetry, drama, prose fiction – we
are asked to see, to comment on and to evaluate literature purely
in terms of rhetoric. Thus Donald Stone, in his *French Humanist
Tragedy* (Manchester, 1974, pp. 12–13), in discussing the
'pseudo treatise' (Stone's own words) of Jean de la Taille, *De
l'art de la tragédie*, seems to miss one of the major points in
tragedy – the appeal to the emotions – which La Taille himself
expresses in this way:

> veu que la vraye et seule intention d'une Tragedie est
> d'esmouvoir et de poindre merveilleusement les affections
> d'un chascun, car il fault que le subject en soit si pitoyable
> et poignant de soy, qu'estant mesme en bref et nument dit,
> engendre en nous quelque passion...[1]

But the didactic predominates over the purely 'tragic' or
aesthetic values in Stone's evaluation of La Taille's tragedy *Saül
le Furieux*. He states, 'when the poets' friends turn to the content
of the tragedies (i.e. in the liminary poems) they see in effect
only one thing – what the play teaches' (p. 17).

Du Bellay's statement in his *Deffence* of 1549, the manifesto
of the Pléiade, is a crucial one for the whole century.

> celuy sera veritablement le poëte que je cherche en nostre
> Langue, qui me fera indigner, apayser, ejouyr, douloir,
> aymer, hayr, admirer, etonner, bref, qui tiendra la bride de
> mes affections, me tournant ça & la à son plaisir.
>
> 　　　　　　　(ed. Chamard, Paris, 1961, p. 179)

The demand that every artist must provoke emotion in the
hearts of his public establishes a fundamental criterion for art.
No emotion stirred means no participation by the reader, no
two-way process between writing–speaking and listening. The
conspiracy between author and reader, without whose relationship there would be no literature, is well expressed by Rabelais
in the poem preceding his preface to *Gargantua* (1534),

> AUX LECTEURS
> Amis lecteurs, qui ce livre lisez,
> Despouillez vous de toute affection;
> Et, le lisant, ne vous scandalisez:
> Il ne contient mal ne infection.
> Vray est qu'icy peu de perfection
> Vous apprendrez, si non en cas de rire;
> Aultre argument ne peut mon cueur elire,
> Voyant le dueil qui vous mine et consomme:
> Mieulx est de ris que de larmes escripre,
> Pour ce que rire est le propre de l'homme.
> 　　　　　　　(*Œuvres complètes*, ed. Jourda)

Of course, Rabelais was writing a comic work, so that there was

---

[1] Jean de la Taille, *Dramatic Works*, ed. by Kathleen M. Hall and C. N. Smith
(London, 1972), p. 20.

no demand for pity or sympathy from the reader. But the fundamental feature is his attitude to the purely didactic, which was basically the same as the Pléiade's – for in spite of their oft-repeated views on the utility of literature they were far more hedonistic, in practice, than didactic. Note the lines

> Vray est qu'icy peu de perfection
> Vous apprendrez...

When Horace says – *Ars poetica*, 99–100

> non satis est pulchra esse poemata: dulcia sunto
> et quocumque volent animum auditoris agunto.
>
> It is not enough that poems be beautiful; they should delight
> and lead the spirit of the listener where they will...

he means that emotional appeal came first in his eyes. And one might add that it does for any reader or writer of poetry. The famous couplet (*Ars poetica*, 343–4)

> omne tulit punctum qui miscuit utile dulci,
> lectorem delectando pariterque monendo
>
> he has gained full marks who has mingled profit with pleasure
> by at once delighting the reader and instructing him.

gave Western Europe a 'teaching' that was (and in many readers' minds, still is) very ambiguous. On the one hand we read in Castor's *Pléiade Poetics*, op. cit. p. 22, 'This recommendation to didacticism was a commonplace of criticism in the sixteenth century, and it occurs quite frequently in the writings of the Pléiade...We have to remember, of course, that Horace was himself much influenced in his ideas by the theories of the classical rhetoricians.' On the other hand, both Quinn and Williams clearly put this position in reverse form. For they treat the whole question of didacticism very subtly. They state that reflection – even abstract reflection – on human behaviour, motives and actions is a legitimate activity for a poet who is interested in the human condition. Thus a poem of Horace might seem at first sight to be nothing more than general moralisations formulated as *sententiae*. But when one looks at the whole poem as a poetic structure, these *sententiae* are embedded in dense poetic contexts. It may be the manipulation of concrete and abstract, or the intensely personal weaving together of general commonplaces and personal feelings put forward at a level which the poet has recreated as universal feeling.

Didacticism is set, therefore, in a new perspective by the studies of Quinn and Williams. The notion that a poem – or indeed any aesthetic work – can present the intelligible, the universal, by way of the particular is basic to our understanding of Horace and the other Roman poets, the French Renaissance and the subsequent centuries in France. Rosemund Tuve in her important book, *Elizabethan and Metaphysical Imagery* (Chicago, 1947) clearly demonstrated that this universal or essence of something is crucial in our understanding of Renaissance poetics. The poet when he writes a poem is much more likely to be thinking of what his words will convey to the mind of the reader rather than going through some personal psychological crisis within himself. To show how communication of the universal is not to be equated simply with didacticism let us examine the famous poem by Ronsard, first published in 1553, *Mignonne, allon voir.*

> Mignonne, allon voir si la rose
> Qui ce matin avoit declose
> Sa robe de pourpre au soleil,
> A point perdu, cette vesprée,
> Les plis de sa robe pourprée,
> Et son teint au vostre pareil.
>   Las, voiés comme en peu d'espace,
> Mignonne, elle a dessus la place
> Las, las, ses beautés laissé cheoir!
> O vraiment maratre Nature,
> Puis qu'une telle fleur ne dure
> Que du matin jusques au soir.
>   Donc, si vous me croiés, mignonne:
> Tandis que vôtre age fleuronne
> En sa plus verte nouveauté,
> Cueillés, cueillés, vôtre jeunesse:
> Comme à cette fleur, la vieillesse
> Fera ternir vôtre beauté.[1]

[1] *Œuvres complètes*, 20 vols., ed. P. Laumonier, I. Silver and R. Lebègue, Paris, 1914–75, vol. v, p. 196.

Donald Stone in his analysis of this ode in his book, *Ronsard's Sonnet Cycles. A Study in Tone and Vision* (New Haven, Conn., 1966, pp. 4 ff) sees it as a didactic lesson. For instance he says (p. 7)

> the shift from first to second person in the poem's imperatives accentuates Ronsard's serious didactic purpose...He has become her teacher...And, of course, the didactic attitude continues through the final imperative, again the second person, 'Ceuillés'. The experiment having been performed, the observations having been made and the results recorded, the poet-philosopher rests his pen.

This is surely a mis-understanding of the poem. For Ronsard is here not a 'poet-philosopher' presenting us with a lesson; *carpe diem* has been a commonplace since men started writing poetry. Nor is the ode a description; the comparison between a rose and a young maiden is a topos, verging on a cliché. The poet's seriousness lies not in the manipulation of mosaics taken from his reading but in the serious view of art that he points to. This is poetry woven around commonplace ideas. And it is the weaving that should be commented on, and not what twentieth-century readers mistake as moralising. We are hardly ever given lessons by Ronsard. What we are always given is the sheer joy of creating.

Simple language in all successful poems depends on conceal-ment. Every part of the linguistic, prosodic and melody-making structure is highly artificial or stylised, and it is for the reader to try and tease out the implications of a highly intricate form. Ronsard's ode starts off with a *Mignonne* – a rather 'light' *m...n...n* conveying 'a sweeting or sweet-hart, a prettie minion, a lovelie delight' (Cotgrave). Ronsard uses the familiar and endearing term three times, thereby setting the light, graceful tone of the poem: a natural invitation to the young girl to come for a walk. When we read the next six syllables, and the eight and eight of the next two lines, and notice the tense-scheme – set back in an earlier time through the use of the pluperfect – we begin to realise that the poem is not as simple as it seemed. The first three lines are followed by a verb in the perfect tense, a past participle acting as an adjective – *pourprée*

– a pause before an imperative, followed by another perfect, a present, a conditional, a present, two imperatives – and the whole ode ends on a future tense. This complex temporal sequence is tightly controlled by the poet. He evokes the morning rose which is already in the past; so an opposition between morning and evening is present throughout. The beauty and freshness of the rose is all the more poignant for being evoked in the past. The first six lines through their rhythmic sequence give the impression of a promenade through time: rather light and tripping. The next six lines almost come to a halt: the repetition of *las* and the placing of the word *mignonne* between the first and second uses hint for the reader at the sadness, the tenderness and the loveliness of the couple looking at the faded rose. The last six lines are more urgent in rhythm, the two imperatives and the future tense express the *carpe diem* satisfyingly.

The visualisation in the first stanza depends largely on the colour crimson: the Augustan poets in Rome had also used *purpureus* in an evocative way. It conveyed something more than redness. It expressed the idea of radiance or richness. Ovid, *Amores* ii.1.38 had even referred to love itself as *purpureus*.[1] Ronsard suggests a concrete delight in colour through the three words *pourpre*. . .*soleil*. . .*pourprée*: a feast of colour, light, radiance and sheen; early morning, dew, the shape of a perfect rosebud, with tightly curled petals, the hint of the wrinkles before they open out wide in the sun. A graceful and lovely vision.

The fusion of the rose and the young maiden is already in our minds. Ronsard then takes up the *robe* theme, and amplifies it in 'les plis de sa robe pourprée'. The folds of the dress give a point of contact between the rose and the girl. Her lips and cheeks, her *teint* – her complexion are all discreetly evoked. One can say that words are in themselves neutral, but there are words in good places and words in bad places. Ronsard knew how to position his language.

---

[1] Horace, *Odes* iv.1.10 had used it with reference to swans and Vergil to spring flowers in *Eclogues* ix.40 and to youth in *Aeneid* 1.591. Also *purpuratus* – dressed in purple – was used of high-ranking officers in a regal court. This suggestion of 'regalness' in its use in Augustan Rome passed over to the French *pourpre*: to be dressed in *pourpre* is a king's privilege.

He very subtly makes us see the invitation through the eyes of the young girl. In 'ses beautés laissé cheoir' the use of an abstract noun *beauté* in the plural endows the word with a certain concrete character – just enough to call up for us the falling petals.[1] Yet there is only a hint of the actual fall or the appearance of the petals. The suggestion of the fall of the petals is, perhaps, there in the repetition 'Las...Las, las': the form and sequence of the poem has established a rose of reminiscence (the morning one) and then invited us, with the girl, to go out and look at the present actual rose. We are in front of it when the first *Las* appears; the second *Las, las* makes us think that two more petals have fallen in quick succession. In other words the flower is disintegrating before our eyes. The *maratre* brings in the half-playful, half-sad note – nature is unkind to let such a beautiful thing die so soon.

When he turns to Cassandra we do not think of the *donc* as a logician's word, nor does it seem an 'experimentation'. Rather the 'moral' rises naturally from the situation. The tone surrounding *donc* is the lover's wistful realism: she has seen the rose and its fading as clearly as he has. Ronsard carries over the image of the flower into the general reflection at the end – 'fleuronne/verte nouveauté/Cueillés vôtre jeunesse.' The only suggestion of physical death is in the word *ternir*.

There is no tragedy, or revolt against the dictates of nature: the poet accepts the natural term of life and all things mortal, but concentrates on the idea of living and loving while one is young. The ode is a perfect blend of personal and abstract, of general reflection and *invitation à la promenade* to a young mistress. The brevity of the ode corresponds well to the delicate emotion and favours the simplicity of image and description. And the tripartite division gives the poem a firm and dramatic structure which is almost madrigalesque. The final impression the ode leaves in our appreciation is natural elegance.[2]

[1] Compare the clever way in which Scève in the first dizain of *Délie* – *L'Œil trop ardent en mes ieunes erreurs* – recasts the Petrarchan *errore* (in the first poem of his *Rime*) and makes it plural. This pluralisation of abstract nouns to make them concrete was a characteristic of Roman poetry. And Scève is not dealing with the abstract fault or error in Petrarch's sense but making us think of the wanderings of carefree youth.

[2] For a full discussion of Ronsard's ode against the background of Roman poetry see H. Weber, *La Création poétique au XVIe siècle en France* (Paris, 1956, vol. I, pp. 341–8).

There is no didacticism in the ode, still less a specifically philosophical lesson to be gathered. Indeed, when critics talk about the philosophy of Horace or Ronsard what they really mean is 'attitude to life' or 'savoir vivre'; for neither was a philosopher in the strict sense. What distinguished Horace for the sixteenth century was his superb gift of creating, and this was what they imitated, not merely his theory or his 'philosophy'. Obviously there are qualities of the imagination, the nature of the world, of beauty and of life itself that Horace moulded in his poetry and we shall see that there is a set of attributes and a 'tone' of voice that Ronsard and his fellow poets used.[1] But it was his power of creativity that made him unique.

We must now turn to the aesthetic values the Roman poets had embedded in their tradition before we can see what particular aspects were important to Ronsard and Du Bellay and everyone that followed them.

[1] See the whole discussion around *moraliste*, pp. 45 ff.

3

Roman aesthetic values

French Renaissance writers took over a whole scale of values from the Ancients – the fact is recognised over and over again. But we do not always realise that the exact meaning underlying these values – which is often glossed over – and exact implications with regard to culture must also be recovered. There are several points that need to be re-stated, for they are vital to our general cultural conception of literary France from the sixteenth to the twentieth centuries. There are, I believe, five points or canons which characterise the Roman tradition: the development of a poetic language, the emphasis on aesthetic values, the allusive nature of poetry, the aristocratic characteristics of literature and the *moraliste* view of the human condition.

Let us analyse first the most important thing: language. Latin, i.e. written Latin, was a form of speech adapted to a 'noble' style. It was stylised in the sense that regular features were imposed on what in effect is non-stylised. There is a distinct cleavage between a non-literary colloquial language and a stylised, noble language, an artificial language – not in the modern pejorative sense of the word, but based on the sense *artifex* – produced by art. L. R. Palmer in *The Latin Language* (London, 1954) speaks of the Romans' apprenticeship in the art and discipline of Greece: they violated their native tradition by having recourse to foreign literature; their approach to literature arose not spontaneously but under the dominance of Greek influence. The upper classes were bilingual and often had formal instruction in Greek before they could speak their own 'vernacular'. Palmer cites Eduard Fraenkel:

again and again it may be shown how Livius [i.e. the 3rd
century B.C. translator of the Odyssey] is at pains by means
of highly archaic forms of speech to lend dignity and
remoteness to his epic, remoteness not only from every-day
language but also from the style of less august poetical genres.
(p. 98)

Palmer remarks that all Livius's successors adhered to this view
of art. The difference was between colloquial conversation –
sermo plebeius, sermo rusticus – and the studied literary style – *sermo
urbanus*. And Cicero has a fine discussion of the sharp differences
between one style and another in a letter to Paetus,

Verum tamen quid tibi ego videor in epistulis? nonne plebeio
sermone agere tecum? nec enim semper eodem modo. Quid
enim simile habet epistula aut iudicio aut contioni? quin ipsa
iudicia non solemus omnia tractare uno modo. Privatas
causas et eas tenuis agimus subtilius, capitis aut famae scilicet
ornatius; epistulas vero cotidianis verbis texere solemus.

(*Epistulae ad familiares*, IX. 21)

But be that as it may, what about my letters? Don't you think
my discussions with you in these are in the popular idiom?
Nor indeed is my manner always the same. For what has a
letter in common with a law-court or a political meeting? For
that matter take just the courts: we don't usually treat them
all in one way. We usually compose speeches in civil actions
and minor cases in a plain style; in criminal cases where life
or reputation are at stake naturally in a more elaborate style;
but letters in ordinary everyday language.

The fine gradations of style are based on evaluative words like
subtilitas, suavitas, acumen, sonitus, vis, gravitas – which are analysed
in a later chapter. Here it is important that we see in what
context language was discussed.[1]

Now in what ways did the Latin language evolve to produce
an artificial or stylised form? Palmer again (*The Latin Language*
p. 123) says that already in the early 2nd century B.C. – he is
presumably thinking of such poets as Ennius – there existed 'a
blend of colloquial speech with the archaic forms of the religious
carmina and the formulae of the law, embellished with native
cosmetics, with the *lumina* of Greek rhetoric, and the flowers of

[1] For examples of the *sermo cotidianus* in Horace's Satires see the survey by D. Bo, *Q.
Flacci Opera* (Turin, 1960), III, 335–50.

contemporary poetic diction'. And it was this 'curious amalgam which during the course of the next century was refined into the language of classical prose. The process was essentially one of selection and rejection, the pursuit of *latinitas* under the banner of *urbanitas*.'

Roman poets could speak, read and write in Greek as well as in Latin. Horace, for instance, 'himself had once tried his hand at Greek verse, but had been deterred by Romulus, who (he says) appeared in a dream and warned him of his folly. Now he writes only in Latin.'[1] The question of language is interesting; it suggests that Roman poets had reached the same stage as French writers had by the seventeenth century: both Roman and French writers stressed the need to prune all excesses and to aim at clarity.[2] In Latin literary prose we can more or less command the chief items that were deemed pure latinity: Cicero, for example, in his *De oratore* states that correct vocabulary and forms with due regard for number and gender and also correct pronunciation are to be sought:

> ut Latine loquamur, non solum videndum est, ut et verba efferamus ea, quae nemo iure reprehendat, et ea sic et casibus et temporibus et genere et numero conservemus, ut ne quid perturbatum ac discrepans aut praeposterum sit, sed etiam lingua et spiritus et vocis sonus est ipse moderandus.
>
> (*De oratore* III. 40)

> in order to speak Latin correctly we must not only be careful both to produce words that no one can justly object to and to arrange them in respect of cases, tenses, gender and number in such a way that there may be no confusion and false concord or wrong order, but we must also regulate our tongue and breath and actual tone of voice.

The fusion of Greek and Roman culture renders Latin a polished and flexible medium of expression, in which intellectual problems can be discussed as adequately as in Greek. (*De or.* III. 95, 96 and 171) In *Brutus*. 138, he even represents Latin as

---

[1] Niall Rudd, *The Satires of Horace* (Cambridge, 1966), p. 94. He is paraphrasing what Horace said in *Sat.* I, 10. 36–9.

[2] Although Peletier (*Art poétique*, 1555), had made clarity his first requirement – 'La première et plus digne vertu du Poème èst la clèrtè' – the sixteenth century did not aim at pruning the French language.

surpassing Greek in resources and expressiveness. The Roman intelligentsia had cut out of their language the rustic, the provincial and the foreign:

> neque solum rusticam asperitatem, sed etiam peregrinam insolentiam fugere discamus. (*De or.* III. 44)

> and learn to avoid not only rustic roughness but also provincial solecisms.

Cicero and Quintilian considered rhythm to be very important in literary prose: praising euphony and harmony, the avoidance of hiatus, the gift of *elegantia, concinnitas* and *numerus* (see for example, Cicero, *De or.* III. 171, *Orator*, 149 and Quintilian, IX. 4. 35).

In poetry it can be shown again and again that all Roman poetical genres made use of archaisms and dialect words (this was in accordance with Greek theory and practice) to lend dignity to the language and remoteness from everyday colloquial speech. Vergil, for example, had brought into the epic genre all the devices of rhetoric, such as rhetorical questions, exclamations, short rapid sentences mutually balancing each other, and symmetry created by features such as antithesis, anaphora and chiasmus. But there were differences between poets and prose writers: Cicero says how in the very composition of words the poets are far freer:

> frequentiores sunt et liberiores poetae; nam et transferunt verba cum crebrius tum etiam audacius et priscis libentius utuntur et liberius novis... (*Orator*, 202)

> the poets are more assiduous and take greater liberties in the former [rhythm]; they employ metaphors more frequently, and also more boldly, and use archaisms and new words more freely.

Or again he says,

> Est enim finitimus oratori poeta, numeris astrictior paulo, verborum autem licentia liberior, multis vero ornandi generibus socius ac paene par; in hoc quidem certe prope idem, nullis ut terminis circumscribat aut definiat ius suum, quo minus ei liceat eadem illa facultate et copia vagari qua velit.
> (*De or.* I. 70)

> The truth is that the poet is a very near kinsman of the orator, rather more heavily fettered as regards rhythm, but with ampler freedom in his choice of words, while in the use of many sorts of ornament he is his ally and almost his counterpart: in one respect at all events something like identity exists, since he sets no boundaries or limits to his claims, such as would prevent him from ranging where he will with the same freedom and licence as the other.

Palmer resolves this apparent difference between poetry and prose by saying (*The Latin Language*, p. 140) 'it is true to say that the classical ideal as manifested in the oratory of Cicero and the Vergilian epic drew a sharp line between the language of prose and that of poetry'. We come to expect that Cicero in his great speeches will be a representative of literary prose just as Vergil will be of poetry. Roman writers were apprentices in the culture, art and discipline of Greece, and this relationship was to last throughout the centuries as an essential trait of Roman civilisation. Furthermore, French gives us a close parallel in the differences between the spoken and the written word – 'langue écrite et langue parlée sont tellement éloignées l'une de l'autre qu'on ne parle jamais comme l'on écrit et qu'on écrit rarement comme on parle'.[1] Of all the Romance languages it is French that has most faithfully reproduced the Latin fixity of tradition.

The artificial style, where remoteness from everyday speech is vital, makes poems difficult for the listener or reader precisely because the writer forces us to do so much of the unravelling of meanings ourselves. It is probable that much of Roman poetry was difficult even in its own time and that the heritage of Renaissance France was essentially one of difficult poetry. In this concept of difficult poetry the question of style and language is crucial.[2]

To take this at the most basic level consider Castor's observations in his *Pléiade Poetics* (Cambridge, 1964, p. 4):

[1] Quoted from Vendryès on p. 3 of M. K. Pope, *From Latin to Modern French* (Manchester, 1934, reprinted 1956).
[2] See the discussion of 'hard' poetry, the *durus/mollis* antithesis in Roman poetry and the way it was transmitted particularly to Scève in D. G. Coleman, *Maurice Scève*, ch. 3, 'Tradition'.

The common reader's reaction to the theoretical work of the Pléiade is often to feel that it is almost trivial, and certainly rather disappointing, compared with the practical achievement measured in terms of excellent poems written. For one thing, a great deal of time was spent on technical matters, on stanza-forms and rhymes, line-lengths, elisions, mute -e's, and so on, but comparatively little attention seems, at first sight at least, to have been given to any general ideas about what poetry is, or should be. Nowadays the position is normally reversed. Technicalities of that sort tend to be either ignored or taken for granted, which simply reflects the interest of modern critics in the problems of imagery and metaphor rather than in those of harmony and rhythm.

But the theoretical bias of 'the common reader' and 'the modern critic' does not correspond to the poets' own attitudes. In the *Ars poetica* of Horace we find elements that are very important to any poet in every age: for instance, the actual forging into use of words, or the juxtaposition of words one with another, or a new rhyme or a new rhythm,

> in verbis etiam tenuis cautusque serendis
> dixeris egregie notum si callida verbum
> reddiderit junctura novum.
> (lines 46–8)

For arranging of words in a phrase you must be precise, attentive and accurate: it will be a great success if you give newness to a term or a word through the clever relationship of the words.

These lines are re-echoed by Dylan Thomas who in his 'Poetic Manifesto' (*Texas Quarterly*, IV, Winter of 1961) said,

> I use everything and anything to make my poems work and move in the direction I want them to: old tricks, new tricks, puns, portmanteau-words, paradox, allusion, paranomasia, paragram, catachresis, slang, assonantal rhymes, vowel rhymes, sprung rhythm. Every device there is in language is there to be used if you will. Poets have. . . to enjoy themselves sometimes, and the twistings and convolutions. . . are all part of the joy.

In *Letters to Vernon Watkins* (London, 1957) Thomas writes to his brother-poet Vernon Watkins to urge him to come to

Carmarthen so that they can discuss poems that they are both writing; Thomas very excitedly tells him that he has two new poems, one with a thoroughly untried rhythm. He wants to discuss prosody with him. There are also poets' letters like the Sitwells' which prove the same point: if you are a poet you are not concerned about *what poetry is*. General theories of poetry do not really interest you. Thomas wrote this advice to a young friend,

> Read the poems you like reading. Don't bother whether they're 'important', or if they'll live. What does it matter what poetry *is*, after all?...Poetry is what makes me laugh or cry or yawn, what makes my toenails twinkle, what makes me want to do this or that or nothing.[1]

It is a matter of knowing the behaviour of words, skilfully making them obey your command, entreating them, forming rhythms around them and *hearing* them. This last point is important: for to Horace reading his poems to a few chosen friends was what counted most. And all Roman poets would expect to have to read their works aloud.[2] Now this question of 'hearing' a literary work raises the problem: how would Ronsard or Montaigne have pronounced Latin? How could they have been sure about the *sound* of Latin poetry? Latin in France must have been affected by native speech-habits. Sidney Allen in *Vox Latina: The pronunciation of Classical Latin* (Cambridge, 1965, p. 102) gives us several examples:

> ...some peculiarities of the French pronunciation of Latin, e.g. the rendering of both consonantal *i* (*iustum*, etc.) and 'soft' *g* (*gentem*, etc.) as an affricate [dz] (as in English *judge*). 'Soft' *c* came to be pronounced as [s] (after the thirteenth century when earlier French [ts] changed to [s]); all vowels

---

[1] *The Colour of Saying*, ed. Prof. Ralph Maude and Aneirin Talfan Davies (London, 1963) Introduction, p. xviii.

[2] Indeed one could argue that every poet expects his poetry to be read aloud in spite of the tendency of much poetry since 1830 or thereabouts to demand in addition silent reading. Take for example Valéry's translation of Vergil's *Eclogues*: he insists on there being no rhyme in spite of his editor's views – 'Sans rimes, est-ce que ça chantera? osai-je lui redemander.' Valéry answers 'Ça, je vous le promets.' He called his editor a month later 'et me lut la première *Bucolique*: Ça vous plait? Vous entendez, ça chante, vous voyez bien que les rimes sont inutiles.' And the editor adds: 'En effet, c'était un enchantement, on croyait entendre Virgile parler en vers français.' (See the notes to *Les Bucoliques* in the Pléiade edition, Paris, 1957, vol. I, p. 1691.)

were shortened before two or more consonants, e.g. in *census*, *nullus*; and Romance practice re-inforced the tendency to lengthen vowels in open syllables (e.g. *tēnet, fŏcus*, for *tĕnet, fŏcus*).

The really important sixteenth-century work on the pronunciation of Latin and Greek was, of course, Erasmus' dialogue *De recta Latini Graecique sermonis pronuntiatione* which appeared in 1528. This sets out to reform national peculiarities and to restore classical Latin and Greek to their true pronunciation. Professor Allen comments,

> The dialogue makes a number of important deductions about the ancient pronunciation of Latin, including the 'hard' pronunciation of *c* and *g* before all vowels, the voicelessness of intervocalic *s*, and the importance of vowel length. (p. 103)

Given that Erasmus was important as a pedagogic master, and given that Dorat was the main teacher of the whole Pléiade one might expect Ronsard and Du Bellay to have benefited from this new restoration. However, since Erasmus in the very same dialogue said that the French pronunciation of Latin was the worst of all European countries, and all attempts at reform since the sixteenth century have been unsuccessful, one might hazard the guess that sixteenth-century France heard a very 'Frenchified' Latin with the *u* (e.g. *tempus*) pronounced *ü* and *qu* pronounced as a *k*.[1]

Nowadays it is the exceptional poem or poet that gets read aloud. The poem is to be *seen* on the page. Yet hearing a poem should, in my opinion, always come before reading the poem. And both demand the participation of the listener–reader.[2]

---

[1] A. Ewert, *The French Language* (London, 1943, reprinted 1964, p. 86), says that 'in the Middle Ages Latin was pronounced as though it were French' and maintains that the sixteenth century endeavoured to correct the pronunciation, but implies that success in this line was never to be won.

[2] Cf. Dafydd ap Gwilym's insistence on the participation of the reader. He superimposes several different meanings upon a word or phrase so that the listener–reader simply has to grapple with the difficulties. His case is particularly interesting as, writing in Wales in the fourteenth century, he was aware of the whole European tradition of writing poetry. He calls himself *dyn Ofydd* (Ovid's man); he was also aware of the love poetry of the troubadours; and yet he could fuse the different threads with his own Welsh tradition which went back to the sixth century. Standing back, for a moment, from our study of the Roman literary tradition, Dafydd ap Gwilym can be said to have assimilated *more* than the French would do for four centuries and the Welsh tradition was very much more 'difficult' than even the Roman tradition.

Later on in his *Ars poetica* Horace states that creating new words is vital in poetry; it may be essential that you create words for thoughts that have not been expressed by anyone before. But it must be *licentia sumpta pudenter* (line 51) and neologisms will be better if they are derived from the Greek.[1] Note how this is again the poet's task, not the theoretician's. And having stated the theory, it comes as no surprise to find that Horace approved of Ennius for having coined new words: for instance, compounds like *altitonans, altivolans, bellipotens* and so on. On a strong passionate note he says,

> Licuit semperque licebit
> Signatum praesente nota producere nomen.
> (lines 58–9)

It always has been so and always shall be so: poets have the right to create new words.

However, a few lines later we come upon the fundamental criterion in creating words, and that is usage,

> multa renascentur quae jam cecidere cadentque
> quae nunc sunt in honore vocabula, si volet usus
> quem penes arbitrium est et jus et norma loquendi.
> (lines 70–2)

> Many words that have today disappeared may be born again, many words that are today in honour will fall out of usage, for it is usage that is the ruler of legitimate language and the norm of the tongue.

This criterion of usage was held from the beginning in the French Renaissance. Du Bellay in his *Deffence* had said,

> use de motz purement François, non toutesfois trop communs, non point aussi trop inusitez...
> (ed. Chamard, Paris, 1961, p. 142)

And he advises poets to coin words from Greek and Latin but to use the judgement of their ear as well as the norm of language:

> Ne crains donques, Poëte futur, d'innover quelques termes, en un long poëme principalement, avecques modestie toutes-

---

[1] Cf. the Pléiade assumption of this right to re-create words from Latin and Greek words.

fois, analogie & jugement de l'oreille...Parquoy je renvoye
tout au jugement de ton oreille.   (ibid. p. 139–42)

This statement is crucial: the whole Pléiade stressed that
musicality, the judgement of the ear, was essential for poets
when writing poetry. And this is surely very important both for
Roman writers, and in Renaissance and post-Renaissance
poetry. But the early works of the Pléiade were too obscure, too
mythological and too rich in allusion for the critics – often poets
themselves – and it was only when Ronsard and Du Bellay
realised this that they changed the tone of their work. In their
later books they work more consciously to Horace's precept –
the criterion of usage. This criterion was to be thoroughly
understood and used by the seventeenth century, and it is
fundamental to our conception of French literature as a whole.

Much has been made of Horace's theory of decorum and
bienséances, his notion of tragedy and comedy, but it seems to me
that this is to stop at some of the most transitory doctrines in
the *Ars poetica*. What is more important lies at the deepest level
of poetry and literary prose: namely language itself.

And it is at this basic level that one can understand Du
Bellay's statements on his own translation–version of two books
of Vergil's *Aeneid*,

> non que ie me vante (ie ne suis tant impudent) d'avoir en
> cest endroit contrefait au naturel les vrais lineamens de
> Vergile: mais quand ie diray que ie ne m'en suis du tout si
> eslongné qu'au port et à l'accoustrement de *cest estranger
> naturalisé*, il ne soit facile de recognoistre le lieu de sa nativité,
> ie croy que les equitables oreilles n'en devront estre
> offensees.[1]   (my italics)

The assimilation of *cest estranger naturalisé* suggests that Du Bellay
is aware of the French language in a creative way. For example,
the precise hints of advice from Horace's *Ars poetica* are followed
when he is forced to coin words,

> quelques motz composez, comme pié-sonnant, porte-lois,
> porte-ciel, et autres, que i'ay forgez sur les vocables Latins,

---

[1] *Deux Livres de l'Eneide de Vergile* (Paris, 1561), the 'dédicace Au Seigneur Ian de Morel', p. 3.

> comme cerve, pour bische... C'est pourquoy ne voulant
> tousiours contraindre l'escriture au commun usage de parler,
> ie ne crains d'usurper quelquefois en mes vers certains mots,
> et locutions, dont ailleurs ie ne voudray user, et ne pourroy
> sans affectation, et mauvaise grace. Pour ceste mesme raison,
> i'ay usé de gallees, pour galleres: endementiers pour en ce
> pendant: isnel, pour leger: carrollant, pour dansant, et autres
> dont l'antiquité (*suyvant l'exemple de mon auteur Vergile*) me
> semble donner quelque majesté aux vers, principalement en
> un long poeme, pourveu toutefois que l'usage n'en soit
> immoderé.   (ibid, my italics)

Thus this first characteristic value of the development of a
poetic language is to be seen as informing the sixteenth-century
outlook on poetry. Of course, there is nothing exclusively
Roman about a preoccupation with language. But in the
Renaissance, France saw that to re-vitalize her own literary
tradition she had to start by renewing contact with the classical
languages of Greece and Rome. It is this which makes Elcock
say:

> From the beginning there probably appeared in Gaul more
> clearly than in other provinces the division into two currents
> of 'learned' and 'popular' speech. Throughout the history
> of French this dichotomy which prevailed in Rome itself is
> continually apparent, and the interplay of these two forces
> naturally divergent but brought to some extent into unison
> by the craft of writers and grammarians, is at every stage a
> vital factor in the formation of the linguistic norm.[1]

It was in the Renaissance that colloquial French speech, or the
speech of the *plebs* became sharply differentiated from literary
speech. And the first explicit mention of this is made by Tory
in his *Champfleury* (1529) where he refers to the pronunciation
of the *dames de Paris* as opposed to the traits of the *menu peuple*
or the *populace*.[2] The reign of François Ier was a turning point
in the development of a 'learned' French.

The second Roman canon is the preoccupation with aesthetic
questions. As I have said, it was not theoretical discussion of
what poetry or literature was about that kindled the minds of

---

[1] E. D. Elcock, *The Romance Languages*, revised by John N. Green (London, 1975), p.
199.

[2] Geoffrey Tory, *Champfleury* (Paris, 1529), unnumbered pages, ca. *b*. i, verso.

these poets. As Professor Brink (*Horace on Poetry*, p. 153) puts it, 'Aristotle is the exemplar of a philosopher who philosophised on poetry...The Aristotelian view is the external view – external, that is, to the poet...It is essentially the reader's or listener's view, writ large and systematized.' Not that the Roman poets were totally unaware of theoretical considerations when they wrote poetry. However in reading them we ought not to be too concerned with how theoreticians solved problems that were inherent in theory in the historical and literary situation of the first century B.C. Thus questions such as 'what was the relationship between aesthetics and philosophy or between aesthetics and history?' are not of prime relevance. What we want to see is where the poets place their view of art in the hierarchy of human activities. Do they have anything to say about the status of literature? Is the artistic or aesthetic the only true evaluation?

Cicero and Quintilian recognised a very important aesthetic concept, namely that of decorum: every word must be appropriate if it is to carry conviction. So they elided utility and function with grace and aesthetic pattern. Quintilian, praising Cicero for his command of language (VIII. 3. 3–4), says,

> Sublimitas profecto et magnificentia et nitor et auctoritas expressit illum fragorem.

And this is the chief style for moving people

> Nam, qui libenter audiunt, et magis attendunt et facilius credunt, plerumque ipsa delectatione capiuntur, nonnumquam admiratione auferuntur. (VIII. 3. 5)

> It was the sublimity and splendour, the brilliance and the weight of his eloquence that evoked such clamorous enthusiasm...For when our audience find it a pleasure to listen, their attention and their readiness to believe what they hear are both alike increased, while they are generally filled with delight, and sometimes even transported by admiration.

This was the 'grand' style, distinguished by dignity of sentiment and expression. It was called *gravis* by Cicero (*Orat.* 5. 20) and it will become the focus of discussion in the next chapter. The two critics also recognised a 'plain' style, commonly called *subtile,* marked by clarity and simplicity; and a *medium* or *modicum* style (*Or.* 28. 98) which has a kind of flowery grace and sweetness which Quintilian (XII. 10. 58) called *floridum.*

Cicero reserves his admiration for the grand style:

> Tertius est ille [the third type of orator] amplus copiosus, gravis ornatus, in quo profecto vis maxima est. Hic est enim, cuius ornatum dicendi et copiam admiratae gentes eloquentiam in civitatibus plurimum valere passae sunt, sed hanc eloquentiam, quae cursu magno sonituque ferretur, quam suspicerent omnes, quam admirarentur, quam se adsequi posse diffiderent. Huius eloquentiae est tractare animos, huius omni modo permovere. Haec modo perfringit, modo inrepit in sensus; inserit novas opiniones, evellit insitas.
>
> (*Or.* 97.)

The orator of the third style is magnificent, opulent, stately and ornate; he undoubtedly has the greatest power. This is the man whose brilliance and fluency have caused admiring nations to let eloquence attain the highest power in the state; I mean the kind of eloquence which rushes along with the roar of a mighty stream, which all look up to and admire, and which they despair of attaining. This eloquence has power to sway men's mind and move them in every possible way. Now it storms the feelings, now it creeps in; it implants new ideas and uproots the old.

This is the style which combines beauty and emotion.

The poetic ideal was purely aesthetic: the satisfaction of finding form in harmony with content. It is not rhetorical moralisations that the poets were aiming at but the use of words to suggest an intuition of life's complexities rather than a rational analysis of some of those complexities. Thence the famous antithesis in Horace of *pulchra/dulcia*:

> Non satis est pulchra esse poemata, dulcia sunto
> Et quocumque volent animum auditoris agunto.
>
> (*Ars poetica,* 99–100)

It is not enough that poems be beautiful; they should delight and lead the spirit of the listener where they will.

Since Latin is an inflected language and lacks articles, the relationship between subject, object and modifiers is defined by their inflexions. Thus poets could afford to override prosaic sense sequence in composing poetry; they could build up stanzas in accordance with their aesthetic idea. The reader had to *feel himself* into the poetry; he had to work out the setting of the poem himself although the good poet gave him all the clues for doing so. He was required to participate in the poet's work and exercise his own imagination. Roman contemporaries would not be disturbed by a play on word-order, since they were used to it to some extent; but the modern reader, if his linguistic experience is in English or Romance rather than in the more highly inflected structures like German or Russian, labours under a double difficulty.

This intellectual element is a constant in the appreciation or criticism of a Roman poet. Thus, for instance, when a twentieth-century reader is faced by a stanza of a Horatian ode he has to let the words, their positions, the prosody and the sound be caught first. Take this well-known stanza of Horace *Odes* 1. 5. (also analysed by Steel Commager, *The Odes of Horace. A Critical Study*, New Haven, Conn., 1962, p. 50):

> Quis multa gracilis te puer in rosa
> perfusus liquidis urget odoribus
>   grato, Pyrrha, sub antro?
>   cui flavam religas comam
> simplex munditiis?

> What slender youth, Pyrrha, bedewed with perfume, presses you down amongst the roses in this delicious grotto? For whom are you binding your yellow hair so simple in your coquetterie?

Quis is the first word of the ode: it announces a question, general and neutral. We notice the position of *te*, in between *gracilis* and *puer*, themselves between *multa...in rosa*: we have a difficult but highly expressive order of words: 'many–slender–you–boy–in–rose'. The apparently arbitrary sequence of words is, of course, a highly sophisticated technique for making the reader work as hard as the poet. So we have a double-line process whenever we read a Latin work.[1] Text and reader must co-operate: the reader must suspend his judgement, the text will come to help

---

[1] For further details of this see D. G. Coleman, *Maurice Scève. Tradition and Originality* (Cambridge, 1975), Ch. 3.

him. The process will depend also on how literate – in the literature of time past and time present – the reader is. For he will ultimately see the text in relation to other texts of other literatures as well as the Roman. Only then will the reader be in a position to judge and evaluate.

This intellectual dimension is coterminate with the poet's own awareness of the language that was available to him, the similes and metaphors – not as ornaments of thought, but as methods of thought – the concrete woven in with the abstract, personal comments slipping into an abstract generalisation; the elevation of certain genres – as for instance military odes or an epic like the *Aeneid* – all of which were used to focus attention on the words themselves and ultimately to relate them to the context of the whole poem.

Admittedly, Aristotle had already given Western Europe one of the best definitions of a metaphor,

> Metaphor consists in giving the thing a name that belongs to something else; the transference being either from genus to species, or from species to genus, or from species to species, or on grounds of analogy.   (*Poetics*, 21. 1457b)

And he had followed this up with a brilliant grasp of its quality,

> But the greatest thing by far is to be a master of metaphor. It is the one thing that cannot be learnt from others; and it is also a sign of genius, since a good metaphor implies an intuitive perception of the similarity in dissimilars.
>
> (*Poetics*, 22. 1459a)

But this eye for resemblances has to work within certain frameworks. After all, no work of literary merit is merely a mosaic of bright ideas, bright metaphors; each one, perhaps, conjuring up a sensuous picture, or making us look at a field of daisies with new spectacles. It has to have coherent shape and form to become an effective poem.[1]

---

[1] It may look here as if I am depreciating movements of poetry like Surrealism and clinging to a far 'easier' poetic tradition which seems to stop with Valéry. But underlying all the statements of Éluard and Breton there is the knowledge that the control of reason has to be present – at some stage – when composing poetry. In Éluard's case, in particular, he does write some exquisite short poems like 'L'extase' or 'Les Yeux' which have very little to do with Surrealism and very much to do with the poetic tradition which is the heart of this book.

Poetry is patterned language. It is the intellectual element that makes the structure of the poem hold together, and in Rome poets had established the role of the intellect in writing poetry.

To see how the intellectual element gives rise to an aesthetic emotion where every sound is highly charged with associations, every word significant and every emotion illuminated with sensation, let us examine briefly the famous poem by Catullus on his mistress's sparrow. Catullus is the first Roman poet to integrate fully the native Latin tradition and the ideals of Hellenistic poetry. And he represents the beginning of the poetic tradition which was to continue through Horace and Vergil until it reached Propertius. The poem is an exquisite one,

> Passer, deliciae meae puellae,
> quicum ludere, quem in sinu tenere,
> cui primum digitum dare appetenti
> et acris solet incitare morsus,
> cum desiderio meo nitenti
> carum nescio quid lubet iocari,
> et solaciolum sui doloris,
> credo, ut tam grauis acquiescat ardor:
> tecum ludere sicut ipsa possem
> et tristis animi leuare curas!

> Sparrow, source of pleasure to her I love,
> with you she often plays and holds you to her breast,
> offering fingertip to eager beak,
> soliciting your darting nip.
> (For there are moments when my radiant love
> Finds a kind of comfort in this idle play.
> You are a consolation in her pain. She hopes
> to soothe, I feel, her brooding love thereby.)
> I wish I could, like her, play and sport with you,
> and lighten trouble's burden in my heart.
> (Translation by Kenneth Quinn, *The Catullan Revolution*,
> Melbourne, 1959, p. 98)

The interplay between the two layers of meaning in this poem is startling. The literal one is a delightful description of Lesbia's pretty pet sparrow. (For, although Classical scholars will continue to argue over what bird is actually meant by the word *passer* I take it to mean a sparrow; but it could be any other small bird that Italians kept as a pet.) The second layer of meaning is a suggestive pattern of a sex relationship. From the second word *deliciae* this pattern is imposed. For *deliciae* was also used of human beings: a darling. For instance Plautus, *Poenulus* 365 has 'mea voluptas, mea delicia', and the emperor Titus was called *deliciae generis humani.* Cicero, *Pro Caelio* 1944. uses *deliciae* with distaste as a fashionable euphemism for the amours of Clodia's set – *amores autem et deliciae quae vocantur.* In Scève's *Délie* there is a constant play on *Délie* and *délices* which is used positively as an appreciation of love. It may have been triggered off by the Catullus poem, and indeed Scève used it first in Latin in an epigram to Ducher

> Delia si laetis blandum mihi ridet ocellis:
> Non mirum: mea nam Delia delitiae est.
> (B. Guégan, *Œuvres poétiques complètes de Maurice Scève*, Paris,
> 1927, p. 312).

To understand this basic notion of allurement is the key to the double pattern of the sparrow and the lover. Other words use the same equivocation: for instance, *quicum ludere* – to play with a lover or a sparrow, *quem in sinu tenere* – to hold the lover/ sparrow to her breast, *appetenti* – to be greedy and to be desirous of sex, *incitare morsus* to incite and provoke little nips, darting kisses and fond pecks. All these phrases apply to the play with the sparrow, but at the same time suggest playing the game of sex in a thoroughly Catullan way – that is in a very passionate *odi et amo* style, especially if *passer = penis*, as Martial clearly took it.

Catullus is the first Roman poet to make love the important feature of his poetry, so that even in this little poem, which at first sight seems to be a précieux one addressed to the sparrow, the underlying pattern is that of love. We notice other words which connote strong passion: for instance, *desiderio meo* and *gravis acquiescat* or *ardor* – all words which were normally used of physical suffering and passion.

He uses the diminutive *solaciolum* – a little comfort or solace – of *sui doloris*, thereby toning the grief down. The use of the diminutive is interesting because the 'affective' tone was a native resource of Latin speech: the diminutive creates an emotional overtone of affection, kindliness or amusement. In literature it is the counterpart of a smile, a tender look, a sigh or a shrug of the shoulders in real life. After Catullus the use of diminutives in Latin poetry diminishes, so that poets like Horace and Propertius are more selective in admitting this affectionate, intimate language into their poetry. But one needs only look at Ronsard to realise how much Catullus influenced him: for instance the *Amourette* in the 1552 *Amours* has an abundance of diminutives – and this was to be one of the central features of 'le stile mignard' followed by all members of the Pléiade. The whole tradition of 'kissing' poems also goes back to Catullus. The very words *basiare*, *basium* and *basatio* are unused by Vergil, Propertius, Ovid or Tibullus. They belonged to Cisalpine Gaul.

The poem also has two tones: a light-hearted one plus an ironic one. In one sense it is an intellectual game, but in the other there is irony underlying the relationship between the poet and his Lesbia. It delicately offers a poem within a poem; for by receiving all the sexual connotations of the words the reader gets the impression of an 'insider' in the game of love. However, the distance created by Catullus invites us to look at the poem at once as an 'outsider' and as an 'insider'. The whole poem is suggestive, and each word is charged with associations which the reader needs to grasp, balancing his knowledge about the tradition of poetry against his associations in the actual experience of his own life. It is in fact an admirable illustration of Winifred Nowottny's assertion that 'if poetry is language at full stretch, the stretching must help us to see more clearly the nature of the fabric stretched'.[1] This value of poetry is a complex, sophisticated and intellectual–aesthetic one and it was passed down to France in the Renaissance.

The third aesthetic value could be expressed as 'allusiveness versus explicitness'. Every great poet uses a special language, one that is allusive rather than explicit, symbolic rather than literal. 'Great literature is simply language charged with meaning to the utmost possible degree' said Ezra Pound, and

[1] *The Language Poets Use* (London, 1972), p. 85.

literal language is the arch-enemy of poetry. In order to see how the Roman poets relied on allusiveness – and handed that art down to France – I concentrate on one poet and critically analyse one poem – Propertius, i. 3.

Qualis Thesea iacuit cedente carina
  languida desertis Gnosia litoribus,
qualis et accubuit primo Cepheia somno
  libera iam duris cotibus Andromede,
nec minus assiduis Edonis fessa choreis
  qualis in herboso concidit Apidano:
talis visa mihi mollem spirare quietem
  Cynthia non certis nixa caput manibus,
ebria cum multo traherem vestigia Baccho
  et quaterent sera nocte facem pueri.
hanc ego, nondum etiam sensus deperditus omnes,
  molliter inpresso conor adire toro.
et quamvis duplici correptum ardore iuberent
  hac Amor hac Liber, durus uterque deus,
subiecto leviter positam temptare lacerto,
  osculaque admota sumere et arma manu,
non tamen ausus eram dominae turbare quietem
  expertae metuens iurgia saevitiae;
sed sic intentis haerebam fixus ocellis,
  Argus ut ignotis cornibus Inachidos.
et modo solvebam nostra de fronte corollas
  ponebamque tuis, Cynthia, temporibus,
et modo gaudebam lapsos formare capillos,
  nunc furtiva cavis poma dabam manibus,
omniaque ingrato largibar munera somno,
  munera de prono saepe voluta sinu.
et quotiens raro duxti suspiria motu,
  obstupui vano credulus auspicio,
ne qua tibi insolitos portarent visa timores,
  neve quis invitam cogeret esse suam:
donec diversas praecurrens luna fenestras,
  luna moraturis sedula luminibus,
compositos levibus radiis patefecit ocellos.
  sic ait in molli fixa toro cubitum:
'Tandem te nostro referens iniuria lecto
  alterius clausis expulit e foribus?
namque ubi longa meae consumpsti tempora noctis
  languidus exactis, ei mihi, sideribus?
o utinam tales perducas, inprobe, noctes,
  me miseram quales semper habere iubes!

nam modo purpureo fallebam stamine somnum,
   rursus et Orpheae carmine fessa lyrae;
interdum leviter mecum deserta querebar
   externo longas saepe in amore moras:
dum me iocundis lapsam Sopor inpulit alis.
   illa fuit lacrimis ultima cura meis.'

Just like the maid of Cnossus, lying languid on the deserted
shores while Theseus' ship went away; and Andromeda, child
of Cepheus, slipping into her first sleep, freed at last from the
hard rocks; and the Thracian maenad, no less weary from the
unending dances, lying down on the grassy banks of Apidanus;
just so, it seemed to me, did Cynthia breathe her gentle rest,
her head propped on faltering hands, when I dragged my
footsteps back, drunk with deep draughts of Bacchus, and the
slaves were shaking their torches late at night.

Not yet were all my senses destroyed, and I strove to
approach her where she lay, and lightly pressed against her
couch. And although a twofold frenzy had laid hold of me,
and on this side Love, on that side Liber – both harsh gods
– urged me to assail her, passing my arm under her where
she lay, and with outstretched hand take kisses and begin the
battle of love; yet I had not dared to disturb my mistress's
rest for I feared the angry quarrels and that savagery which
I had endured so often, but fixed my gaze upon her with fixed
eyes, even as Argus looked on the strange horned brow of the
daughter of Inachus. And now I took off the chaplet of flowers
from my brow and placed it, Cynthia, about your head and
now took delight in composing your loose hair; and stealthily
with hollowed hands gave you apples, and on your thankless
sleep lavished all my gifts, gifts that kept rolling from your
breast as you lay there. And every time you sighed, sometimes
moving, I was amazed – though vain was the omen that I
believed – lest what you were seeing brought you strange
terrors or that someone was forcing you to be his against your
will.

At last the moon, hastening past the window opposite,
officious with its fading light, opened her fast-closed eyes with
its gentle rays. Then with elbow propped firmly on the soft
couch she cried: 'At last another's scorn, respectful of my bed
has driven you out and closed the doors against you. For
where have you spent the long hours of the night – that was
meant for me – ah me, you come back tired out when the stars
are driven from the sky? May you, cruel one, endure nights
such as you're always bidding me keep, broken hearted that
I am. For just now I was beguiling my eyes from sleep with

purple embroidery, and then, work-wearied, with the music of Orpheus' lyre. And now and again, left thus forlorn, I made gentle moan to myself that you were often lingering long in another's love, till at last I sank down and sleep fanned my limbs with pleasant wings. That was my last thought amid my tears.'

This magnificent poem on Cynthia asleep shows the intellectual strength, compressed craftsmanship, ambivalence, allusiveness, irony and emotional awareness of Propertius. In one sense the structure is divided into two parts: first Cynthia is asleep and unconscious, with the poet the only person conscious; then Cynthia is awake and doing the talking. But to present this division as clear, unilinear and straightforward would be to sense no nuance in the poem, to cancel out the distance and nearness of vision, to undermine the mythology which carries a great deal of emotion, to be unaware of sensations, to misundertand the sleep–love leit-motif and to miss the whole irony.[1]

The opening of any poem is important. Propertius' openings sometimes plunge the reader *in medias res*, as for instance the first elegy of the first book,

> Cynthia prima suis miserum me cepit ocellis
>   contactum nullis ante cupidinibus.

> Cynthia first ensnared me, wretch that I was, by her dear eyes; till then I was not caught by any passions.

Or it can be a sudden semi-colloquial address as in 1. 5.

> Invide, tu tandem voces compesce molestas
>   et sine nos cursu, quo sumus, ire pares!

> Envious man, now at last suppress your unwelcome prayers and let us go hand in hand along the path that now we tread.

But in our elegy the opening (1–6) is immediately literary; the allusions are to mythology; the distance of the poet is striking. The effect of a camera, focussed on the background, comes through the repetition of *qualis...qualis...qualis*. The three

[1] For a different analysis of this poem see R. O. A. M. Lyne, 'Propertius and Cynthia: Elegy 1. 3.', in *Proceedings of the Cambridge Philological Society*, No. 196 (New Series, No. 16), 1970, pp. 60–78.

mythological figures have one element in common: all three are sleeping beauties, but the legends individually carry different implications which Propertius is putting into our minds. The first of these is love: Ariadne in love with Theseus; Andromeda delivered from the monster by Perseus; a Bacchante, a slave to a very emotional religion, whose orgiastic ceremonies worked to an intense pitch of ecstasy – whose feelings and sensations could be sexual orgasm. The order primarily suggests the vicissitudes in human love: Ariadne abandoned; Andromeda about to be happy after her ordeal chained to a rock; the Bacchantes possessed. Ariadne is characterised by the adjective *languida*: faint, weak in a physical sense, though not here, I think, sexually weak. Andromeda is *libera*: freed from, independent from. (Possibly *Libera* = Proserpina, daughter of Ceres and Liber – the Italian God of wine – which was often used as an attribute of Ariadne and which, perhaps, is subtly hinted at here. See Ovid. *Fasti* 3. 512). The Bacchante is *fessa*: worn out, fatigued, tired out.

Then their background is stressed. Ariadne is on the shores of Naxos: *desertis litoribus*, shores that have been deserted by the man she loves. Andromeda has been on harsh, flint-like rocks: *duris cotibus*. And the Bacchante is sleeping in *herboso...Apidano*. The Bacchic legend is mentioned last and for this reason it remains in the reader's mind: he thinks of orgies when women would abandon their houses, dance around, swing torches, dismember animals or even children, and eat them.

Into this varied background is set the *talis visa* of line 7. It has changed from being a poem very rich in mythological associations to being abruptly a poem of sensation and sight,

> talis visa mihi mollem spirare quietem
> Cynthia non certis nixa caput manibus...

The phrase – *mollem spirare quietem* – miraculously puts the reader in the picture, enabling him to see Cynthia's body, to hear her breathing and even to smell the sound. She seems to breathe forth *quies*. She embodies the softness of sleep, when the watcher is alone and watched unconscious. Do we not have something of the feeling that Marcel has when watching Albertine asleep?

> En le tenant sous mon regard, dans mes mains, j'avais cette impression de la posséder tout entière que je n'avais pas quand elle était réveillée.[1]

Propertius is violently aware of the real physical attraction of Cynthia. This is not an idealised woman he is seeing. This is Cynthia unconscious; and she is powerfully seductive. Nowhere does he tell us what she is like; nowhere do we see how she is dressed or whether she is dressed. All we visualise are parts of a female body and we can feel the extreme excitement of the male.

Now we are given the narrative details of the poet's finding Cynthia in bed: it is the dead of night, he has been to an orgy and is tottering in tipsiness,

> ebria cum multo traherem vestigia Baccho
> et quaterent sera nocte facem pueri.

Bacchus alludes to the Bacchante of lines 5–6; the *pueri* are at the same time slaves fanning torches to light their master's way home and little cupids fanning the torches of love. The whole tone is of kindling physical desire: wine increases lust and the lust doubles when the desired one is seen asleep. This becomes explicit in the next line with a *nondum etiam sensus deperditus omnes*, and the suggestion of getting closer to Cynthia,

> molliter inpresso conor adire toro

'pressing her bed just lightly as I bent over her'.

The distance of the poetic vision in the first six lines has now been cancelled, so that the reader, like the poet himself, is simply touching a lovely body. From line 13–30 the nearness of the vision is the powerful mark which succeeds so well that it makes this poem perhaps unique among Roman poems – sensuality, tenderness, pathos, self-pitying attitude, wonder and amazement and extreme sexual desire are mingled to induce a perpetual emotion, which is aesthetic and not just biographical. The

---

[1] *A la recherche du temps perdu*, Pléiade edition (Paris, 1954), vol. III, p. 70.

'sincerity' of the poet is irrelevant here: what he does is to produce a state of emotion for the reader to experience.

The two gods – Love and Liber, the Italian god of wine – are introduced as third persons interfering. But on another level, we know that in literal terms, his desire is strong and he is intoxicated. Another layer of meaning is that the intoxication by wine is transferred into sensations in his body called forth by the sight of the sleeping Cynthia. At yet another level of meaning the two Gods are *durus uterque deus* – thus taking our attention back to the first six lines of the elegy. This brings in *languida* – in the sexual sense, and *accubuit* and *fessa* – both with underlying sexual connotations. And it may be a hint at the phenomenon that, as Shakespeare put it, wine promotes the desire but takes away the performance. Thus by introducing the two gods Propertius calls on multifarious associations.[1]

At this point we have the poet trying out sensations in order to possess Cynthia physically without her knowing it,

> subiecto leviter positam temptare lacerto
> osculaque admota sumere et arma manu...
> (lines 15–16)

The words here are sensual. *Temptare* – to fondle her, but *leviter* so lightly that she will not wake up. The sensual meaning works at two different levels: literally *feeling* her, and *assailing* her – for *temptare* usually suggests brutal aggression. Similarly, *admota manu* – caressing her, and in fact distinctly erotic, perhaps – though this remains implicit – caressing the nipples of her breast; furthermore the phrase *admovere manum* can have a military sense – to lay violent hands on, to attack or assault. Proust's description of the movements of Marcel in response to the same situation is more explicit and rather less beautiful than Propertius,

> délibérément je sautais sans bruit sur le lit, je me couchais
> au long d'elle, je prenais sa taille d'un de mes bras, je posais
> mes lèvres sur sa joue et sur son coeur, puis sur toutes les
> parties de son corps posais ma seule main restée libre et qui

---

[1] For a discussion of *Amor* in Propertius see Kenneth Quinn, *Latin Explorations*, pp. 173–4.

était soulevée aussi, comme les perles, par la respiration d'Albertine.

(Pléiade ed., vol. III, p. 72)

The next two lines express the side of love uppermost in the poet's mind; the phrase *dominae turbare quietem* – two people both awake, restlessly aware of desire. This is followed by the poet's fear,

expertae metuens iurgia saevitiae.

Here the *saevitiae* suggests the true madness of love: the *odi et amo* feelings, the violence of both partners, the undying vicissitudes of human life, the almost anti-human element in a love-relationship and the completely irrational path that love makes us take. The *metuens* is the poet's fear, the fear that lovers have of each other when faced with this irresistible force. *Expertae* is Propertius being intellectually aware that this savagery is indeed love. It is a *iurgia*, a strife, the quarrel of two bodies and the altercation between the soul and body of two people, at once unified and disunified – which is love. In the context of the whole poem, this line is the first hint of irony. Propertius knows what a shrew Cynthia can be. He shows in this elegy the contrast between the exceptional moment, the subtly tender and sensual idealisation (both helped and complicated by a slight drunkenness) and the awakening. It is the beginning of the interweaving of themes like the *moment privilégié* and the reality of this love relationship – this *expertae... saevitiae*.

Then, sharply and immediately, Propertius moves from this intellectual narration to the reader – which is half-mocking – to show what a love relationship is, and we have the wonderment, bewilderment and astonishment in simply gazing at Cynthia. This is introduced via the Argus allusion,

sed sic intentis haerebam fixus ocellis,
Argus ut ignotis cornibus Inachidos.

The vision is intense: *fixus* – immovable, fixed. *Intentis... ocellis*: often Propertius calls Cynthia's eyes *ocellis* – for instance, in the first line of the first elegy – a term which is both poetic and endearing; here he calls his own eyes *ocellis*; *intentis* – attentive upon, eagerly waiting for something. Argus, also called in Greek

Panoptes 'the all-seeing one', had a hundred eyes, some of which were always awake. It is this aspect the reader must have in mind here: the vision, the looking at the strange sight of Io changed into a heifer.[1] The poet is as if he were Argus, looking at Cynthia with a hundred eyes. *Ignotis* – unknown; Cynthia, a heifer and therefore 'other', is an identity bearing no name, but who is 'toute une existence physiologique qui était devant moi, à moi' (Proust, Pléiade ed., III, p. 73). It is the purely physiological effect of Cynthia on the poet that is brought out, and the strangeness is effected by the Argus allusion. The astonishment is like a leit-motif in this section of the elegy: we shall meet it later in the words *obstupui* and *credulus*.

Time seems to have stopped. This we can see by the use of tenses in the verbs. From *haerebam*, through *solvebam, ponebamque, gaudebam, dabam* to *largibar* – all the verbs are in the imperfect. This suggests that time and again, always, he went on *doing* this. Furthermore, notice the adverbs which qualify these verbs: *et modo* is repeated – so that now he was doing this and now he was doing that. Propertius' imagination then enters as he describes removing a garland from his own brow and putting it on Cynthia's temples: it is a visual gesture but also a sensuous and intimate one. Cynthia being asleep, an aesthetic picture or tableau is created: the poet possessing her now in an artistic now in a sexual way. His forming ringlets in her hair suggests the poet's 'playing with' various features of her anatomy as if in the act of possessing her when she is awake. These two gestures are of a different quality from the caresses we have seen earlier. They are on an artistic and almost 'playful' level.

Then comes an almost laughing tone of voice as Propertius says,

> omniaque ingrato largibar munera somno,
> munera de prono saepe voluta sinu...
> (I. 3, lines 25–6)

All these things were useless *munera*; 'I was a large benefactor, and what a poor fool I was, because even these apples just rolled around and off her breast. How ungrateful sleep is, so useless

---

[1] For a full description of Juno, Io and Argus see Ovid, *Metamorphoses*, I. 601–746.

is it for me to do such loving things with an unconscious person.'
There is just one other touch of wonder,

> et quotiens raro duxti suspiria motu,
>   obstupui vano credulus auspicio...

and this section of the poem is ended.

The rest of the elegy is powerfully intellectual. Irony is the
main weapon: irony at Cynthia's words; irony towards himself.
The description of the moon is the antithesis of its natural
function in Propertius – and indeed in all Augustan poets:
instead of being the guarantee of safety for lovers, here the moon
shatters Propertius' dream world, for it is now *moritura*. Instead
of being sacred, it is a *luna sedula*.

The speech of Cynthia is arresting. All the points that are
obviously out of character with the previous presentation are
given full effect. The bitchy, hen-like wifely rights are referred
to – the other woman's *iniuria*; the *clausis...foribus* – Cynthia
laughing at the thought of the poet being shut out of a mistress'
house; the *meae...noctis* – as though she owned his time, particularly the night-time; the obvious deceptions about her
wife-like activities – for instance, the allusion to Penelope, who
is an emblem of fidelity, and to Orpheus in the single love-
relationship with Eurydice. The repetition in her mouth of
languidus...fessa...deserta... makes us now see that the first six
lines had sexual connotations. Through all Cynthia's words, an
intellectual irony acts like a lighthouse, shining back over the
first part of the poem. We know from other elegies that Cynthia
was promiscuous. We know that her sexual talent was ambiguous. From the very first elegy Love taught the poet to hate
castas...puellas and to live *nullo...consilio*. The very vocabulary
in that first elegy was ambiguous; the words *saevitiam, amens
errabat, saucius* could be applied to the poet's own feelings but
by an artistic illusion were put within Milanion's story and only
reflected indirectly on Propertius himself. The poet attempts to
domuisse puellam and says *quaerite non sani pectoris auxilia*. We see
what kind of love-relationship Propertius has with Cynthia. But
to give his mistress all the terminology of a wife is masterly; and
the reader can see the irony from the word 'tandem'. Thus he
reacts in a cerebral way to this break-up of the sensuous

dream-like world that the first half of the poem describes so beautifully.

The poem as a whole is complex: sustained by extremely intellectual principles and imbued with the joy of creation. The interweaving of themes – for example, love, fantasy world, sleep and awakening – is controlled by the poet's intellect and is calculated to stir up the emotions of the reader. It is like a dance and an incantation through linguistic formulae. Indeed, Georg Luck[1] sees the dance as characteristic of Propertius' poetic creation; 'The appeal of a ballet performance consists in the perfect co-ordination of music, movement and gesture. The choreography may be complex and difficult, but the final impression must be one of natural elegance.' This comment is suggestive of Propertius' poetry, and of Ronsard's too, where the dance, the movement, the continual to-and-fro are traits of the basic musicality that characterises all good poetry.

What in the end matters for Propertius? How is one to evaluate this elegy? Is it not the situation of man? Basically every man is alone. He knows this, but desperately tries to make a relationship with others. It can be done in dreams; it can be done in fantasy; as it was done in the first section of the elegy. But the lucid way in which Propertius has made us see that this relationship exists only in the mind of an individual is akin to the notions of Montaigne and Proust. The individual is encased in his own skin, and relationships are merely mirror-images of the individual. In very different ways, the three writers are saying the same thing. We can say with Belleau, in his comments on Ronsard's love poems, 'pren peine de lire...une elegie de Properce (Poëte sur tous les autres le plus passionné ...)' and the most intellectual too.

This analysis leads firmly into the fourth aesthetic canon that France derived from Ancient Rome. That is the *moraliste* tradition.[2] We begin by looking at Horace as a *moraliste*. The famous lines,

[1] Georg Luck, *The Latin Love Elegy* (London, 1959, 2nd ed. 1969), p. 133.
[2] By *moraliste* I mean a writer who is concerned with the nature of man. He presents us with a knowledge of the human mind, a vision of human life as it is in the universe. It does not imply 'moralising' in the ordinary sense of drawing morals or preaching sermons.

> aut prodesse volunt aut delectare poetae
> aut simul et jucunda et idonea dicere vitae
>
> (*Ars poetica*, lines 333–4)

> Poetry seeks either to instruct or to please; or is instructing
> and pleasing at the same time.

Plaire et instruire: can one see in these lines of the *Ars poetica* the start of the *moraliste* trend – a trend which was to flourish more in France than in any other Western European country? Or is Horace presenting a general doctrine applicable to all literature?

In the last chapter we analysed Ronsard's ode *Mignonne, allon voir* and concluded that its purpose was not didactic. We can now go forward from that point. Horace believed that his poetry had moral value, but this is very different from moralising, and far removed from didacticism in the strict sense of the word. He showed all the different aspects of the human condition, without necessarily teaching that this way of behaving was right and that way was wrong. Commonplaces like death are not treated so as to enlighten disciples with a systematic philosophy but to make his readers experience the fact of death with the same immediacy as we see a red daisy on a field of green. Thus for instance the *carpe diem* theme in *Odes* I. 11, is seen in the present; there is no metaphysical framework, for that is denied; man can know nothing, except how to live life and accept death when it comes.

Then there is the very famous poem in *Odes* I. 24, written to Vergil on the death of their common friend Quintilius. The first question that opens the poem is unlimitedly rhetorical,

> Quis desiderio sit pudor aut modus
> tam cari capitis?
>
> (lines 1 – 2)

how can one express the grief a friend leaves after him? it is unconceivable; it is far beyond any sign of language. What conceivable limit should there be to our grief?[1] The vicissitudes of nature are inevitable and to be accepted as such; nature

---

[1] See how Montaigne uses this rhetorical question in the essay *De l'amitié*, analysed in Chapter 7 of this book.

abides only in its illogic. In the case of death the change is inevitable and irrevocable. And so, it is

> durum; sed levius fit patientia
> quicquid corrigere est nefas.
>
> (lines 19–20)

> A hard law; but patient resignation makes it easier to suffer those ills that the gods do not permit us to put right.

We see that the emotional content is strong, but the appeal is aesthetic and not didactic. The ode is exquisitely shaped, with an alternation between the general and the personal, between the abstract and the concrete, between the mythological allusions and the down-to-earth facts. For example, following the first question, there is a formal address to the Muse,

> praecipe lugubris
> cantus, Melpomene, cui liquidam pater
> vocem cum cithara dedit.
>
> (lines 2–4)

> Teach me songs of grief, Melpomene, you who have been given by your father a limpid voice and a lyre...

This is immediately followed by a strong emotional statement of fact,

> ergo Quintilium perpetuus sopor
> urget!
>
> (lines 5–6)

> Thus the everlasting sleep weighs on Quintilius.

The words *ergo* and *urget* and the exclamation stress the emotion. Similarly after the lines concerning Quintilius' honour and good faith and so on there is this line

> nulli flebilior quam tibi, Vergili.
>
> (line 10)

The very placing of the *heu* in the next line, not at the beginning but after *tu frustra pius*, is significant, because the emotional and rhetorical effects are diminished and the artistic impact is strengthened. The very emphatic *durum* in the last line but one is part of the artistic handling of the thought that resignation is needed, not an excess of grief. The ode does have moral value:

it is a clear look at the human condition, without illusion and without theoretical pre-assumption. But it is not didactic.[1]

In Horace's case all the seeming 'didacticism' was simply read into the poetry by later ages for whom this was the way to read all poetry. Scholars take such lines as,

> omne tulit punctum qui miscuit utile dulci,
> lectorem delectando pariterque monendo
> (*Ars poetica*, lines 343–4)

> He has gained full marks who has mingled profit with pleasure by at once delighting the reader and instructing him.

to prove that he was didactic. But it is important to realise that Horace counsels not simply a 'return to nature' but rather an acceptance of the human condition; that his *nil admirari* ('wonder/be surprised at nothing') is a phrase which accommodates him (and by implication every man) to the vicissitudes of life; that he teaches others only indirectly, by practising self-examination; that he achieves a kind of self-regulation which suggests not an evasion of responsibility but a higher kind of responsibility, to life itself as lived in and through the present.

I have taken Horace as the chief poet of the Roman *moraliste* tradition mainly because he above all other poets was given the tag of didacticism. It would have been easier, of course, to point to Vergil, whose *Eclogues* were interpreted allegorically from a few years after his death and were so read throughout the Middle Ages right up to the Renaissance. Similarly Ovid, whose works were moralised and reformulated in the Middle Ages and the moralisations and works went through several editions during the sixteenth century.[2] The allegorical interpretation of every Roman poet in the Middle Ages is well attested. But the Renaissance saw a dramatic volte-face: the pagan universe of Rome starts to be established in its own right and the divorce

---

[1] This theme of the law of transience applied to nature and man is a particularly Roman one and is passed over to France in the sixteenth century. Even Cicero stresses the willing submission to the pattern of nature. For example, in *de Senectute*, 5, he says, 'sed tamen necesse fuit esse aliquid extremum et, tamquam in arborum bacis terraeque fructibus, maturitate tempestiva quasi vietum et caducum, quod ferendum est molliter sapienti.' The death of youth is violent and unnatural; the death of old age is in complete accord with the laws of nature.

[2] See *Ovide moralisé*, ed. C. De Boer, in *Verhandelingen der Koninklijke Akademie van Wetenschappen te Amsterdam*, 15.

between religion and literature begins. With this came the *moraliste* tradition – through the Roman poets.[1]

And fifthly, the *vulgaire* is not the audience of the writer. French writers took over from Rome the notion that a writer rejected the *vulgus* – the 'fickle multitude' – as an audience. Let only a handful of learned and civilised friends approve of one's work. Horace, for instance in *Odes* II. 16, 37–40 says,

> mihi parva rura et
> spiritum Graiae tenuem Camenae
> Parca non mendax dedit et malignum
> spernere vulgus.

> for myself I have only a poor little country property and the gentle breath of the Greek Muse; these are the gifts of honest Fate which at the same time teaches me to disdain the spiteful crowd.

His *spiritum...tenuem* is too fine for public consumption. Now the word *tenuis* is a literary cult word: for example in Vergil's *Eclogues* it occurs in the first two lines of the first eclogue,

> Tityre, tu patulae recubans sub tegmine fagi
> siluestrem tenui Musam meditaris auena...

and in VI. 8 it occurs again. Robert Coleman in his recent edition of the *Eclogues* (Cambridge, 1977, pp. 176–7) says: 'The metaphor is commonly used of literary style...As a term of approval the adjective connotes the polish and refinement of neoteric personal poetry in the *genera tenuia* of elegy and lyric.' It is part of Vergil's *recusatio* of epic themes and it is similarly used by Horace.[2] Horace wants his poetry to stand the scrutiny of a few chosen friends. Behind this lies the conviction that the awareness of the public can never be adequate to the peculiar quality of his own experience. A good writer must be content with few readers. But they must be the right readers: as Horace says, they must be '*doctos...et amicos*' (*Sat.* I. 10. 87).

---

[1] See the different opinion about the sixteenth-century attitude to antiquity in Donald Stone's article, 'The Sixteenth century and antiquity: a case study', in *The French Renaissance Mind, Studies presented to W. G. Moore*, edited by Barbara C. Bowen, *L'Esprit Créateur*, vol. XVI, No. 4. Winter 1976.

[2] We shall see, in a later chapter, Montaigne's use of *recusatio* in his preface to the *Essais*.

If we are to understand the aristocratic characteristic of French poetry from the Pléiade onwards – a characteristic that no-one denies – then we must see that the rejection of the *malignum vulgus* was one of the first things that ancient poets established as an essential part of their poetic tradition. Furthermore, the whole concept of the *vates*, the divinely inspired prophet–poet – prominent in the first century B.C. – suggests that poets thought that poetry had a special dignity and seriousness of purpose. Their main audience, at base, was composed of people with taste, a feeling for the human condition, and stylistic and aesthetic awareness, all of which corresponded to the poet's own. Readers would be as civilised as writers. This may be seen as a very narrow range of appeal, but one must remember that the lettered public was until the nineteenth century a minute portion of the population in any Western European country (it still is, for that matter, if we are talking about a public for poetry).

Nowadays post-Romantic assumptions about poetry condition our thinking about Roman and French Renaissance poetry. Twentieth-century readers expect the poet to reveal his own experiences, thereby discovering for them new and complex ranges of feeling. There is an intense interest in the processes of the mind, in human feelings and human sensations. We like to see a poem about 'a man having thoughts more than a poem about the thoughts a man had'. So that when the poet is speaking about the thoughts he has, we assume that he is really speaking about himself in the process of having them. As a result any writer who *seems* to be analysing the turns and twists, the complexities and contradictions in his own make-up has a sympathetic hearing. On the contrary, there is very little sympathy for a writer who *states*. He must discover. Poetry, according to this view, deals with problems: not so much resolving them as expounding them, 'working them out' via poetry. Poetry is conceived as an exploration, a discovery, and the result is that the audience is the least important element of the triangle – poem, poet, audience.

Poetry is largely a matter of myth and symbol; and since it is almost impossible to develop one's own language and still be understood, it follows that communication and intelligibility depend largely on the assumptions shared by poet and reader. And it is precisely this heritage – in Rome in the first century – that was shared by so few. Thus there is no surprise that great poets spurned the *vulgaire* – the unlettered ninety-nine per cent of the population, and counted instead on a few chosen and civilised friends as their audience and as their critics.

The concept of the *vates*, which corresponds to the 'divine fury' of the Pléiade, meant that inspiration was posited as giving peculiar weight to the words of the poet. In this concept where was the theory of the Muses which every Roman poet exploited? It can be seen even in the Epicurian Lucretius, 1. 926–7 as well as in Vergil, *Georgics*, 3. 10–12 and in Propertius, 3. 1. 17–18 a generation later – they all employ the visit to Helicon to announce that they were the first Latin writers to attempt their specific genres. But it can best be seen once again in the ode of Horace (III. 1, 1–4) where he warns the reader of the public role he adopts in writing the odes,

> Odi profanum vulgus et arceo;
> favete linguis: carmina non prius
>   audita Musarum sacerdos
>   virginibus puerisque canto.

> I despise the profane mob and I keep them at a distance; speak no ill-omened words; I, priest of the Muses, sing to boys and girls songs never heard before.

Horace hates the profane populace, i.e the uninitiated, the majority audience again, and keeps them at a distance; he is going to sing songs for the innocent boys and girls who have never heard such songs before, and therefore need to be instructed, initiated. Vergil in his *Eclogues*, *Georgics* and *Aeneid* – though with a different tone in the three genres – shows the same attitude and his position is again that of a *vates*. And similarly – though he has a slightly different attitude to the *vates* – Tibullus shares this view of the *vulgus*. (For a more detailed analysis see the two books by Gordon Williams mentioned in the last chapter.)

This opposition of *vulgus* and *vates* is crucial in Rome. For it opens the way for poets to write political poems as well as the semi-chatty *Epistles* or *Satires* of Horace or the love elegies of Propertius, and to make heard the new voice of Italy in Vergil's *Georgics* and *Eclogues*. There is a passage in a letter addressed by Horace to Augustus (*Epistles*, II. 1, 124–33) which shows the position of the poet in society extremely well:

> Militiae quanquam piger et malus, utilis urbi,
> si das hoc, parvis quoque rebus magna juvari.
> os tenerum pueri balbumque poeta figurat,
> torquet ab obscoenis jam nunc sermonibus aurem,
> mox etiam pectus praeceptis format amicis,
> asperitatis et invidiae corrector et irae;
> recte facta refert; orientia tempora notis
> instruit exemplis; inopem solatur et aegrum.
> castis cum pueris ignara puella mariti
> disceret unde preces, vatem ni Musa dedisset?

> Though he may only be a half-hearted and bad soldier he is useful to his city, that is if you grant that great activities are helped by small ones. A child's tender stammering of speech is shaped by poets; even at that early stage they direct his ear from language that is unseemly and subsequently have a formative influence on his sensibilities by their kindly precepts, correcting faults of harshness, envy and anger. The poet tells of upright deeds and trains the earliest years by employing well known models; he comforts the under-privileged and the sick. Where would innocent boys and unmarried girls together learn how to pray to the gods, if the Muse had not given them an inspired bard?

This passage conveys the feeling that a great poet is needed by society to sing of men's actions and magnify the importance of their works, not only in war or valiant deeds, but in every aspect of living. The child, the boy, the unmarried girl – all look to the bard, it is he who shapes communication and attitudes. The bard, then, is proud of his calling, proud of his profession.

We have summarised in this chapter five distinct concepts: five Roman aesthetic values which are crucial to our under-standing of French Renaissance literature. It was by creatively devouring Roman literature that the urge and excitement to compose poetry was born in France. These concepts can be seen as five columns which stand supporting the structure of French literature from the Renaissance to the twentieth century.

4

The establishment of the grand style in poetry

'For what is rhetoric', Yeats asked, 'but the will trying to do the work of the imagination?' But, as we have seen in earlier chapters, this view of rhetoric is misconceived, partly no doubt because Yeats stands in the English tradition of poetry which is slightly different from the French. Yet many twentieth-century readers would perhaps agree with him and imply that imagination entered poetry in the eighteenth century. Our sense of the imaginative element in Renaissance thinking and writing is blurred. Indeed we have for a long time almost refused to see that all good poetry must rely heavily on imagination as its inspirer. For in whatever age, in whatever country, in whatever terminology, the creative process opposes rationalism – be it that of Aristotle or Plato. To quote Professor Cocking in his very interesting essay on imagination:

> But imagination came into the foreground of men's thinking about art, and particularly about literature, at the time of the Renaissance. It existed in happy ambiguity with imitation in the Renaissance notion of invention. The subsequent competition between imitation and imagination seems to be related to the competition between reason and imagination, or between the reason of rationalism and the reason of noûs.[1]

And later on he remarks that 'Imagination depends on culture; it is not simply native, even in the poet'.[2] This is crucial when we consider the Roman tradition in sixteenth-century France. For we must posit the rule that Vergil, Propertius, Horace and

[1] 'Imagination as Order and as Adventure' in *Essays presented to C. A. Hackett*. Edited by E. M. Beaumont, J. M. Cocking and J. Cruickshank (Oxford, 1973), pp. 257–69.
[2] Ibid. p. 261.

53

so on were obviously using their imagination in creating poetry. They may not have called it 'imagination' but

> While they [i.e. the Ancient writers] affirmed that his [i.e. man's] arts are the products of naturally given faculties, imitate natural processes, use natural material, and assist natural evolutionary tendencies, they recognised a point where the conditioning influence of nature ends (both within and outside human beings) with man's free and rational creative power coming into play.[1]

Horace's odes are virtually a biography of his imagination. The most important fact of Horace's life is his poetry, and we must see as secondary – as product or material – the 'philosophy', the urban conviviality and the worldly career of Horace; for the poet was a historian of his imaginative consciousness and not of anything else we can attribute to him.[2] We accept his lines,

> mediocribus esse poetis
> non homines, non di, non concessere columnae.
> (*Ars poetica*, lines 372–3)

> Neither God nor men nor the pillars of the peristyle have ever allowed poets to be mediocre.

Mediocrity is allowed in things which are necessary to life, but it is not allowed in things which are produced only to give pleasure. No-one should write poetry without the requisite skill. The inspired poet is separated from the vulgar throng to whom the world of the imagination is unknown and he is only so when the Muses are favourable to his call.

This is setting poetry's case very high.[3] So high that Mon-

---

[1] A. J. Close, 'Art and Nature in Antiquity and the Renaissance' in *Journal of the History of Ideas*, xxx, no. 4, 1969, p. 483.

[2] It is true of his criticism also. Commager *The Odes of Horace* (New Haven, Conn., 1962), p. 48 says 'Informing his criticism is a concern with the physical act of writing rather than with any metaphysical concept of literature, a perception into means rather than a vision of ends.'

[3] Grahame Castor in his *Pléiade Poetics* (Cambridge, 1964), pp. 54–5 sees Horace's concept of imitation as the false mimesis and views it as a 'trivialisation' of the true Aristotelian mimesis. But so far as poets in the sixteenth century were concerned they would not have agreed with the taking of literary mimesis as a thing so trivial and worthless. And in any case would have quarrelled with Castor's remark (p. 67) about 'Imitation of this sort, whose aim was to achieve as nearly as possible identity with the author imitated...' Du Bellay would have pointed out that the words tradition and imitation for him really meant assimilation.

taigne, after experimenting in writing Latin verses, saw lucidly that he would be a mediocre poet and stopped writing verse. Horace's lines force us to recognise that his art is supreme: ironic, witty, serious and conversationally stylised. Later in the *Ars poetica* he speaks on a very strong, passionate note saying, as near as may be: 'Hide away your manuscript for nine years; break it up; destroy it; but once you have published it you have no longer any force against or for your work.' Any attempt at 'putting down' experiences is 'true' in the sense that they accurately represent the author's reaction to experience.

Now Marcel Raymond in his anthology of sixteenth-century poetry called *La Poésie française et le Maniérisme* (London, 1971) argues that the concept of mannerism introduces in French poetry a notion of style and a consciousness of the fundamental ambiguity of fiction. He takes Ronsard as an example and asks whether the truth or verisimilitude of his poetry made it valid. He quotes two statements: the first from a sonnet to Cassandre,

> Je ne crois plus tant d'amours que les vieux
> Chantent de Toi: ce n'est que poésie.

And the second from *Discours en forme d'elégie*,

> O beau visage feint
> ...ton faux m'est gracieux...

He concludes: 'Le mensonge peut donc être le lieu de la beauté, de la grâce. Ou je me trompe, ou nous assistons à la formation d'une "catégorie" de l'esprit qui est celle de l'esthétique.' (p. 24) I am not convinced that this category comes about as a consequence of the *maniera/mannerism* of the visual artists. Indeed I think that parallels between the fine arts and literature have a very transitory value: see how Marcel Raymond's earlier book on Ronsard, *Baroque et Renaissance Poétique* (Paris, 1955) has given way this time to a term like *Maniérisme*.[1] I think however that the critic has touched on a very important change: the concept of aesthetics and of style at the time of the Pléiade. My hypothesis – and it implies a more remote effect than that of

---

[1] Fashions change rapidly in twentieth-century literary criticism: in the 1950s the thing to look for in Renaissance literature was the baroque; in the 1960s and 1970s it is mannerism.

mannerism – is that to a large extent one can find in Roman literary tradition the elements that explain and elaborate this concept.

There are traces of it earlier than Marcel Raymond demonstrates. For instance, there is Marot. Thanks to Professor Mayer's enormous work in producing a critical edition we now have a clearer picture of Marot's position. We can understand his hesitation over the genres of poetry: for example, many of the *epigrammes* were already written and published before they were, in 1538, put in a category called *epigrammes*. There was his determination to recreate Graeco-Latin genres such as the elegy or the epithalamion and his clear awareness of the Roman/Italian tradition in love poetry – all these points are important in his experimental renovation and reformation of poetry.

Marot constantly lets us see his own consciousness of style in the *Epitres*. For instance, he is aware that they are not written in a high, heroic style: in xv he uses the simile of a bell to bring out this point,

> car petite Clochette
> A beau branler, avant que ung hault son jecte,
> Puis qu'il n'a donc que humble & basse value,
> Par ung bas stile humblement vous salue.[1]

Or he tells a lady what type of thing he would have written in the grand manner if he had had more time on his hands (xvi). Or the very fine parody of a grand style that he composes at the end of the epistle addressed to the King (xxv),

> mon stile j'enfleray,
> Disant: O Roy amoureux des neufz Muses,
> Roy en qui sont leurs sciences infuses,
> Roy plus que Mars d'honneur environné,
> Roy le plus Roy qui fut oncq couronné,
> Dieu tout puissant te doint (pour t'estrener)
> Les quatre Coings du Monde gouverner,
> Tant pour le bien de la ronde Machine,
> Que pour aultant que sur tous en es digne.

[1] *Les Epitres*, ed. C. A. Mayer, (London, 1958). All quotations are from this edition.

This is also a parody of bombastic flattering letters written to the King by other versifiers. The fact that Marot knew exactly the style and could use it wittily is significant. The letter to the King written from exile at Ferrara is, as Mayer has pointed out, thick with passages imitated from Ovid's *Tristia*, another work dependent on exile. For instance,

> O que je n'ay le cheval Pegasus,
> Plus hault volant que le mont Pernasus
> Ou les dragons avec lesquelz Medée
> Est de la tour de Corinthe evadée.
> De Dedalus ou Perseus les esles
> Vouldroys avoir, il ne m'en chault lesquelles!

The last phrase is Marot's humorous aside on the very style he has just been using. The King alone can choose to give him inspiration so that he will write in a different way; a month before he was exiled he was on the point of writing to the King for 'ung lieu plaisant et coy':

> Ma nef legiere osoit bien presumer
> De faire voille en ceste haulte mer.

These lines are almost translating Horace, *Odes*, iii. 29.

> tunc me biremis praesidio scaphae
>   tutum per Aegaeos tumultus
>   aura feret geminusque Pollux.
>   (lines 61–3)

> Then my little two-oared boat will be sufficient, and I shall sail over the waves of the Aegean sea, blown by the breeze and guided by the stars of the Divine Twins.

Horace takes 'the tiny skiff sailing on the tumultuous sea' as one of his leit-motifs: and it is a stylistic one. The fact that he is humble, honest and free in writing poetry is his way of saying that he does not want to be a war poet, nor an epic poet. What he is doing is 'low'. Marot is saying the same. And in his last *epitre* to Monsieur d'Anguyen he promises to write heroic poetry,

> S'ainsi advient, sortez de ma pensée
> Tristes ennuictz qui m'avez fait escrire
> Vers douloureux. Arriere ceste lire

Dont je chantois Venus mettre en avant,
Ne de Flageol soner chant Bucolique,
Ains soneray la Trompete bellique
D'un grand Virgile ou d'Homere ancien:
Pour celebrer les hautz faictz d'Anguyen,
Lequel sera (contre Fortune amere)
Nostre Achiles, & Marot son Homere.

A recent book on Clement Marot by P. M. Smith, *Clément Marot. Poet of the Renaissance* (London, 1970), gives detailed discussions of his variety of genre and style. Yet in the 'Conclusion on Marot and the Pléiade' no mention is made to Marot's awareness of the possibility of the grand style as given in the epistles.

But the best example of a person who was aware of the concept of style before the Pléiade is, of course, Scève. In Chapter 3 of my book on him (*Maurice Scève*, Cambridge, 1975) I tried to clarify what the phrase *durs Epygrammes* in the preliminary huitain to *Délie* really meant. The word *durs* derives from Roman literary tradition. Briefly it entailed three different things. First, it is a rhetorical term opposed to *enervis* and *effeminatus* and related to *asper*. The style of a writer could be held to be *durus*. Secondly, it is a term denoting a genre, opposed to *teneri versus* or *teneri modi*. It is the opposite of elegiac verses and metres specially devoted to love. Catullus and Propertius are writing *teneri modi*. Lastly, it suggested the seriousness of the writer of the high style. Now I can add more to that argument. As it was in Roman practical criticism that the term *durus* was used, we see the *mollis/durus* juxtaposition in literary works. Furthermore *mollis* is not only opposed to *durus* but also to *fortis* or *gravis*.[1] Poets such as Ovid (*Tristia*, 2. 307) call an elegiac or amatory poem *mollis versus* and Propertius alleges his unfitness 'in heroic verse' (*duro versu*). Not only is this juxtaposition – the *mollis/durus* one – common, but there are others such as Horace's double adjective phrase – *molle et facetum* – applied in this case to the bucolic poetry of Vergil to denote a quality of *compositio*, the euphonious or rhythmical collocation of words. *Dulcis* is

---

[1] *mollis* is associated with *perlucens* 'translucent', *tener* and *flexibilis* 'supple' (e.g. Cicero, *Brutus*, 274) and contrasted with *durus, fortis; facetus* associated with *elegans* (ibid. 292) and *urbanus* (Cicero, *de Or*, 1. 159), contrasted with *gravis, severus*.

applied to oratory and orators: for example, Quintilian, x. 1. 77,

> Dulcis in primis et acutus Hyperides...

where the meaning is that he was eminently pleasable, or xii. 10.44,

> et loquendo dulcis magis.

Gravis means weighty, important, grave, with the dignity of authority: thus for Cicero in *Brutus*, 95. 325, one of the Attic styles is 'sententiosum et argutum, sententiis non tam gravibus et severis...' and so the antithesis *douce gravité*, or the two nouns *douceur* and *gravité* – which were to be used evaluatively by all critics of poetry in sixteenth-century France – are implicit in this juxtaposition. This also comes out in the Italian tradition of Petrarch: for instance, Petrarch in *Rime*, 125 (ed. Carducci, Florence, 1957) states that because of the nature of his passion he cannot always write *dolci rime*,

> Però ch'Amor mi sforza
> E di saver mi spoglia,
> Parlo in rim' aspre e di dolcezza ignude.

The contrast is between *dolce* and *aspre*, and in his poetry there are some *gravi* and some *dolcissimi versi*.[1] But whether this evaluative juxtaposition came straight from Rome or through Petrarch to France is, I think, unclear at this moment. My hypothesis is that the notion came from Ancient Rome and modern Italy.

The *gravité* is seen almost without the *douceur* in Scève. His poetry was evaluated by Charles Fontaine within a year of *Délie*'s publication. In an epigram he picks out the qualities of Scève,

---

[1] Dante too and Boccaccio are involved with this. A sixteenth-century commentator has a delightfully unknowing attitude as to where this connexion is hidden. He implies the opposite: 'Dante, il Petrarca, il Boccaccio... hanno ne' gravi et dolcissimi versi et orationi loro mostro assai chiaramente, con molta facilità potersi in questa lingua esprimere ogni senso... Chi negherà nel Petrarca trovarsi uno stile grave, lepido et dolce et queste cose amorose con tanta gravità et venustà trattate, quante senza dubbio non si trova in Ovidio, in Tibullo, in Catullo, in Propertio, o in alcun'altro Latino.' (Lorenzo de Medici, *Commento sopra alcuni de'suoi sonnetti*, ed. Venice, 1554, fol. 119 ro). Evaluative terms such as *dolcezza, facilità, gravità* and *venustà* are all terms from the Roman poets and critics.

Tes vers sont beaux, & bien luysants,
Graves, & pleins de majesté:
Mais pour leur haulteur moins plaisants,
Car certes la difficulté
Le grand plaisir en a osté.
Brief, ilz ne quierent un Lecteur,
Mais la commune autorité
Dit qu'ilz requierent un Docteur.

(La Fontaine d'amour,
contenant Elegies, Epistres & Epigrammes, Paris, 1545, miiij vo)

Graves, majesté, beaux and *bien luysants* are all elements of the *haulteur* of Scève's style. Charles Fontaine does not find the verses *doux*. And perhaps his evaluation fits at least a large minority of the dizains. But we can say that Scève chose to characterize his genre by implying that it was a tough, heroic and harsh style. Propertius alleges his unfitness for heroic verse by using the terms *duro versu*, but Scève alleges the opposite in the terms *durs Epygrammes*. Scève was indeed the first French poet to be aware of the aesthetic Roman concept of a grand style, a heroic style, and unlike Marot, to use it. Marot was obviously conducting his poetry from a wide public platform, an experimental platform. And like Scève he is in a position that is pre-Pléiade in theoretical terms; they were both writing before the (real) beginning of vernacular criticism of poetry.

Since the dramatic upheaval of French Renaissance poetry criticism – an upheaval which started with Alan Boase's article 'Then Malherbe came' published in *The Criterion* (x, 1930–1, pp. 287–306) – which has concentrated on the 'difficult', 'committed', 'serious' aspects of poetry it is, I suppose, inevitable that Marot, for whom the traditional epithets had been 'naïf', 'witty' and 'élégant badinage', was damned. And like Scève, his break with the *Grands Rhétoriqueurs* is unsung by the Pléiade who take for themselves the golden mantle of poetry and claim that they are the only poets that France has had. The first-rate poets in France – and this includes Marot, Scève and Louise Labé, each one outside the Pléiade clique (Marot by chronology, the other two by being Lyonnais) – were not thinking in terms which were primarily metaphysical; they were pragmatists in the theory of criticism. They knew perfectly well what they were trying to do: to re-graft the tradition of Graeco-Roman culture on to the tree of French poetry. The tradition they were grasping towards was neither Platonic nor Aristotelian. It was literary. The first attempts at reform or criticism are bound to be concerned with technical details rather than with general principles.

Now the Pléiade's mesmerised worship of the Ancient civilisation is so well-known that it needs no comment, but the enormous ramifications of this awe have yet to be traced either through the smallest or the largest details of their linguistic and literary theory. The oft-asserted statements about the necessity for a poetic style 'éloingné du vulgaire' (Du Bellay) or that 'le style prosaïque est ennemi capital de l'éloquence' (Ronsard) will stand closer analysis, for they are embedded in particular contexts and are tied to particular literary problems.

We start with Du Bellay's comment on Marot in the *Deffence*:

> Marot me plaist (dit quelqu'un) pour ce qu'il est facile, & ne s'éloingne point de la commune maniere de parler... Quand à moy, telle superstition ne m'a point retiré de mon entreprinse, pour ce que j'ay tousjours estimé nostre poësie Françoise estre capable de quelque plus hault & meilleur style que celuy dont nous sommes si longuement contentez.
>
> (ed. Chamard, Paris, 1961, p. 91)

Du Bellay is not condemning Marot for writing in multifarious genres but condemning him for writing nothing else. Marot was aware of the 'grand style'. He was the founder of the French epigram in that he was really the first to write them. He had, no doubt, the classical model – for example Martial – in mind. He was copied, in a very different tone however, by Scève who used the form and the term of *Epygrammes* for his dizains. Marot was the first writer to introduce Martial to the French public. And he was the first to be aware of styles.[1] But he had not,

---

[1] Of course, the *grands rhétoriqueurs* had been aware of different styles, and indeed the whole of the Middle Ages had commented on Cicero and his followers. But it was only in the decades from 1520 onwards that the desire to have *un plus hault style* was strong. It could be argued that the *grands rhétoriqueurs* did have a desire to develop *un plus hault style* but went about the job in an idiosyncratic fashion. It was not ambition they lacked but literary insight. Furthermore, the idea of a noble, lofty style is something that underlies the provençal poets like Rambaut d'Orange and Arnaut Daniel with the opposition of *clus trobar* and *leu chanso*. See the article by S. C. Aston,

fundamentally, altered the tone of French poetry. It is only now that we can see how he had experimented with the Roman tradition – and that was implicit, that is, without writing an *art poétique* or singing in his poetry of his efforts at assimilating Roman tradition. He is condemned by Du Bellay for his *facilité*. But we can – more fairly and perhaps more convincingly – say that the characteristics of his poetry are the *douceur*, the *dolci rime* and the *élégant badinage*. Left out is the *gravité* of Scève.

Scève had changed the tone of French poetry. Not only in the seriousness of the task of composing love poetry in 'heroic verse' – *durs Epygrammes* – but also in a number of different ways. In the first French *canzoniere* he had introduced allusiveness of language to the French public. Through contextual linguistic formulae he *created* love within the poems themselves. The intensity and complexity of the human experience of love is brought out by the allusiveness, by intellectual vigour, by tautness and the juxtaposition of words, by voluptuous images and by exploiting the European tradition of love poetry. But Scève did not altogether succeed in these *durs Epygrammes*: there is an over-complication in structure in many dizains (e.g. 448), a heaviness in the syntax, a certain schematic abstraction, and a tendency toward materialisation of metaphor, as in 'L'humidité, Hydraule de mes yeulx' in dizain 331. Furthermore his whole *préciosité* – his attachment to a social world that he shared with Marot – is important.[1] Professor Odette de Mourgues in her *Metaphysical, Baroque and Précieux Poetry* (Oxford, 1953, p. 26) writes that: 'The Pléiade brought forth a new kind of poetry, the aesthetics of which were incompatible with the tenets of Scèvian "metaphysical" poetry.' This seems to me to be true only for a minority of dizains in *Délie*. When we consider the whole cycle of love poems I think we can see more clearly how Scève and Marot are closer to each other than is often thought. If we forget, for the moment, the 'metaphysical' element in

'The Troubadours and the concept of style' in *Stil- und Formprobleme in der Literatur. Vorträge des VII. Kongresses der Internationalen Vereinigung für moderne Sprachen und Literaturen in Heidelberg* (Heidelberg, 1959), p. 142–7, and the book by Roger Dragonetti, *La Technique poétique des trouvères dans la chanson courtoise. Contribution à l'étude de la rhétorique médiévale* (Bruges, 1960).

[1] See D. G. Coleman, *Maurice Scève* (Cambridge, 1975), Chs 4 and 5 for a fuller discussion of précieux elements in *Délie*.

Scève, we can view the *gravité* and the *durus* quality of his verse alongside the *facilité* and *douceur* of Marot's verse, and can conclude that neither had in fact put the *douce gravité* into poetry. It remains implicit, and it is not until the coming of the Pléiade that the antithesis entered into the criticism of poetry, becoming explicit in the *Deffence*.

Du Bellay puts forward the case for the development of French language and literature on the assumption that French is naked and this is a cause of weakness not of strength; a sign of poverty not of elegant simplicity. Whether this was the case or not is irrelevant; what is relevant is that his whole view of his native tongue is coloured by the Romans' view of their language *vis à vis* Greek. Quintilian, for instance, was acutely aware of the limitations of Latin as compared to Greek, and he insisted on the need to use all the resources of the language to show it at its best advantage. Latin, according to him, could not afford to aim at simplicity or bareness of style,

> Sensus sublimes variique eruantur: permovendi omnes ad-fectus erunt, oratio translationum nitore inluminanda. Non possumus esse tam graciles, simus fortiores: subtilitate vin-cimur, valeamus pondere: proprietas penes illos est certior, copia vincamus. (XII. 10. 36)

> We must discover sentiments full of loftiness and variety, must stir all the emotions and illuminate our style by brilliance of metaphor. Since we cannot be so delicate, let us be stronger ...that grace of language, which our words cannot provide, must be secured by the admixture of foreign ingredients.

In order to rival Greek, Latin had to use ornament, since it did not possess the innate charm of Greek:

> verborum gratia, quam in ipsis non habemus, extrinsecus condienda est. (ibid.)

Since the French theorists and practitioners of poetry and prose in the sixteenth century have a similar inferiority complex vis à vis Italian as well as vis à vis Latin and Greek, this theory seems an appropriate principle for their times. The loss of *subtilitas* will be compensated by *pondus* and *copia*: hence the rather *simpliste* (to twentieth-century eyes) assumption that the more words a language possesses, the richer will be its powers of expression.[1] The equation of strength with quantity is partly accounted for by the heavy reliance on Cicero and Quintilian, and partly by the very clear-sighted sense that French had not been stretched at all – yet.

It is no secret that Cicero and Quintilian reserved their most enthusiastic praise for the grand style in oratory. Thus Cicero (*Orator*. XXI. 69), listing the traditional three aims of the orator and the three different styles to which he has access, says

> Sed quot officia oratoris, tot sunt genera dicendi: subtile in probando, modicum in delectando, vehemens in flectendo; in quo uno vis omnis oratoris est.

> For these three functions of the orator there are three styles, the plain style for proof, the middle style for pleasure, the vigorous style for persuasion; and in this last is summed up the entire virtue of the orator.

The distinction between the plain and the grand style is not as far removed from Mallarmé's and Valéry's attempts at theorising about poetic language as one might think. Thus the main object of a plain style was thought to be a practical one – that of communicating something specific to the reader or listener, while the main object of the grand style was aesthetic.

How closely did Du Bellay's terms of praise and blame, admiration and disapproval of style correspond to Cicero's terminology in particular, but also to Quintilian's? Apart from the occasional respect paid to a 'perfect' simple style the Romans' ecstatic wonder goes always to the first-rate manipulators of the grand style. Thus Cicero in his *Orator* v. 20. says,

> cum ampla et sententiarum gravitate et maiestate verborum, vehementes, varii, copiosi, graves, ad permovendos et convertendos animos instructi...

> [The orators of the grand style] showed splendid power of thought and majesty of diction; they were forceful, versatile, copious and grave, trained and equipped to arouse and sway the emotions.

---

[1] *subtilitas*, as glossed in Peterson's edition of Quintilian, Book XII means a plain style. The metaphor taken from textiles refers primarily to its dialectical quality rather than to its simplicity. *Copia* – the great literary concept which we shall return to later.

It is perfectly clear at the end of the *Deffence* that Du Bellay aligns himself with Cicero – his *sole* ecstatic idea of a poet corresponds exactly to the sublimity of the grand style in oratory,

> saiches, Lecteur, que celuy sera veritablement le poëte que je cherche en nostre Langue qui me fera indigner, apayser, ejouyr, douloir, aymer, hayr, admirer, etonner, bref, qui tiendra la bride de mes affections, me tournant ça & la à son plaisir. Voyla la vraye pierre de touche, ou il fault que tu epreuves – en tous poëmes, & en toutes langues.
>
> (ed. Chamard Paris 1961, pp. 179–80)

Chamard in his edition of the *Deffence* refers to Cicero, *De Oratore*, I. 8. 30 and XII. 5. 3, to his *Brutus*, L. 188 and to his *Orator*, XXXVIII. 131, but he does not seem to have grasped the implications of this – that is, the clear correspondence between Cicero's comments on the grand style and Du Bellay's ideal poet.

Ideas, emotional appeal, metaphors, forcefulness, the flood of language – all the qualities of the grand style will display Latin and French at their best. Terms of appraisal in the *Deffence* are, of course, linked closely to Cicero and Quintilian. Thus, for example, p. 22 *copieuse/riche*; p. 33 *cete copie* and *richesse d'invention* and

> l'office doncques de l'orateur est de chacune chose proposée elegamment & copieusement parler.

Now all criticism pre-supposes a certain degree of culture – whether it be a mere groping around among a few ideas or the grasping of a fully-fledged civilisation; it pre-supposes also a certain advance in self-consciousness and above all a standard of comparison. And it is this last quality that the poets of the Pléiade valued above all. So that when we read their theories after having read their poetry we realise that the basic elements in their aesthetics came from Ancient Rome.

Take as an example a poet talking of his epic, and note how everything he says corresponds to the concept of *un style élevé*. Ronsard in several prefaces to his *Franciade* takes up the question of manipulating alexandrines so that they do not *raser la prose*. In the 1587 preface he says,

> Au reste, ils ont trop de caquet, s'ils ne sont bastis de la main
> d'un bon artisan, qui les face autant qu'il luy sera possible
> hausser, comme les peintures relevées...
> (Ronsard, *L'art poétique, Cinq préfaces*, Cambridge, 1930, p. 41)

Already one has the sense of something which is *relevée* as in
painting and epic poetry. He goes on to say 'et quasi separer
du langage commun'. The separation of literary prose or poetry
from prosaic discourse underlies this statement and, as usually
happens, the phrase was to be torn out of its context and used
for any type of poem, any type of literary prose. It originally
had a precise context: epic poetry. But then Ronsard goes on
to say,

> les ornant et enrichissant de Figures, Schemes, Tropes,
> Metaphores, Phrases et periphrases eslongnées presque du
> tout, ou pour le moins separées de la prose triviale et
> vulgaire...

By this time Ronsard has shifted his position slightly; the first
part of the statement was specifically speaking about epic. It
seems that the conclusion is saying that all poetry is to be
removed from the triviality and the vulgarity of prosaic prose.
Horace's *malignum vulgus* is felt just below the surface. For the
next comment – in parenthesis – is

> (car le style prosaïque est ennemi capital de l'eloquence
> poëtique)...

And this sentence is a crucial one for French poetry. Implicitly
French poets will always bear it in mind, so that Valéry's
remarks on language, style and poetry are to all intents
sophisticated re-workings of this essential sentence in the Renaissance. And the concept of *copia* almost covers the concept of
a grand style. It is easy to prove this by comparing the *Deffence*,
Ronsard's *Art poétique* and Peletier's *Art poétique*, and seeing the
link with Cicero and Quintilian and – more importantly – with
Horace and Vergil.

Much work has been done on *copia* in the sixteenth-century
and I am assuming that this is known.[1] The most influential

---

[1] Lee Ann Sonnino, *Handbook of Sixteenth-Century Rhetoric* (London, 1968); Robert J.
Clements, *Critical Theory and Practice of the Pléiade* (Cambridge, Mass. 1942); Grahame
Castor, *Pléiade Poetics* (Cambridge, 1964); Alexander L. Gordon, *Ronsard et la*

book was in Latin: Erasmus' *De duplici copia verborum ac rerum commentarii duo* (1511). This teaches the poet how to write eloquently and persuasively by selecting the right words, the right phrase, the right tone for a particular work – whether in prose or poetry. When we combine *copia* with the necessity for *un plus hault style* we find that here lies the beginning of French Renaissance and post-Renaissance aesthetics. Most of the major borrowings from Ancient rhetorical and detailed poetic theory are concerned with the heroic genre, and this influences the whole way in which poetics is conceived in the sixteenth century. When Du Bellay praises poetry it is in terms of

> grandeur de style, magnificence de motz, gravité de sentences, audace & varieté de figures, & mil' autres lumieres de poësie: bref ceste energie...que les Latins appelleroient *genius*.   (ed. Chamard, Paris, 1961, p. 40)

Such terms are inherent in a *plus hault style que celuy dont nous sommes si longuement contentez* and this is the sublimity of the grand style. By implication Du Bellay's ideal poet behaves like the ideal orator of the third style in Cicero's theory: he behaves in a fiery way among coldly sober people.[1] We have already met this juxtaposition when we discussed the *vates* opposing the *vulgus* in Horace's poetry. A sixteenth-century edition of Quintilian's Book X has a commentary by a number of people, among whom is Stigel. His paragraph on Bk. 10. 1. 119 will properly bring out the attributes and qualities in this grand style:

> sublimis oratio est fusa et ampla, plena liberioribus figuris, splendida gravitate sententiarum, et ornamentis schematum, ardens affectibus, crebra locis communibus, ampla circuitu

Rhétorique (Geneva, 1970); R. R. Bolgar, *The Classical Heritage and its Beneficiaries* (Cambridge, 1954); E. Curtius, *European Literature and the Latin Middle Ages* (New York, 1953); Yves Le Hir, *Rhétorique et Stylistique de la Pléiade au Parnasse* (Paris, 1960).

[1] Cicero, *Orator*, 99. 'Qui enim nihil potest tranquille, nihil leniter, nihil partite, definite, distincte, facete dicere, praesertim cum causae partim totae sint eo modo, partim aliqua ex parte tractandae, *si is non praeparatis auribus inflammare rem coepit, furere apud sanos et quasi inter sorbios bacchari vinulentus videtur.*'   (my italics)
For a man who can say nothing calmly and mildly, who pays no attention to arrangement, precision, clarity or pleasantry – especially when some cases have to be handled entirely in this latter style, and others largely so, – if *without first preparing the ears of his audience* he begins trying to work them up to a fiery passion, he seems to be a raving madman among the sane, like a drunken reveller in the midst of sober men.   (my italics)
Cf. *Brutus*, 233, where *furere* and *insanus* are used of an *orator omnia magna voce dicens*.

periodorum. Haec cum rerum copia, tum cursu ac sonitu
verborum dignitate affectuum admirabilis est.
(the approximate date of the edition is 1550, n.p. p. 196)

The elevated style is expansive and profuse, full of uncon-
strained figures resplendent in both the weight of its ideas and
the decorative qualities of its devices, fiery in its emotions,
packed with commonplaces and expansive in the well-
rounded shape of its periods. This style is to be admired not
only for the abundant wealth of its subject matter but also
for the sweep and sound of its diction and for its impressive
emotional content.

Thus the poet will reject the *submissa* and the *media oratio* and
choose the *sublimis* as his model. The *gravitas*, the *ardens*, the *ampla
circuitu periodorum* and the *sonitas verborum* can be paralleled in any
sixteenth-century criticism of Ronsard and Du Bellay's poetry.
For instance, in the 'Privilège' to the *Bocage* of 1554 it is claimed
that Ronsard has equalled the Ancient poets,

> Lequel...a de si pres suivy les anciens & excellens poëtes
> Grecz & Latins, tant en subtilité de poësie & gravité de
> sentences, qu'en propriété, doulceur & grace de langage, que
> tous les doctes de nostre temps...le confessent meriter non
> moins que Pindare...[1]

Gravity implies especially the seriousness of the poet's purpose
and the dignity of his profession and this provides a link between
Scève's *durs* and the *gravité* of Du Bellay and Ronsard. Similarly
Peletier in his *Art poétique* (ed. Boulanger, Paris, 1930, Bk. 1. Ch.
v, p. 95) talks about imitation and how Homer and Vergil are
to be read. He adds,

> (car j'examplifirè par tout pour l'Euuvre Heroïque *sus lequel
> s'antandront les autres g'anres*)   (my italics)

He goes on to say,

> les èt comme incorporèz an sa memoęre pour son principal
> fons, e comme pour son ordinere patron: afin que quand ce
> viendra a lire les autres Poëtes, il soęt preparè a an pouvoęr
> convertir la lecture an cete felicite premiere imbue: a la sorte
> des vins excęlans, qui se ramplicęt, non de pareilh vin, quand
> il ne s'an trouve point, męs du meilheur qui se puisse

[1] *Œuvres complètes*, ed Laumonier (Paris, 1914–67), vol. VI, p. 3.

rɇcouvrer. Car lɇ tonneau etant bien auinè, lɇ vin d'infusion se reduìt facilɇmant a la saveur dɇ la principalɇ bonte.

Through a delightful simile of wine-making Peletier makes us see that our literary barrel must be soaked with Homer and Vergil – the best Ancient models – so that our reading and writing bottles come out equal to the best. In ch. viii of book two he states categorically

> l'Euure Heroïquɇ ɇ̀t cɇlui qui donnɇ lɇ pris, e lɇ vrei titrɇ dɇ Poëtɇ. (p. 194)

And that is the feeling of the Pléiade as a whole: that only in the heroic genre can literature be stretched. Ronsard writes, that writing (or elocution)

> n'est autre chose qu'une propriété et splendeur de paroles bien choisies et ornées de graves et courtes sentences, qui font reluyre les vers comme les pierres precieuses bien enchassées les doigts de quelque grand Seigneur... Pour ce tu te doibs travailler estre copieux en vocables, et trier les plus propres et signifians que tu pourras pour servir de ners et de force à tes carmes, qui reluyront d'autant plus que les mots seront significatifs, et choisis avecques jugement.
>
> (*Art poetique*, p. 9)

This *gravitas* leads us to the structural metaphors underlying Renaissance theory which have been borrowed from the Romans. Take two familiar statements by Ronsard and Du Bellay:

> car tout ainsi qu'on ne peut dire un corps humain beau, plaisant et accomply, s'il n'est composé de sang, venes, arteres et tendons, et sur tout d'une nayve couleur, ainsi la Poësie ne peut estre plaisante, vive ne parffaite sans belles inventions, descriptions, comparaisons, qui sont les ners et la vie du livre.
>
> (Ronsard, *Art poetique*, p. 5)

and

> (eloquence) dont la vertu gist aux motz propres, usitez, & non aliénes du commun usaige de parler, aux methaphores, alegories, comparaisons, similitudes, energies, & tant d'autres figures & ornemens, sans les quelz tout oraison & poëme sont nudz, manques & debiles.
>
> (Du Bellay, *Deffence*, ed. Chamard, p. 35–6)

These are often taken as illustrations of an essentially 'decorative' theory of poetry. Odette de Mourgues, analysing a number of dizains in Scève which have a rather 'metaphysical' quality, remarked that Scève's imagery was functional, 'an imperious necessity of thought which cannot express itself otherwise.'[1] This approach to the best dizains of Scève is suggestive, but it clearly sets up the antithesis between the 'functional' and 'decorative'. As twentieth-century readers we tend to admire flashes of light in a poem for their own sake, because they set in motion a free play of associations, transcribe sense impressions or describe aspects of nature and mythology which seem 'delightful' and 'fresh' to us.

Now the theory of ornamentation and the sixteenth-century understanding of decorum have been fully analysed – though only for English literature – by Rosemund Tuve in her book, *Elizabethan and Metaphysical Poetry* (Chicago, 1947). But the implications of the metaphors used above by the two giants of the Pléiade have not been followed through, and the fact that these metaphors, and the whole theory of *copia*, are essential to the French idea of Renaissance and post-Renaissance poetry is rather ignored by French scholars and critics.

The metaphors reveal fully the rhetorical assumptions and the classical view of the nature of poetry which the Pléiade subscribed to and took so much for granted that the various mental habits underlying them are largely invisible to the modern reader. What is particularly interesting about these two statements is the way the analogy between a healthy body and good poetry puts the emphasis on health and proper functioning rather than on decoration and superficial beauty.

The analogy itself is a commonplace of Roman rhetorical and poetic theory, and it is given one of its clearest expressions in the form of a simile by Tacitus,

> Oratio autem, sicut corpus hominis, ea demum pulchra est in qua non eminent venae nec ossa numerantur, sed temperatus ac bonus sanguis implet membra et exsurgit toris ipsosque nervos rubor tegit et decor commendat.
>
> (*Dialogus*, xxi)

[1] *Metaphysical, Baroque and Précieux Poetry* (Oxford, 1953), p. 19.

No, it is with eloquence as with the human frame. There can be no beauty of form where the veins are prominent, or where one can count the bones: sound healthful blood must fill out the limbs, and riot over the muscles, concealing the sinews in turn under a ruddy complexion and a graceful exterior.

The description of the elements of the human body is full but the tenor of the comparison (the elements of poetry) is merely mentioned. Can we press the analogy further to make it reveal the precise ways in which the blood, muscle, strength and healthy functioning of the body correspond to particular elements in an organised piece of poetry or prose? I think we can.

Terms of approval in Roman practical criticism reveal the writers' constant mental habit of regarding details of a particular man's style in terms of this analogy. Thus for example Quintilian praises Demosthenes

> tanta vis in eo, tam densa omnia, ita quibusdam nervis intenta sunt. (x. 1. 76)

Or he qualifies Aeschines as having 'carnis tamen plus habet, minus lacertorum' (x. 1. 77) or Archilochus 'plurimum sanguinis atque nervorum'. (x. 1. 60)[1] He sees that the fullness and richness of thought and style, the force of the persuading are like the sinews, arteries and tendons of an athlete's body. (x. 1. 4, cf. x. 1, 33; x. 3, 7; x. 4. 4; x. 7. 1 and 23) Elsewhere he demonstrates that the metaphor is taken from a living organism which gathers strength from the nourishment supplied to it. The joints of a human body must not lose their suppleness (x. 2, 12).

Conversely, terms of disapproval echo the same analogy: Cicero, for example, castigates philosophers' style thus:

> tamen horum oratio neque nervos neque aculeos oratorios ac forensis habet. (*Orator*, xix. 62)

> yet the style lacks the vigour and sting necessary for oratorical efforts in public life.

Quintilian often applies to style terms such as *nitor, nitidus, nitere*, and they carry with them the full associations of the sheen and glow of health. A further extension of the metaphor – an

[1] Cf. Cicero, *Ad Atticum* iv. xvi, 100, 'amisimus...omnem non modo sucum ac sanguinem sed etiam colorem et speciem pristinae civitatis'.

extension that radically alters our view of the 'decorative' and 'functional' antithesis – is the element of virility, of masculinity even, approved of in style. Quintilian speaks with pleasure of

> hic ornatus...virilis et fortis et sanctus sit nec effeminatam levitatem et fuco ementitum colorem amet: sanguine et viribus niteat.   (VIII. 3. 6)

> But such ornament must be bold, manly and chaste, free from all effeminate smoothness and the false hues derived from artificial dyes, and must glow with health and vigour.

The athletic form lingers in our mind – the wrestling for words and the harmonious movements together with the vigour and tough vehemence that is required to exercise and to be fit. Muscularity, health, brilliance, texture and clarity shine forth in the whole of Quintilian's brilliant passage in the Proemium to Book VIII. He assimilates grace and aesthetic pattern to the functioning of an athlete's body, appearing at its most splendid. Cicero and Quintilian speak with distaste of an anaemic, flabby, soft, sinewless style (e.g. Quintilian, XII. 10. 25). A brilliant style must wear a manly dress, 'et nitor ille cultum virilem' (XII. 10. 79.). So the opposition is between a manly and an effeminate style. Even a simple style, devoid of vehemence and the full rush of blood through the veins, must be a healthy, well functioning one: thus Cicero in the *Orator*, XXIII. 76, says

> Etsi enim non plurimi sanguinis est, habeat tamen sucum aliquem oportet, ut, etiam si illis maximis viribus careat, sit, ut ita dicam, integra valetudine.

> For although it is not full-blooded, it should nevertheless have some of the sap of life, so that, though it lacks great strength, it may still be, so to speak, in sound health.

In this *ut ita dicam* there is an apology for the metaphor, a hint perhaps of Cicero exploring the possibilities of the healthy body analogy to express fully what he has in mind about style. Evaluative selection is always in terms of *sanguis, nervi, caro, sucus, lacerti, robus, vires, virilitas, robusta*. Similes are military, athletic, physical and bodily. And terms of disapproval are also derived from the look and bearing of a male physique: thus for instance the word *ieiunus* or *aridus* refers to the lean and shrivelled Attic style; the meagreness of the style is a metaphor taken from physical leanness.

These metaphors in the works of the rhetoricians also underlay the work of the poets of Rome. In the *Ars poetica* of Horace there are numerous examples of this: words like *nervi* denote the sinews or tendons of a body – in the literal and metaphorical sense; *asper* and *levia* – the rough as opposed to the smooth – all make one think of a human body.

But how literally did Ronsard and Du Bellay understand these terms? How far did they appreciate the wealth of implications in the metaphor which they use so naturally? A glance at Stigel's commentary on Quintilian, which appeared around 1550, illuminates the extent to which these metaphors were discussed and literally interpreted in the sixteenth century. Stigel in his discussion of imitation says,

> . . . et in optimis optima, quaeque maxime excellant, quantum fieri potest, persequi atque excerpere, excerpta non in sanguinem modo, sed in sucum quoque convertere, quo ali et iudicium et peritia in dicendo possit. . . Videndum itaque qui nervi ac lacerti sustineant corpus scripti. Nam hoc non pigeat nos saepius inculcare adolescentibus: sicut in animato corpore musculi et nervi et lacerti vocantur ea, quae sustinent universum corpus, caro item et sanguis, quae alunt, spiritus hoc ipsum, quod movet, et tanquam aura quaedam impellit, ita ab harum rerum similitudine, viribus quoque Eloquentiae appellationes esse additas, ut distingui inter se virtutes possint. Nervi namque et musculi ipsa argumenta vocantur et substantia totius negotij quibus nititur et fulcitur oratio. Caro atque sanguis, cum loci communes, tum utriusque generis affectus dicuntur, quibus in oratione fusis atque sparsis ipsum corpus quasi nutrimento quodam refertum completur. Spiritus vero in ornatu est elocutionis motus, videlicet, ex tropis et schematis additus. Igitur nervi, hoc est praecipua argumenta, quae docendi ac probandi causa comparata sunt. . .   (p. 149)[1]

. . . and in the best authors to hunt down and excerpt, so far as one can, what is best and most outstanding and having

---

[1] This is typical of all sixteenth-century editions and commentaries of Quintilian – the text being reproduced at least a hundred times in the course of the century. For example, Aldus, Ascensius, Petrus Mosellanus, Gryphius, Joachim Camerarius (even the edition with MSS. notes by Jean Passerat, Paris, 1522) were all following a literal *explication de texte*.

excerpted them all to convert them not only into blood but also into that juice by which judgement and accomplishment in speaking can be nourished...And so we must see what sinews and tendons support the body of a written work. For we must not feel sad about inculcating this again and again into young pupils: just as in a living body muscles, sinews and tendons are what we call the things which hold up the whole body and in the same way flesh and blood those things which nourish it and spirit the very force which moves it, driving it along like some breath of wind, so by analogy with these things names have been assigned to the strength of Eloquence as well, to enable us to distinguish its qualities one from another. For sinews and muscles are what we call the actual arguments and the substance of the whole business on which discourse rests and is supported. Flesh and blood the commonplaces and also the feelings of both kinds which once they are scattered and diffused in discourse ensure that the actual body of it is, as it were, stuffed full of nourishment. But spirit is the movement of style in ornament, added of course from the store of tropes and figures. Hence, the sinews, that is the particular arguments which have been brought together for the purpose of instruction and proof...

We must imitate the best things in the best authors. We must not only take the blood but also the *succum*, the marrow and pith out of the work and convert it into our own work. The rest of the paragraph demonstrates fully just how literal a transcript Stigel was making – body/health/virility/blood equals good writing. For the *nervi* and *musculi* are really the arguments which make the speech shine with light. The *caro atque sanguis* are the *loci communes* or commonplaces, and the *spiritus* is the tropes and schemas, the figures of speech in a work. Running through Du Bellay's *Deffence* is the same muscular imagery – the *chair, oz, nerfs et sang* – and this suggests that the same mental habit was inherent in him. Even in sound-play he insists that it should be *viril, non effeminé* as does Peletier (*Art poétique*, ed. Boulanger, p. 143)

> Qui veùt ètrɇ facilɇ, il dɇvient moɸ, efeminee sans ners. (Cf. Horace, *Ars poetica*, lines 25–30.)

Peletier further suggests that invention

ęt repanduę par tout le Poęmę, comme lę sang par le cors dę l'animal: de sortę qu'ęle sę peùt apęler la vię ou l'amę du Poęmę. (ibid., p. 88)

This virility, or masculinity, this muscular image of poetry, must be linked with the Roman juxtaposition – *mollis/durus* or *mollis/gravis* – and must be looked at carefully in the Pléiade works. The famous statement of the *Deffence*, a statement made within the context of the Ode, a high genre, says:

> prens garde que ce genre de poëme soit eloingné du vulgaire, enrichy & illustré de motz propres & epithetes non oysifz, orné de graves sentences & varié de toutes manieres de couleurs & ornementz poëtiques.(ed. Chamard, p. 113–14)

This has been interpreted as proof of the 'decorative' intention of the whole Pléiade theory of poetics. For instance Odette de Mourgues (*Metaphysical, Baroque and Précieux Poetry*, p. 27) comments on the above quotation: 'With the Pléiade imagery tends to become decorative instead of functional, and also to be more lavishly used because it is a means of enriching, illustrating and adorning.' Du Bellay's statement does not put delightfulness and intrinsic prettiness first, and functional quality second. If we analyse it in terms of Roman theory, and the metaphor of full health and glowing vigour in the human body, we shall see it in a different way. '*Eloingné du vulgaire* – we have already seen that this is a crucial concept in the aesthetics of Rome and of the Pléiade. '*Enrichy* & *illustré*:' this is Cicero's notion of *evidentia* which is achieved by a brilliant image or an apt, powerful metaphor coupled with rich language. The phrase as a whole means the bringing of lustre, light and richness to the text, as befits that kind of poem. We fundamentally misunderstand Du Bellay if these are thought of as rich ornaments 'stuck on' for pretty, decorative value.[1] Stigel explains what is meant by 'Illustratio' (*Quintilian*, Book x, ed. of c. 1550, p. 32)

> splendor in elocutione cum gravitate rerum coniunctus, qui fere ex verbis sonantibus bene translatis, ex epithetis et ex ijs figuris constat, quae addunt lucem et splendorem orationi...

[1] Cf. *illustratio* and *evidentia* in Quintilian VI. ii. 32 and VIII. iii. 61. And see Rosemund Tuve (*Elizabethan and Metaphysical Imagery*, p. 29) for a discussion of these qualities.

> Radiance in style combined with weighty subject matter...is
> generally based on fine-sounding words well adapted in
> tropes, on the use of epithets and those figures which add
> clarity and radiance to discourse...

The *gravitas* gives dignity to the style; and in Roman criticism *gravis* is added to the adjectives *durus* and *fortis* as a means of discriminating between literary forms. Opposed to *gravis* is *mollis*, often serving as the stock epithet of the elegiac mode; it defines the simpler and lighter forms of verse as contrasted with the more ornate and elevated. And so this statement of Du Bellay and the commentator on Quintilian make it clear that the juxtaposition *gravis/mollis* is at the base of the sixteenth-century *douceur/gravité* concept. Where *douceur* stands in opposition to *gravité* is in the way the sublime style of the heroic work contrasts with the familiar and the informal.[1]

We can see how the Odes of Horace have a certain *gravitas*, whilst the Epistles or Satires have a lighter, more conversational *douceur*. We can see the *Aeneid* of Vergil as strictly *gravis* whereas the Eclogues are *molles*. Propertius called the love elegy *mollis*. But in all these poets there was a serious purpose, a forceful dignity to the profession of poetry. There is in the same way in sixteenth-century France an evaluation of poets according as to whether they are *grave* or *doux*: the sonnets to Cassandre were *graves* whereas he changed the style in the sonnets to Marie. Belleau comments on this change

> tant pour satisfaire à ceux qui se plaignoient de la grave
> obscurité de son style premier, que pour monstrer la gentillesse
> de son esprit, la douceur & fertilité & diversité de ses
> inventions...[2]

There is thus an evaluation implicit in the terms used, and they

---

[1] Professor M. A. Screech has brilliantly shown how the differing styles of Du Bellay in *Les Regrets* and in *Antiquitez de Rome* come directly out of Horace and relate specifically to the *gravis/mollis* antithesis. In the introduction of the edition of *Les Regrets et Autres Œuvres Poëtiques*, *Textes Littéraires Français* (Geneva, 1966, p. 31) he shows how the distinction that Horace made between his odes and his Epistles and Satires is there in the forefront of Du Bellay's mind: 'Si Horace s'est permis d'écrire en deux styles, l'un élevé, l'autre bas, Du Bellay peut faire de même...S'il adopte un autre style pour un autre genre, c'est qu'il se plie aux exigences des différentes conventions.'

[2] *Les Œuvres de Pierre de Ronsard Gentilhomme Vandosmois Prince des Poetes François. Reueues et augmentees* (Paris, 1617), p. 253.

are so flexible that they can change according to the style of the poet; for example Du Bellay was usually regarded as having *douceur* and Ronsard *gravité*, but often the terms were put together as *douce gravité* to qualify a certain style.

To proceed in the analysis of Du Bellay's statement, what do we understand by *motz propres*? This tends to be interpreted as the equivalent of twentieth-century readers' *mots justes*. But this phrase too closely follows Ciceronian definitions. For instance we read in *De Oratore*, III. 37. 149.

> Ergo utimur verbis aut iis, quae propria sunt et certa quasi vocabula rerum, paene una nata cum rebus ipsis; aut iis, quae transferuntur et quasi alieno in loco conlocantur; aut iis, quae novamus et facimus ipsi.

> The words we employ then are either the proper and definite designations of things, which were almost born at the same time as the things themselves; or terms used metaphorically and placed in a connexion not really belonging to them; or new coinages invented by ourselves.

In poetry one can have *mots inusités* (*De Oratore*, III. 38. 153) and metaphoric language is born of necessity. We see with delight that Cicero uses the body/health metaphor in dealing with words,

> Nam ut vestis frigoris depellendi causa reperta primo, post adhiberi coepta est ad ornatum etiam corporis et dignitatem, sic verbi translatio instituta est inopiae causa, frequentata delectationis. (III. 38. 155)

> For just as clothes were first invented to protect us against cold and afterwards began to be used for the sake of adornment and dignity as well, so the metaphorical employment of words was begun because of poverty, but was brought into common use for the sake of entertainment.

And Cicero follows this with an analysis of the pleasure afforded by metaphoric language (III. 40. 160). Quintilian goes further than this in book x. 2. 13, suggesting that words are not beautiful or ugly in themselves but that their function and their appropriateness depend on the context in which they are used,

> eaque non sua natura sint bona aut mala (nam per se soni tantum sunt), sed prout opportune proprieque aut secus

> collocata sunt, et compositio cum rebus accommodata sit, tum ipsa varietate gratissima.

> and they are not good or bad in virtue of their inherent nature (for in themselves they are no more than mere sounds), but solely in virtue of the aptitude and propriety (or the reverse) with which they are arranged, while rhythmical composition must be adapted to the theme in hand and will derive its main charm from its variety.

Du Bellay ties his *motz propres* to *epithetes non oysifz* and we may infer that these are French terms for evaluating epithets according to Roman theory. They are. Epithets are transliterations of sense impressions – qualities that are added to the noun – and they are judged by their aptness and their function. Quintilian in book x. 1. 76 disapproves of *otiosus* epithets; he calls them useless and vacant in the same way as Ronsard does in his *Art poétique*

> Tes epithetes seront recherchez pour signifier, et non pour remplir ton carme, ou pour estre oyseux en ton vers.
>
> (Cambridge, 1930, p. 10)

Or again in the 1587 preface to his *Franciade* he says,

> Epithetes significatifs et non oisifs, c'est à dire qui servent à la substance des vers. . .   (ibid., p. 44)

Du Bellay in the *Deffence* comments on epithets which are significant, II. ch. 9.

> Quand aux epithetes. . .je veux que tu en uses de sorte, que sans eux ce que tu dirois seroit beaucoup moindre, comme la *flamme devorante*, les *souciz mordans*, la *gehinnante sollicitude*; & regarde bien qu'ilz soint convenables, non seulement à leurs substantifz, mais aussi à ce que tu decriras, afin que tu ne dies l'*eau undoyante*, quand tu la veux decrire *impetueuse*, ou la *flamme ardente*, quand tu la veux montrer *languissante*.
>
> (ed. Chamard, pp. 162–3)

These are very precise pieces of advice. We are again – as we were with Horace – eavesdropping on a poet who brings to the surface what any poet needs to hear. If the advice is followed well, then you may be a poet.

He follows this advice with the mark of authority,

Tu as Horace entre les Latins fort heureux en cecy, *comme en toutes choses*. (my italics)

And so for the whole Pléiade *non oysifz* means epithets that are apt, not redundant, functional and assisting in the logical structure of the poem rather than merely picturesque, decorative, non-significant, or used to fill out the measure.

'*Ornés de graves sentences*' is another phrase embedded in Roman theory, and is again evaluative. The *sententiae* are like points, expressions of some universal truth, put forward as pieces of advice or which would lead a person towards a decision. Quintilian, x. 1. 60 says

> Summa in hoc vis elocutionis, cum validae tum breves vibrantesque sententiae, plurimum sanguinis atque nervorum, adeo ut videatur quibusdam, quod quoquam minor est, materiae esse, non ingenii vitium.

> For he [Archilochus] has a most forcible style, is full of vigorous, terse and pungent reflexions, and overflowing with life and energy: indeed, some critics think that it is due solely to the nature of his subjects, and not to his genius, that any poets are to be ranked above him.

But in book viii. 5. 28 he is harsh about the author who brings in indiscriminate *sententiae*,

> ut adfert lumen clavus purpurae loco insertus, ita certe neminem deceat intertexta pluribus notis vestis.

> A purple stripe appropriately applied lends brilliance to a dress, but a dress decorated with a quantity of patches can never be becoming to anybody.

Quintilian illustrates this point with metaphoric terms culled from hairdressing,

> ne intonsum caput, non (ut) in gradus atque anulos comptum, cum eo quod si non ad luxuriam ac libidinem ⌐eferas, eadem speciosiora quoque, sint, quae honestiora.
>
> (xii. 10. 47)

> I agree that the hair should be cut, but not that it should be dressed in tiers and ringlets, since we must always remember that ornaments, unless they be judged from the standpoint of the fop and the debauchee, are always effective in proportion to their seemliness.

This is fine, for the words have a metaphoric bearing which leads the reader to a notion of effeminacy in style. Quintilian loathed this quality, and so did the French authors of the sixteenth century. It was commonly termed *calamistratus* – 'crimped' by the Roman writers. Thus the *gravité* of the *sententiae* is part and parcel of the *style hault*.

Finally we have the '*couleurs et ornementz Poetiques*', which are clearly the images, the figures of speech or the metaphors. Now the kind of enquiry one must make before one can call images[1] 'embroidery' or 'lavish' or 'delightfully decorative' is to ask whether or not they are separable from the poem's full conceptual meaning. If you are able to abstract the images in a sonnet praising the lady, the praise is not effectively there. We must distinguish between irrelevance of ornament and basic structural flaws. As Rosemund Tuve said (*Elizabethan and Metaphysical Imagery*, p. 33): 'Modern misrepresentations of the Renaissance writers' theory of the didactic usefulness of poetry have intervened to blind us to the extreme complexity and flexibility of their definitions of the functional image.' Lustrous splendour is praised as an accompaniment to structural lucidity. The whole point of the word *illustré* was the light, the illumination brought to a work and the harmony, order and proportion revealed therein. This was above all traditional in Roman poetic theory as seen in Cicero, as seen in Vergil and as seen by Horace.

The problem raised here is this: if the antithesis functional/decorative is invalid, we have somehow to provide different terms to describe the functions of an image. Each image may be thought of in quite specific terms; each image has a function to play within the context of the work itself. The context is overridingly important. Thus, when speaking of the imagery of Scève's *Délie* we are thinking of an image within one dizain. We are analysing the function it plays in a particular context. The word *decorative* has been frequently used to evaluate rather than to describe and, as this is dangerous, I shall not use

---

[1] I am using the word *image* to mean all the figures in which a comparison of two terms is implied for example, simile, metaphor in its strict sense, personification, allegory and symbol. For detailed discussion of these points, see W. Nowottny, *The Language Poets Use* (London, 1972).

the term *decorative* at all with regard to images of style. Each image has a specific purpose and it is the multifarious functions of imagery that will later be analysed.

In all the theory, the whole point about *ornatus* was that it was a means of moving, and of inducing approval, enthusiasm and passion in the reader. It was merely a tool-of-the-trade, and whether a poet was good or bad he did consciously use the tool. It was not a matter of 'being decorative'; it was a function-full literary theory, and the constant use by the Romans of the blood and muscle metaphor suggests that health, brilliance, vigour, movement and clarity were essential in their view of literature.

Finally this metaphor underlies one of the most important Roman concepts: that matter and style are inseparable. If you are foolish enough to try to separate them, you are like a man trying to separate body and soul – they cannot be separated,

> et qui tamquam ab animo corpus, sic a sententiis verba seiungunt, quorum sine interitu fieri neutrum potest...
> (Cicero, *De Oratore*, III. 6. 24)

> who separates words from thoughts as one might sever body from mind- and neither process can take place without disaster...

We have seen how the French writers aimed at *un plus hault style*, how this involved *copia*, and how the style that emerged was not decorative but functional. We have seen that the heroic style was regarded as the best one, and how germs of it were in Marot and certainly in Scève. To trace all the movements between the different styles that poets used is not the task of this study but we hope to have shown, at least, that those writers who followed the Ancient theory would do so

> cum ampla et sententiarum gravitate et maiestate verborum, vehementes varii, copiosi graves, ad permovendos et convertendos animos instructi. (Cicero, *Orator*, V, 20)

> [The orators of the grand style] showed splendid power of thought and majesty of diction; they were forceful, versatile, copious and grave, trained and equipped to arouse and sway the emotions.

And the *gravité* was there in all Roman writers. Like most elements of their poetic theory the French simply adopted the juxtaposition *mollis/gravis*; and it ended as the *douceur* and the *gravité* of their practical criticism.

In the next chapter I analyse examples of the basic allusiveness in poetry, a concept which applies equally to Scève, Ronsard and Du Bellay. Of course, allusiveness does not do away with the different functions of an image. It is an altogether different aspect of imagery. But we shall see that it is not the antithesis between 'functional' and 'decorative' imagery that distinguished between these three poets. It is something far deeper.

5

Scève, Ronsard and Du Bellay: allusiveness

Allusiveness is one of the main literary qualities of sixteenth-century poetry. With Scève, Ronsard and Du Bellay there started the habit of allusiveness which was to become a feature that would descend to later generations. Bi-lingualism and bi-literacy were obviously the base of this habit. Every reader of Rimbaud or Mallarmé or Nerval recognises that allusions are part and parcel of literary technique, and every scholar devoted to the task of exegesis is unflaggingly tied to an effort to identify allusions. What has been called 'imitation' in Ronsard's poetry must not, in the light of the previous chapters, be simply thought of as literal imitation. For as we have seen, the creative process, in which imagination, sensitivity, perceptivity and intelligence are fused, is further deepened by re-creating through another literature or another language. In other words, the reader has to consider sometimes two or three poems – Greek, Latin, or French – before he can evaluate the Ronsard poem. This two-way line – between author and reader – is exciting and intellectual; and the participation of the reader is surely the beginning of the long train of *doctes amis*[1] who are ready to read 'aristocratic' poetry.

Allusions may be of different kinds: for example in Nerval's *Les Chimères* there may be topographical, biographical, alchemical, literary, allegorical, geographical, social, historical and tarotic allusions. But no reader – even after teasing out the various hints – could reduce the sonnet simply to a recital of

[1] The adjective *doctus* in Augustan Rome means learned, taxing, full of allusions, demanding a high degree of intelligence, taste and literary appreciation from its reader. A person who was *doctus* may be translated as a 'person possessing good taste'. It is in this sense I use it.

allusions. The reader has to grasp all the complex details, to organise the separate elements and to judge the validity of the 'focus' of Nerval's sonnet as a fully organic structure. What Eliot said so shrewdly about a poet's mind is vital:

> When a poet's mind is perfectly equipped for its work, it is constantly amalgamating disparate experiences; the ordinary man's experience is chaotic, irregular, fragmentary. The latter falls in love, or reads Spinoza, and these two experiences have nothing to do with each other, or with the noise of the type-writer, or the smell of cooking; in the mind of the poet, these experiences are always forming new wholes.
>
> (*Selected Essays*, p. 287)

Similarly, with sixteenth-century poets we can load the exegesis with valuable explanations which help us to work out the multifarious allusions and references, but in the last analysis we must judge it.

Images are always envisaged as presenting thoughts ready for grasping and holding, helping us to apprehend thought with immediacy. An idea which we might not grasp is put into an analogical relationship with another idea we probably will grasp – maybe because of the simplicity and familiarity of a concrete situation – this is a perfectly traditional, ordinary but important role of any image. And it is as true of Horace and Valéry's images as it is with Ronsard's or Scève's. The combination of abstract and concrete language is basic in poetry of any age. And the relating of any experience to personal experience is crucial. What we are doing when writing a poem, is seeking the 'objective correlative' of a mood, an experience, a thought – which Eliot thus defined,

> The only way of expressing emotion in the form of art is by finding an 'objective correlative'; in other words, a set of objects, a situation, a chain of events which shall be the formula of that *particular* emotion; such that when the external facts, which must terminate in sensory experience, are given, the emotion is immediately evoked.
>
> (*Selected Essays*, p. 145, Eliot's italics.)

It is not claiming to enter into a new range of feelings or

attitudes, hitherto concealed, to analyse the emotion conjured up by one single poet – in France or anywhere. Take a line from Baudelaire's *Au Lecteur*:

Et nous alimentons nos aimables remords

where on the one hand the realm of food and nourishment is evoked and on the other the realm of thought, and balance it with a phrase from Pascal's *Pensées – un roseau pensant* – both show the clash in the structure of language. They are dealing with well-known feelings and ideas, but they are conveyed with immediacy, bite and force: there is a natural controlled suggestion given by the context; if there are images in a poem or a piece of literary prose they are logically relevant and assist in the development of the reader's general interpretation of the 'objective correlatives' in the two authors' work. We tend in the twentieth century to overread a man's interest in his own psychological complexities rather than analysing the particular effect or emotion that he is giving his reader. It is not the poet's reactions to episodes or events that directly concern us. As Eliot said in his essay 'Tradition and the Individual Talent' – 'Honest criticism and sensitive appreciation is directed not upon the poet but upon the poetry.'

It is rare for an image in Ronsard and Du Bellay to demand to be admired for its own sake regardless of its link with the subject matter of the poem. What strikes the twentieth-century reader as a delightful (because it evokes accurately and suggestively sights and sounds of nature or the physical beauty of a female's body) yet gratuitous (because it is out of proportion with the argument and only tenuously connected with it) series of images is, on closer analysis, an essential part of the poem. Thus, for example, one of our greatest difficulties is to accept the lavish use of imagery in 'simple' poems praising a lady's beauty. But it is our unwillingness to accept the seriousness and worth of the subject matter of these poems that conditions our response to the images.

Professor Odette de Mourgues in her *Metaphysical, Baroque and Précieux Poetry* (pp. 27–8) takes Du Bellay's sonnet, *Deja la nuit en son parc amassoit* and comments on it in this way.

The imagery is effective not because it helps us more adequately to grasp the subject-matter (which is no more than a praise of his lady's beauty worked out through a conventional petrarchan fiction), but because it sets the imagination wandering along many different paths which are not closely connected with the subject.

It seems to me that this demonstrative kind of poem sets out to pay homage to the lady and to convince the reader of her superlative beauty: no element of description or narrative, no simile or metaphor will be irrelevant to this task. It does not 'set the imagination wandering' freely; the whole suggestive control of the structure, the linguistic formulae, the harmony of the line, the fluidity and the images are not 'free'. They weave a texture in which the reader and the poet are present. The intrinsic coherence of the poem is controlled.

It can be shown that in Scève, Ronsard and Du Bellay, poems in praise of beauty depend largely on beautiful images and hyperbolical statements. Take dizain 124 of *Délie*:

> Si Apollo restrainct ses raiz dorez,
> Se marrissant tout honteux soubz la nue,
> C'est par les tiens de ce Monde adorez,
> Desquels l'or pur sa clarté diminue.
> Parquoy soubdain, qu'icy tu es venue,
> Estant sur toy, son contraire, enuieux,
> A congelé ce Brouas pluuieux,
> Pour contrelustre à ta diuine face.
> Mais ton tainct frais vainct la neige des cieulx,
> Comme le iour la clere nuict efface.
>
> (ed. I. D. McFarlane, Cambridge, 1966)

The basic formula of the poem is to compare Délie's radiance with hypothetical perfection – the brilliance of sun and the whiteness of snow. Scève chooses to organise events that will prove Délie's quality in a narrative, descriptive framework. Lines 1–4 give, in a timeless present, the cause of the sun's disappearance: Délie puts Apollo to shame. Lines 5–8 narrate a specific event, Apollo's attempt at vengeance, turning the storm clouds into snow 'Pour contrelustre à ta diuine face'. But this in turn is merely the occasion for another triumph of Délie: the last line is the climax of the praise, as it presents Délie on the same level as the natural phenomenon of day's regular victory over night. We may regard the whole conception of the poem as exaggerated or artificial but we cannot deny that the pictures of nature and hyperbolical devices have a function – indeed they contain the meaning of the poem and are in no way separable from it.

Du Bellay's famous sonnet can be considered in the same way

> Deja la nuit en son parc amassoit
> Un grand troupeau d'etoiles vagabondes,
> Et pour entrer aux cavernes profondes
> Fuyant le jour, ses noirs chevaulx chassoit:

> Deja le ciel aux Indes rougissoit,
> Et l'Aulbe encor' de ses tresses tant blondes
> Faisant gresler mile perlettes rondes,
> De ses thesors les prez enrichissoit:

> Quand d'occident, comme une etoile vive,
> Je vy sortir dessus ta verde rive,
> O fleuve mien! une Nymphe en rient.

> Alors voyant cette nouvelle Aurore,
> Le jour honteux d'un double teint colore
> Et l'Angevin et l'Indique orient.
>
> (*L'Olive*, E. Caldarini, Geneva, 1974, no. 83)

It is a poem of praise, similarly based on the concept that his lady surpasses the beauty of natural phenomena. As it is a sonnet, he divides it into the octave – describing deliciously the natural scene – and the sestet – the transcendent beauty of the woman. Obviously, he has a longer poem than Scève's dizain and he has more scope in which to build up an allusive, dramatic and descriptive framework. The great beauty of the night-scene described in the first quatrain is in direct contrast to the quality of the scene in the second quatrain: the emergence of dawn is set against the giant blackcloth of night so that the colours, the freshness and the shimmering figure of Dawn herself stand out all the more sharply. The description of the personified *Aulbe* is a judicious combination of the recherché, artificial qualities of jewels (through the choice of works like *perlettes*, *thesors*, *enrichissoit*) and the natural dewy freshness of early morning. The rich rhymes of *amassoit*, *chassoit*, *rougissoit* and *enrichissoit*; the very firm control of the syntax, for example the double *Deja...Deja...* beginning each quatrain; the repetition of a present participle in each quatrain – *Fuyant...Faisant...*; the alternation of blackness with whiteness, of night-time and daylight; the suggestiveness around *vagabondes* – the giant figure of night as the shepherd, calling his flock of sheep to rest from every corner of the mountain/sky; the choice of words like *gresler*, suggesting a delicate *hail* of a thousand small and pretty pearls: all these individual details make the octave dense and suggestive. But they also prepare us for the quality of the second apparition, which far outshines such natural and beautiful phenomena. *Une Nymphe en rient* and *une etoile vive* are endowed with the lingering beauty of the earlier description, but the antithetical value judgement, which has been hinted all along, is at last made explicit in the phrases *nouvelle aurore* and *le jour honteux*. If we accept the kind of poem that Du Bellay is writing, then we must also accept the function of the images and sensuous description – to magnify and amplify the physical beauty of his mistress and convince the reader of her quality. The greater amplitude offered by the sonnet form allows Du Bellay to impress on the reader the concrete details of this beauty, whereas Scève's poem cannot achieve this degree of expansion.

The question 'what do the images mean in the poem?' needs to be answered via an exploration of the associations – semantic, symbolic, historical and mythological – attached to words; and this is not only true of the three poets we are discussing here but every poet. Furthermore, the meaning of an image is not just a matter of teasing out the associations; the function of an image – i.e. its relation to the subject-matter – is vital. To quote Professor L. C. Knights on literary criticism:

> We start with so many lines of verse on a printed page...We have to elucidate the meaning...and to unravel ambiguities; we have to estimate the kind of quality of the imagery and determine the precise degree of evocation of particular figures; we have to allow full weight to each word, exploring its 'tentacular roots', and to determine how it controls and

is controlled by the rhythmic movement of the passage in which it occurs.[1]

The meanings of words in a given poem are modified or re-created by the poet, and it is for the reader to recognise them. The real effort in literature is one of putting words together in precise ways. And our interpretation must be made in the light of all the literature we know, our personal experience of life and our struggle to understand what literature is all about. If I start to evaluate the Scève dizain and the Du Bellay sonnet I am trying to see the two poems in a new light. The practical analysis permits a new view of the relationship between the two poems: the one giving praise rather baldly, the other condensing sixteenth-century language into a 'poetic language', with its imagery embodying a deviation from the norm. But this is a skeleton-like evaluation.

Our knowledge of the two poems is only a starting point in judging them. For understanding their allusiveness means a knowledge of the whole tradition in which they are set, of the body of knowledge we can expect them to control, and of the prosody of the French language. Thus for example many of Scève's images which seem startling to us (in that the tenor and the vehicle of the metaphor or comparison start far apart, but are welded together by a highly personal act of perception or intellection) would reveal their meaning immediately to the sixteenth-century reader. For instance, the famous hare image of dizain 129:

> Car dès le poinct, que partie tu fus,
> Comme le Lieure accroppy en son giste,
> Ie tendz l'oreille...

relies on the common stock of knowledge of the fixed symbolic attributes of animals, so that the hare would be readily understood as a symbol of timidity and of frightened apprehension. This use of brief, unexplained symbols accounts partly for the taut and dense effect of some of Scève's dizains. And the

---

[1] *Explorations. Essays in criticism mainly on the literature of the seventeenth century* (London, 1963), p. 16.

fact that Scève relies more on images of this kind than do the Pléiade poets accounts for some of the differences between his poetry and theirs. We shall return to this point, for there are other differences which have little to do with allusiveness but rather with the kind of dizains he is composing. On the other hand, brief allusions to classical mythology or biblical episodes, which have expected and traditionally controlled associations and connotations, are akin to the technique employed by Ronsard and Du Bellay. The 'Serpent esleué' of dizain 143 is on the same level of 'obscurity' as Du Bellay's allusions to 'les fleurs du sang amoureux nées' in sonnet 45 of *L'Olive*. Both allusions ask the reader to use his memory and knowledge more than his freely wandering imagination, and once the allusion has been grasped no intellectual gymnastics need be performed. Images, allusions, parallels from Ancient literature or mythology, play their part in awakening the *right* body of associations needed to understand the piece of communication.

Both Scève and the Pléiade poets use traditional images in a traditional way – for their efficacy towards a given end. The differences between the poets lie rather in their natures, in what interests them in poetry, in syntax, and in linguistic formulae; thus the best of Scève for example, is tied to an intense intellectualisation of experience and the metaphysical problems which surround love. This is quite unlike Du Bellay's interest; yet one aspect – his allusiveness – is shared by all three poets.

There is nonetheless an antithesis betwen the ways in which any image of the three poets works. In practical criticism, we always have to look at the context, the kind of relationship of the two parts of the metaphor or image – the tenor and the vehicle – the problems the poet is investigating, the syntax he uses, the allusiveness, the elliptical, the discursive, the descriptive poems and the linguistic formulae he is 'founding'. One of the difficult problems in dealing with imagery of any period is that of classification and of the use of descriptive terms. Christine Brooke-Rose in *A Grammar of Metaphor*[1] discusses the various merits and disadvantages of the traditional methods of classification, ranging from the species/genus rule of Aristotle to the

[1] London, 1958.

analysis by dominant trait of the modern German school. One clear point that emerges is that we must think about what questions one is asking the poet or his work. What we really want to see is the function of each image within the poem. In each case, the function of the image must be related to the argument of the poem as a whole.

In descriptive poems or in poems in praise of a lady the image suggests to the reader in which direction his mind is to focus: for example, the admiration of the lady is related to natural scenery and we are meant to admit that she transcends everything that nature has created. But in dialectical poems the image has a powerful logical-plus-emotional effect. Actually, both types of image may be allusive and one can perhaps, see the relationship in this diagram:

allusiveness

descriptive $\times$ dialectical

So that although in a number of Scève's dizains there may be the same kind of allusiveness as we find in Ronsard or Du Bellay, one has to go further and find out what type of function that image has.

Look, for instance, at the two examples quoted earlier: the 'Serpent esleué' of Scève and the 'fleurs du sang amoureux nées' of Du Bellay.

> Le souuenir, ame de ma pensée,
> Me rauit tant en son illusif songe,
> Que n'en estant la memoyre offensée,
> Ie me nourris de si doulce mensonge.
>   Or quand l'ardeur, qui pour elle me ronge,
> Contre l'esprit sommeillant se hazarde,
> Soubdainement qu'il s'en peult donner garde,
> Ou qu'il se sent de ses flammes greué,
> En mon penser soubdain il te regarde,
> Comme au desert son Serpent esleué.
>
> (dizain 143 in Délie.)

> Ores qu'en l'air le grand Dieu du tonnerre
> Se rue au seing de son epouse aymée,
> Et que de fleurs la nature semée
> A faict le ciel amoureux de la terre:

Or' que des ventz le gouverneur desserre
Le doux Zephire, et la forest armée
Voit par l'épaiz de sa neuve ramée
Maint libre oiseau, qui de tous coutez erre:

Je vois faisant un cry non entendu
Entre les fleurs du sang amoureux nées
Pasle, dessoubz l'arbre pasle etendu:

Et de son fruict amer me repaissant,
Aux plus beaux jours de mes verdes années
Un triste hiver sen' en moy renaissant.

(sonnet 45 in *L'Olive*.)

Both allusions play a role in their respective poems which is strictly controlled by the context of the argument and by the traditional associations they bear. When we have discovered that the 'Serpent esleué' is the Brazen Serpent of Moses (Numbers 21. 4–9; John 3. 14–15), and the 'fleurs' are the flowers that sprang from the blood of Adonis after his death, we can move on to consider their function. Neither is a periphrasis nor a straightforward equivalence. Both bring certain associations to bear on the argument of the poem. The Du Bellay allusion brings into play the tragic love affair between Venus and Adonis, ended abruptly by the brutal killing of the youth by the boar. The love between an immortal goddess, patron saint of love, and a mortal man; the poignancy of the end, and the perennial commemoration of the affair by the immortal flowers are resonances which greatly enrich the subjective plane of the poem. So the melancholy state of the dejected lover is juxtaposed with harmonious love in the external world, so brilliantly described in the octave, and suggestively linked to the destruction and suffering of love in the Venus and Adonis story. The allusive phrase 'les fleurs du sang amoureux nées' ensures the correlation between the private and the mythical places.

The phrase 'Serpent esleué' is allusive; but when we look at the whole context we see that it functions in a totally different way from 'les fleurs' of Du Bellay. We have an immediate sense in this dizain, of the expression of psychological and sexual difficulties. It is a dizain of compressed, passionate reasoning, where the poet is moving through an analysis of his memory in a constrained way. Whereas the Du Bellay sonnet expressed the conventional petrarchist theme of the dejection of the lover, the Scève dizain goes very much further in trying to reason out the dissociation of all his faculties in the human experience of love.

The second thing that strikes one is the position of 'Serpent esleué' in the last line. This, inevitably, in a good Scèvian dizain is a signal to the reader to treat this line as a first line and read the poem through again. This is a particular technique in Scève's dialectic: the position is so strained that it needs a leap on to another field of poetic structure: a metaphor or a simile. The reader is reminded of a picture of a serpent on a pole. The associations present through the Biblical allusion are of curing and healing and life. There are also opposite typological associations of the serpent and Eve; this links with the sexual frustration tormenting the poet to create a complex of serpent associations.[1]

There is a three-fold ground-plan in the dizain: first memory soothes him in a dream-world (lines 1–4); then sexual passion takes over completely his thoughts, reasoning and memory (lines 5–8), leading to a static, fixed look at the cure – thinking intellectually of his love. This ground-plan is quite unlike the Du Bellay sonnet where there is a simple contrast between the octave and sestet.

Thus, although the two examples are allusive they have different functions to play in their context. For Scève is expressing one of the paradoxes of love: thinking of the person you love creates the disturbance, and yet cure and order can only work through continued thinking of her (or him).[2] Du Bellay, on the other hand, is not concerned with psychological problems and has no need of a complex ground-plan. Through the use of the well-known Biblical story and the familiar associations of the Serpent image Scève is able to go beyond the recording of experience to an evaluation of them.

---

[1] For an excellent analysis of Scève's dialectic in several poems see Odette de Mourgues, *Metaphysical, Baroque and Précieux Poetry* (Oxford, 1953), pp. 16–22.

[2] For a fuller and somewhat different analysis see D. G. Coleman, *Maurice Scève*, (Cambridge, 1975), pp. 146–8.

We have established a common point between Du Bellay and Scève – both use allusiveness as a logical or structural principle. And we have delved a little further, to see that the allusions played different parts in their particular contexts. We were not at the time evaluating their role but simply describing them more accurately. We have seen that allusiveness is controlled by the context of the argument and it is the context that is overridingly dominant. In any anthology of Scève's best dizains the images would act in the same way as the one just analysed. But if we read the *Délie* as a whole, the striking thing is that whether Scève is writing a précieux dizain or whether he is composing 'difficult', 'metaphysical' or psychological poetry – the allusive turn of mind is inherent in him, just as it is inherent in Du Bellay or Ronsard.

Now take Scève's allusions to 'les tristes Soeurs' in dizain 31: they do not stand in isolation but serve to set in motion the whole argument of the poem. The evocation of the classical legend of Philomela and Procne establishes a sympathetic background for the poet's melancholy and cannot be reduced to the simple equivalence, *Printemps*. It calls to mind associations of tragedy, love, jealousy and calumny which are relevant to an argument concerned precisely with *desdeing* and *calumnie*. Similarly the first line of Du Bellay's sonnet in *Les Antiquitez*,

> Telle que dans son char la Berecynthienne...

brings to mind the lines from Vergil where the allusion to Berecynthian Cybele takes place:

> qualis Berecyntia mater
> invehitur curru Phrygias turrita per urbes
> laeta deum partu, centum complexa nepotes,
> omnis caelicolas, omnis supera alta tenentis.
>
> (*Aeneid*, VI. 782ff)

It serves to set the sonnet in a Vergilian perspective.[1]

---

[1] Du Bellay had already translated this fine passage in the sixth book of the *Aeneid* but in Vergil the description of the procession of the *Magna Mater*, mother of the Gods, takes three and a half lines whereas Du Bellay devotes nine lines to it:
> Elle emmurant sept montaignes ensemble,
> Grosse d'enfans à Cybele ressemble,
> Mere des Dieux, qui de tours couronné,
> Et sur un char de triomphe menée,
> Des Phrygiens traverse les citez,

And again the first line of dizain 369, 'Plongé au Stix de la melancolie' relates the subjective world of the poet to mythical reality.[1] Each of the rivers of the Classical Underworld was thought to have a connection with the moods and emotions of man, Styx being the river of melancholy. Now the allusion in this first line permeates the rest of the dizain and clarifies its content. For the account of the poet's emotions, progressing from melancholy, through anger, to actual weeping, can be seen as a dramatic progress across the clearly chartered rivers of Hell. Boccaccio's description makes clear these points,

> primo recti iudicii perturbata laeticia Acherontem transeunt, qui carens gaudio interpretatur, et sic pulsa laeticia, ut eius occupet moesticia locum necesse est, ex qua ob bonum laeticiae perditum persaepe vehemens nascitur ira, a qua in furorem impellimur, qui Phlegeton est, id est ardens, ex furore etiam in tristitiam labimur, quae Styx est et ex tristitia in luctum et lachrymas, per quas Cocytus accipiendus est quartus fluvius.[2]

> First the happiness that belongs to sound judgement is disturbed and they cross the Acheron, which means 'lacking in joy', and once happiness is driven out, it is inevitable that melancholy should take its place. From melancholy because the boon of happiness is lost vehement anger is very often born and this drives us into fury which is the Phlegeton, i.e. 'blazing'. From fury also we slip into grief, which is the Styx, and from grief into tears and lamentation, which are the reasons why Cocytus must be taken as the fourth river.

S'esjouissant de tant de deitez,
Et de se voir cent nepveuz autour d'elle,
Tous jouissans de nature immortelle,
Tous possedans le hault sejour des cieux.

Du Bellay uses the first line in the *Antiquitez* sonnet to *convertir en sang et nourriture* this Vergilian passage.

[1] Plongé au Stix de la melancolie
Semblois l'autheur de ce marrissement,
Que la tristesse autour de mon col lye
Par l'estonné de l'esbayssement,
Colere ayant pour son nourissement,
Colere aduste, ennemye au ioyeux.
    Dont l'amer chault, salé, & larmoyeux
Créé au dueil par la perseuerance
Sort hors du cœur, & descent par les yeulx
Au bas des piedz de ma foible esperance.

[2] *De Genealogia Deorum* (Basel, 1532), Book 1, p. 17.

The allusion to the Styx brings into play the rest of the psychological geography of the Underworld, and the pattern of the poem is controlled by this mythological correlative to the poet's emotional attitude and situation.

Dizain 143 brings in another sphere of resemblance between the three poets: mythology and the Bible. They do pre-assume that the reader possesses a classical background; they are writing for the cultured man. Now this is important for the understanding of the nature of French poetry for the next four centuries: it too calls upon classical training, love of classical mythology, the knowledge of the Bible – and, crucially, a feeling for French literature of the past. The objective correlatives that Scève, Ronsard and Du Bellay can draw on are the same.

Take for instance Ronsard's famous sonnet to Cassandre praising and magnifying her beauty:

> Quand au matin ma Deesse s'abille
>   D'un riche or crespe ombrageant ses talons,
>   Et que les retz de ses beaulx cheveux blondz
>   En cent façons ennonde et entortille:
> Je l'accompare à l'escumiere fille,
>   Qui or peignant les siens jaunement longz,
>   Or les ridant en mille crespillons
>   Nageoyt abord dedans une coquille.
> De femme humaine encore ne sont pas
>   Son ris, son front, ses gestes, ny ses pas,
>   Ny de ses yeulx l'une & l'autre chandelle:
> Rocz, eaux, ny boys, ne celent point en eulx
>   Nymphe, qui ait si follastres cheveux,
>   Ny l'oeil si beau, ny la bouche si belle.
>
>   (ed. Lemonier *et al.*, vol. IV, sonnet 39, p. 42)

Ronsard gives visual and concrete proof of his hyperbolical assertions about his goddess-mistress. The quatrains develop two different pictures: of the mistress herself, and of Venus. But the central point of their beauty is the long waving golden hair whose colour, movement and curling length are imprinted on the reader's mind. The Botticelli-like picture of Venus in the second quatrain conveys the double emotion present in the poet: admiration and desire. The mistress is at once divinely ethereal and, because of the sensual suggestions of the hair image, physically present and desirable. The tercets state and describe the superhuman quality of Cassandre; the general value judgement 'De femme humaine encore ne sont pas/Son ris, son front, ses gestes ny ses pas' is supported by the visual proof we have had in the quatrains. The sonnet-form allows Ronsard to describe with a fullness and voluptuousness that permeate both quatrains.

Look now at another sonnet on Cassandre's hair:

> Soit que son or se crespe lentement
>   Ou soit qu'il vague en deux glissantes ondes,
>   Qui cà qui là par le sein vagabondes,
>   Et sur le col, nagent follastrement:
> Ou soit qu'un noud diapré tortement
>   De maintz rubiz, & maintes perles rondes,
>   Serre les flotz de ses deux tresses blondes,
>   Je me contente en mon contentement.
> Quel plaisir est ce, ainçoys quelle merveille
>   Quand ses cheveux troussez dessus l'oreille
>   D'une Venus imitent la façon?
> Quand d'un bonet son chef elle adonize,
>   Et qu'on ne sçait (tant bien elle desguise
>   Son chef doubteux) s'elle est fille ou garçon?
>
> (*ed. cit.* vol. IV, sonnet 76, p. 79)

This is almost a *blason* (i.e. a poem describing one aspect of the lady's beauty) on Cassandre's hair. Many critics have analysed it and demonstrated the richness of the evocation: the colour of the hair, the association with the waves of the sea, the slowness of the movement, the associations of the hair and breast of the mistress, the parallel with Botticelli's famous 'Birth of Venus'; or how the jewellery she wears in her hair enables Ronsard to continue to evoke the waves in *serre les flotz*. It is pointed out that there is an uncertainty through the whole sonnet from *Soit que...ou que...* and this rises to a climax of ambiguity – not knowing whether she is a woman or a boy. It is this climax that I want to deal with as, it is an example of allusiveness very tightly controlled and a fine example of *contaminatio*.

The term *contaminatio* is certainly post-classical; the verb *contaminare* was used to mean to mingle, to blend together or unite. When Terence blended scenes from two or more Greek originals to form his own plays he presumed that his viewers would recognise the original and then be able to bring to the new work the harmonics of the old. Quintilian in book XII. 10 puts forward the germ of a comparative method when he sees Roman literature not as a copy of the Greek but as the distinctive product of a different race. In fact all the writers in Rome used *contaminatio* over and over again though the term itself was not explicitly used. Nonetheless it was an established principle in Roman criticism and was taken over by France in the sixteenth century.

The last three lines of the Ronsard sonnet were inspired by these lines (20–4) from Horace's *Odes*, II. 5:

> Cnidiusve Gyges,
> quem si puellarum insereres choro,
> mire sagaces falleret hospites
>   discrimen obscurum solutis
>   crinibus ambiguoque vultu.

> [Lalage will be cherished more than] Cnidian Gyges who, [when] mingled in the chorus of young girls, would absolutely deceive their wise minds, and whose long flowing hair and ambiguous features would hardly let people recognise whether it was a girl or a boy.

The context is rich: Lalage is still too young to love; she is like a green, unripe grape; like a she-goat, she likes to play in the green forests with other she-goats; the poet must wait for her love; and then there comes a list of people that she will be adored more than; in this list appears Gyges.

The theme of sexual ambiguity used by Horace was a convention among Roman poets. They were assimilating Greek literature, which had abounded in homosexual poetry: in Sappho, Callimachus, Meleager and, of course, the dialogues of Plato. Catullus, Vergil, Tibullus, Horace and Propertius wrote a small number of homosexual poems – but this did not necessarily spring from their experience. It was used as a convention – a literary one – and as such, made no claim to be treating life or reality or real experience. The same is true of

Ronsard. He is assimilating Roman poetry and he uses the convention allusively. He uses Horace just as the Roman poets used their Greek models: Catullus 'translates' Sappho and uses the Sapphic metre to compose in. Ronsard's classical training let him see the richness of the principle of *contaminatio*.[1] He expects the Horatian poem and the Roman conventions to be in the reader's mind when he is reading this sonnet. The main mood of the sonnet is admiration; the main line which tells us this is

> Je me contente en mon contentement

The two quatrains weave concrete associations between the mental uncertainty and the ambiguous movement of the hair. The admiration is based on words like *follastrement*, *vagabondes* and *tortement*. They create the fascination that the reader is meant to feel. The sestet starts with a strong emphasis on *merveille*, leading into a comparison with Venus. This in turn gives way to the Adonis allusion, and the story comes to life – not the death-in-love theme that Du Bellay had been using[2] – but the alive-in-love aspect: the astounding beauty of Adonis, the infatuation of the goddess and the intimacy between them.

The allusion in Horace to Gyges of Cnidus is rich: Venus was worshipped in that town, which was one of her favourite abodes: Gyges is a most beautiful youth, and could be compared to Venus or to her son. Ronsard adds another connexion – that of the love between Venus and Adonis. Se we read the ambiguity in two ways: the mistress is so beautiful that she is sexually ambiguous; Gyges was an adolescent boy with fine flowing hair and the association with him runs right through the sonnet. It is both clever and sensuous; witty and sexual; good technique and good content.

In the same way Scève can in three lines open up a wide vista of associations by allusion to an author in the past. For example dizain 308,

---

[1] For details of Ronsard's learning of the classics see P. de Nolhac, *Ronsard et l'humanisme* (Paris, 1921), I. Silver, *The Intellectual Evolution of Ronsard*, volume I: *The Formative Influences* (St Louis, 1969), M. Morrison, 'Ronsard and Catullus: the influence of the teaching of Marc-Antoine de Muret', *BHR*, 18 (1956), pp. 240–74.

[2] See the analysis, pp. 91–2 above.

> Le seul vouloir petitement idoyne,
> A noz plaisirs, comme le mur s'oppose
> Des deux Amantz baisé en Babyloine.

The two terms of comparison are the *vouloir* of the lover and the wall which separated Pyramus and Thisbe in legend. The basic likeness between the two terms is readily apparent, namely their quality as a barrier to passion, but the particular associations cannot be understood without having in mind aspects of the story related by Ovid. The role played by the wall is that of a 'physical barrier to physical union'. Ovid elaborates this point by describing the meeting and conversations of Pyramus and Thisbe,

> tutaeque per illud
> murmure blanditiae minimo transire solebant.
> saepe, ut constiterant, hinc Thisbe, Pyramus illinc;
> inque vices fuerat *captatus anhelitus oris*
> 'invide', dicebant, paries, quid amantibus obstas?
> quantum erat, *ut sineres toto nos corpore jungi*
> aut, hoc si nimium est, *vel ad oscula danda pateres.*
>
> (*Metamorphoses* IV, lines 69–75. My italics.)

Physical frustration is stressed above all else in this account. The pattern of the Scève poem is this: fear, desire and hope are the three forces which urge the lover on towards the attainment of a physical goal. And the result is that his liberty (or the liberty of his *ame*) is attacked and invaded. In the last three lines he states that the only remaining force (or rampart, from the point of view of his *ame*, which is resisting the physical attack) is his *vouloir*, which sets itself against purely physical desire in the same way as the wall separated the bodies of Pyramus and Thisbe. By using allusively the Ovidian account Scève can imply the physical passion within him. Thus the function of the allusion is both to illustrate the argument with an example from mythology and to evoke the associations of physical desire and physical frustration, thereby endowing the abstract *vouloir* with living quality.

Finally let us glance briefly at two examples of this line of allusiveness in two sonnets by the great giants – Du Bellay's first sonnet from *Les Antiquitez* and a famous one in Ronsard's *Sonets pour Hélène*. We start with Ronsard:

> Laisse de Pharaon la terre Egyptienne,
> Terre de servitude, & vien sur le Jourdain:
> Laisse moy ceste Cour, & tout ce fard mondain,
> Ta Circe, ta Sirene, & ta Magicienne.
> Demeure en ta maison pour vivre tout tienne,
> Contente toy de peu: l'âge s'enfuit soudain.
> Pour trouver ton repos, n'atten point à demain:
> N'atten point que l'hyver sur les cheveux te vienne.
> Tu ne vois à ta Cour que feintes & soupçons:
> Tu vois tourner une heure en cent mille façons:
> Tu vois la vertu fausse, & vraye la malice.
> Laisse ces honneurs pleins d'un soing ambitieux,
> Tu ne verras aux champs que Nymphes & que Dieux,
> Je seray ton Orphée, & toy mon Eurydice.
>
> (*Œuvres*, ed. Lemonier *et al.*, vol. xvii, sonnet 22, p. 264)

This organ-sonnet starts with a brilliant chorus, where all the stops are pulled out, figuring two tonal contrasts: reference to Biblical episodes and mythological allusions. This mixture of pagan and Biblical elements is vital: Scève had already, in dizain 143 for example, taken from the Bible the Brazen Serpent of Moses and used it as he used images taken from Classical literature, for example dizain 308, the wall which separated Pyramus and Thisbe. Ronsard, in 1578 – that is in the middle of the Religious Wars – does exactly the same in his sonnet. Later Montaigne will 'prove' very conclusively that pagan and Christian elements can be part and parcel of Renaissance man, but that in a writer the values are aesthetic and not religious. These contrasts in the Ronsard sonnet are underlain by the swell organ, sounding the note of actual events of the time.

The first quatrain has a tonal structure which is superb: the first note is loud and clear, the imperative *Laisse*. The implication is both an invitation and an adieu; this leads into the darkness of Egypt, ruled by Pharaohs, conjuring up the exile of the Israelites in Egypt, suffering curse after curse, held in slavery. The note then changes, and with soft mutation chords Ronsard calls up the whole of Jordan to set in front of Hélène; *sur le*

Jourdain – the land over and beyond the Jordan, a land of milk
and honey, the Promised Land, a land that Hélène could come
to. Between the two imperatives of *Laisse* and *vien* we have
imprinted in our minds the slavery, which in the third line is
linked specifically with the Court – characterized by *fard
mondain*. *Fard* in Cotgrave's translation means 'Fard; painting
(properly Ceruse, or white lead), also, any coloured, or adul-
terate beautie; a deceit, pretence, falsehood, cousenage, blearing
of the eyes.' This Court image is linked backwards to the *terre
Egyptienne* through the adulterous paint, the idol-worship, the
flattery and the lies. The last line of the quatrain parades a series
of mythological figures who have one thing in common: they
are all sorcerers. Furthermore they are qualified possessively: *Ta
Circe, ta Sirene, ta Magicienne*. The allusions are double ones
– to Circe who changed Ulysses' followers to pigs; to sirens
singing on the waves of rocky shores – alluring, enticing men
to their deaths; to the magician of incantatory evocation; and
on another level they are allusions to great figures of Court
divertissements in which Hélène participated. The language, the
allusions, the repetition of *terre*, the position of the caesuras, *&
vien... & tout... & ta Magicienne*, the sibilants in the line – *Ta
Circe, ta Sirene, & ta Magicienne* – the word *mondain* contrasting
strongly with *le Jourdain* in the rhyme – all these features make
it quite an astonishing quatrain.

The second quatrain is like a quiet but firm choir organ, with
comparatively little increase in the ground tone but with a
gradual addition of harmonics. The poet speaks a simple
message in terms of commonplaces such as the Horatian theme
of peace and security in your own house, moderation – do not
seek ambition or wealth or position – the inescapable flight of
time, possessing tranquillity in your own mind and the ever-
favourite theme of *carpe diem*. The *moraliste* is here doing what
he always does – seeing life as a whole with man limited to the
human condition, without any illusion and with lucid
perceptivity.

The first tercet makes a volte-face into an attack on the court
with all the verve of a satirist; the repetition three times of *Tu
vois*; very few concrete suggestions; moral words like *vertu* and

malice formulated like a maxim of La Rochefoucauld (e.g. 'La simplicité affectée est une imposture délicate') in the line *Tu vois la vertu fausse, & vraye la malice* and the whole gathered together with an attacking firmness.

In the last tercet the organ moves towards its climax, the dimension is larger and the sound louder. We are back with the first imperative again – *Laisse*, but then there is a change of tense to the future, a vision of green fields peopled by Gods and nymphs who are the moving, animated people of legend conjured up by Ronsard so often in his poetry. The last line comes as the final climax. But with the mention of this legend he alludes to the most perfect lovers, the whole tragic story of Eurydice's death, the Underworld venture by Orpheus to bring her back to earth, and her final loss, leaving the figure of Orpheus alone and pathetic, but gifted in poetry and song. We know that the poet will never create in reality the *solitude à deux*, but he has created it in imagination. We go back to the ballet figures and we add Orpheus and Eurydice to Circe. The ballet has been performed; the organ fugue is at an end; the love is imaginary; but the incantation is superb. The movement, the alternation between highly allusive terms and the simple language, the harmony of the lines – the aphorismic and the taut, the *moraliste* and the imaginary – all combine to make this sonnet a striking illustration of allusiveness.[1]

Du Bellay's sonnet cycle *Antiquitez de Rome* is the very height of allusiveness, and I want to analyse the first sonnet to demonstrate his mode within his own poetic principles:[2]

> Divins Esprits, dont la poudreuse cendre
>   Gist sous le faix de tant de murs couvers,
>   Non vostre loz, qui vif par voz beaux vers
>   Ne se verra sous la terre descendre,
> Si des humains la voix se peult estendre
>   Depuis icy jusqu'au fond des enfers,

---

[1] See the good analysis of this sonnet in A. M. Boase, *The Poetry of France*, vol. 1, *1400–1600* (London, 1964), pp. lxxvi–lxxvii.

[2] The edition used is that of J. Joliffe and M. A. Screech (Geneva, 1966). I cannot accept Professor Screech's statement that 'Les *Antiquitez* n'ont pas le charme des *Regrets*; elles sont trop marquées par une certaine emphase.' My opinion is that as opposed to the diffusion of *Les Regrets* Du Bellay gives a dense and suggestive coherence to the cycle of *Antiquitez*.

> Soient à mon cry les abysmes ouvers,
> Tant que d'abas vous me puissiez entendre.
> Trois fois cernant sous le voile des cieux
> De voz tumbeaus le tour devocieux,
> A haulte voix trois fois je vous appelle:
> J'invoque icy vostre antique fureur,
> En ce pendant que d'une saincte horreur
> Je vays chantant vostre gloire plus belle.

Confidence in the power of poetry is the starting point of the cycle. Words may bear a whole range of meaning according to the way they are fitted to other words. Allusion provides a grave resonance, and this is one of the main features of *Les Antiquitez*. Du Bellay has chosen to write in the heroic style, evoking the *Aeneid* of Vergil, the *Odes* of Horace and the *Pharsalia* of Lucan: their seriousness of purpose and gravity of style.

The first words *Divins Esprits* are the invocatory entry into a ritual. We recall the invocation to the Muse as used by the Roman poets[1] and see Du Bellay alluding to that motif but giving it a twist. For instead of invoking the lively Muses he invokes the shades of the dead Romans; in fact we are going through a ceremony of calling up the dead souls or spirits of those whose invocation we are imitating. The three words *la poudreuse cendre* govern the whole cycle: weighted by a load of literariness, for it is not the shades of Roman grandeur that are being called but specifically Roman poets. The adjective *poudreuse* becomes a leit-motif in the poems: for instance, Du Bellay had already hinted at it in sonnet 181 of *Les Regrets*, 'Et des vieux murs Romains les poudreuses reliques' and the sonnet to the King before the *Antiquitez* begins – 'des vieux Romains les poudreuses reliques'. When it enters the *Antiquitez* the adjective is recalled again and again: in sonnet 7, line 4 'Honneur poudreux de tant d'ames divines'; in sonnet 14, line 13 'Sur ces pouldreux tombeaux exercent leur audace'; in sonnet 15, line 1 'Umbres pouldreuses' and the last line 'une pouldreuse plaine'; in sonnet 27, the last line 'ces pouldreuses ruines'; and finally in sonnet 28, the last line 'Ce viel honneur pouldreux est le plus honnoré.' The pale grey colour and the

---

[1] See above, p. 51.

crumbling dustiness suggested by the word *pouldreux* give one dimension to the poems as a whole.

Du Bellay then alludes to the poetry of Rome – *vif par voz beaux vers* – the beautiful verse of Vergil, Horace, Propertius, Tibullus, Ovid and Catullus that he knows so well and has assimilated so well. This remark sets the tone for the cycle: it is via re-creation, the converting of the rich splendour of Roman literature to his own *sang et nourriture* – as he had announced nine years earlier in the *Deffence* – that Du Bellay is famous.

The second quatrain calls forth the *fond des enfers* and the *abysmes ouvers* which suggest the classical Underworld and the Manes he is ritually invoking and the poem opens on to another vista: the dimensions are vast, the harmony is broader and the vowel sounds are open. The invocation becomes more dense in the sestet. The three-fold call to the Underworld, the repetition of the three in 'A haulte voix trois fois je vous appelle', the *devocieux* – which Cotgrave translates under *devotion* as 'devotion, zeale, holinesse, conscience, godlinesse; a religous awe, reverend feare, scruple, curiositie' – suggesting a reverence for the works of Antiquity – give an aesthetic perspective to the past of civilisation. In the last tercet the confident statement of *J'invoque* and *Je vays chantant* is balanced against *vostre antique fureur* – the divine fury of inspiration – and *une saincte horreur* – the awe-struck fear that the poet feels within him. *Vostre gloire plus belle* suggests that they will be refurbished in a different language and in a different age.

The suggestiveness of this sonnet is both created and limited by its structure and language. The first eight lines are one sentence: the main clause 'Soient à mon cry les abysmes ouvers' is led up to by a series of secondary clauses – *dont...non...qui...si...* and followed by another secondary clause – *tant que*. This contrasts strongly with the four main clauses of the sestet: confidence and awe at the task are the chief emotions formulated by the timeless present of the tenses. The language has rich but exact connotations: shades, greyishness, blackness, the impression of an underworld and the presence of hallucination, the supernatural, the hovering between death and life. It is as if he were standing near their altar and evoking them to appear. The suggestiveness will be even denser in the famous sonnet 'Palles Esprits, & vous Umbres pouldreuses' – which is far more complicated allusively than this first sonnet and incidentally better.

But the sustained cadences, the repetitions, the complicated syntax are all controlled by the poet: the heroic genre at its best. Screech (Du Bellay, *Les Regrets*, p. 272) quotes an interesting remark by Vauquelin de la Fresnaye which suggests the procedure of Du Bellay's best poetry:

> ceulx-là ne meritent de louange qui, escrivant des satyres, usent de stile trop élevé, car ce seroit faire des vers Heroïques, qui requierent un air haut & magnifique. Ce qui fait qu'au commencement de ces graves poésies on invoque quelque Deité, quasi confessant que ce qu'on doit chanter surpasse les forces de l'entendement humain.

Such is this initiation into a ritual through the incantatory evocation of the *Divins Esprits*.

We have seen in this chapter that it is precisely on the point of allusiveness that we can bring together Scève, Du Bellay and Ronsard. Given the allusiveness traditionally ascribed to great poets, there is not so much a hermetic quality in their poetry as an indirect subtlety akin to that of Horace and Vergil. They rely on classical allusions, for instance: awakening the reader's knowledge and memory so that the full impact of the associations controls the tenor of the argument. Yet the fact that all three are allusive poets does not make them identical. The best of Scève's dizains, especially those that Odette de Mourgues calls 'metaphysical', have a concentration and complexity of argument that makes them very taut. He is passionately interested in the problematic situations that occur in love, and uses syntax, imagery, vocabulary and rhythm to express them.

Throughout this chapter we have been looking at the key concept of *choice* in style: the choice of words, the order of words, the form and shape of the sentence, the structure of the sentence and the shape of the imagery. Everything that transcends the purely referential side of language is stylistic. We cannot talk in polarities like the out-dated *forme/fonds*, since that would imply that our thoughts in the abstract exist in the mind before we have chosen a suitable linguistic expression for them. The meanings, the choice, the style are created by the poets themselves; but it was the presence of a civilisation with a rich poetic tradition that was recovered in France in the sixteenth century that made her so rich in turn. The next person to whom the presence of Rome was crucial was not a poet. It was Montaigne.

6

Montaigne and Rome

In talking about poetry, Montaigne sums up his evaluation of Ronsard and Du Bellay in these words:

> je pense qu'ils l'ont montée au plus haut degré où elle sera jamais; et aux parties en quoy Ronsart et du Bellay excellent, je ne les treuve guieres esloignez de la perfection ancienne.
>
> (II. 17, a I passage)[1]

Yet in an essay which forms an attack against the vanity of rhetoric he states

> Oyez dire metonomie, metaphore, allegorie et autres tels noms de la grammaire, semble-il pas qu'on signifie quelque forme de langage rare et pellegrin? Ce sont titres qui touchent le babil de vostre chambriere. (I. 51, a II passage)

In the first statement Montaigne means that the two poets used rhetorical technique in the same way as the Ancients – Vergil and Horace. In the second statement he means on over-use of rhetoric where the glittering cover hides no thought. The mental habit of seeing the readers in front of one was taken to an extreme by the minor poets of the Pléiade; so much so that it encouraged them to be utterly subservient to audience reaction. A symptom of this phenomenon can be seen in the colossal number of petrarchist sonnets written from 1550 (not only in France but in the whole of Europe) as a result of

---

[1] The I, II, III passages correspond to the 1580, 1588 and 'the exemplaire de Bordeaux' editions. It will be vital in places in the argument that we take notice of these strata-indicators. Montaigne's own copy known as the 'exemplaire de Bordeaux', is the 1588 edition with his manuscript marginalia on it. It is in the Bibliothèque Municipale of Bordeaux. An edited 'exemplaire de Bordeaux' came out in 1906–33 at the hands of Strowski, Gebelin and Villey. When I refer to the actual copy of Montaigne I refer to it as 'his own copy'.

Ronsard's and Du Bellay's experiments with that form of amatory verse. The audience was by far the most important factor in Latin and French rhetorical treatises. Montaigne reversed this relationship, moving into a creative re-texturing of French and Latin in a way that, as we shall see later, is poetic. According to the seventeenth-century critic Guez de Balzac, Montaigne was not a good literary critic because he set Lucretius beside Vergil and classed Seneca before Cicero. Balzac expressed his assessment of Montaigne's classical knowledge thus:

> Quoique le pays latin ne lui fut pas inconnu, il était néanmoins étranger et hôte en ce pays là. Par conséquent, il devait y aller plus retenu et se donner moins de liberté qu'il ne s'en donnait. Il ne devait pas faire le Magistrat où il n'avait pas droit de bourgeoisie. Pour décider des vers latins comme il prétendait de la pouvoir faire il n'entendait pas assez ni le latin ni les vers. Aussi en pareilles occasions, combien d'équivoques et de méprises de son jugement. Je ne vois presque autre chose dans les Essais.[1]

The patronising tone of voice and the arrogance of his social and literary views do not mask the perverseness of the judgement. Like any literary critic with no sensitivity to poetry, he takes what Cicero says about lyric poetry seriously. Seneca, in his *Epistles* XLIX. 5, remarks of Cicero's poetry reading,

> Negat Cicero, si duplicetur sibi aetas, habiturum se tempus, quo legat lyricos.[2]

Montaigne knew the Senecan passage well, for in I. 26, he uses the same view of Cicero's acquaintance with lyric poets,

> Cicero disoit que, quand il vivroit la vie de deux hommes, il ne prendroit pas le loisir d'estudier les poëtes lyriques.

And he adds in the next sentence a damning conclusion on Cicero

> Et je trouve ces ergotistes plus tristement encores inutiles.
> (both being III passages)

---

[1] Cited by A. M. Boase, *The Fortunes of Montaigne* (London, 1935), p. 297.
[2] *Ad Lucilium Epistulae morales*, ed. A. Beltrami (Rome, 1949), p. 171.

The two sophists in question are Aristotle and Cicero.[1]

Even in the twentieth century, over seventy years after Villey's reconstruction of Montaigne's library,[2] the classical knowledge that Montaigne commanded still seems a troubled area. Bowman, for instance, states that 'he overcame his dislike'[3] of Cicero and that 'Montaigne regards his intelligence as critical rather than creative' that 'he possesses no adulation for classical authors', that 'the antiquity of a source [does not] give it any greater venerability' and that Montaigne went 'even to the point of wilfully mistranslating...happily quotes out of context'. These statements are crude and mistaken as generalisations on Montaigne's evaluation of the Classical Tradition.

Another twentieth-century scholar[4] corrects this biased view by saying

> What is most striking about his use of the classics is the way in which, seen through his eyes, antiquity is made alive. Even when he is imitating most closely, he is always aware of ancient life as it was lived, never slipping into the arid lists or scholia characteristic of much classical scholarship in his time and since.

From an early age Montaigne had an emotional link with Latin. It is the starting point of my study. He had the dimension of literary art closely woven into his day-to-day existence. Thanks to the very eccentric methods of education that his father – after coming back from the Italian Wars – was experimenting with, Montaigne did not have French as his mother tongue,

> Quant à moy, j'avois plus de six ans avant que j'entendisse non plus de François ou de Perigordin que d'Arabesque.
>
> (I. 26, a I passage)

Before he had uttered a syllable in any other language he heard conversations in Latin in his home. The German doctor who

---

[1] Montaigne has a quite damning conclusion on Cicero's poetry in II. 10. *Des Livres:* 'Et si ne sçay comment l'excuser d'avoir estimé sa poësie digne d'estre mise en lumiere; ce n'est pas grande imperfection que de mal faire des vers; mais c'est à luy faute de jugement de n'avoir pas senty combien ils estoyent indignes de la gloire de son nom' (a I passage).

[2] Pierre Villey, *Les Sources et l'Evolution des Essais de Montaigne* (2nd edition, 2 vols, Paris, 1933).

[3] F. P. Bowman, *Montaigne: Essays* (London, 1965), pp. 13, 15.

[4] R. A. Sayce, *The Essays of Montaigne: a Critical Exploration* (London, 1972), p. 31.

had been appointed by his father to be his governor did not know any French. Everyone in the household was expected to use or to acquire a few Latin phrases – even housemaids and valets. We can imagine them saying things as *haud scio an* or *sane* or *non satis intellego*. Montaigne's first sentiments were couched in Latin,

> sans art, sans livre, sans grammaire ou precepte, sans fouet
> et sans larmes. (1. 26, a 1 passage)

The particular language to which the child is exposed implies syntactic structures and also intonation patterns. At the age of six, therefore, Montaigne had the pattern of one language in his mind, and that was Latin. Then he went to the college of Guienne at Bordeaux, and the books he learned to love there were books of Latin poetry – Ovid's *Metamorphoses* and Vergil's *Aeneid* for instance – because they were poetry, and poetry, he says, *j'ayme d'une particuliere inclination* (1. 26). He describes his own devouring of Latin poetry, for instance Ovid:

> je me desrobois de tout autre plaisir pour les lire; d'autant
> que cette langue estoit *la mienne maternelle*.
> (1. 26, a 1 passage. The italics are mine.)

Other books were sought after, his college tutor *aiguisoit ma faim* and let him only *à la desrobée gourmander ces livres*. Note the culinary associations behind his whole vocabulary here: he sniffs, smells, yearns physically for dishes that are exotic.[1]

Let us think back to our own childhood reading: remember the excitement of discovering things, remember the impatience when we could not snuggle under the bedclothes with a torch and get on with the story because our mothers would not go away. Remember the absorption, the silence-filled hours and remember the awe and rapture when something in the book matched something we had come across in life. This was the overwhelming experience of Marcel reading Bergotte:

> il me sembla soudain que mon humble vie et les royaumes
> du vrai n'étaient pas aussi séparés que j'avais cru, qu'ils
> coïncidaient même sur certains points, et de confiance et de

---

[1] For details of Montaigne's childhood and adolescence, see Roger Trinquet, *La jeunesse de Montaigne* (Paris, 1972).

joie je pleurai sur les pages de l'écrivain comme dans les bras
d'un père retrouvé.   (Pléiade ed., vol. I, p. 96)

And this was what excited Montaigne in his reading of Latin
poetry. Through him we can begin to see that a personal, bi-focal
attitude to culture and language could be rooted in a French
person of the sixteenth century, even though few people literally
spoke Latin before hearing French. Latin poetry made Montaigne feel as much at home in the first century B.C. – *ce
bienheureux siècle d'Auguste* as Du Bellay calls it – as he did in
sixteenth-century France. The Latin language was his mother
tongue and the link between a child and the language he speaks
is a fundamental one. His *sensibilité*, however crude and rough,
is one of the first qualities to develop. He learns the rudiments
via the tongue that he speaks.

Montaigne quickly lost the ability to converse and write in
Latin,

> Mon Latin s'abastardit incontinent, duquel depuis par desac-
> coustumance j'ay perdu tout usage.   (I. 26, a I passage)

When he reaches a milestone in his autobiography he puts the
point even more clearly,

> Quant au Latin, qui m'a esté donné pour maternel, j'ay
> perdu par des-accoustumance la promptitude de m'en pou-
> voir servir à parler.   (I. 17, a I passage)

But he never lost the ability to read and comprehend his
'mother tongue'. And he never lost the adulation for the Latin
poets: Vergil, Catullus, Propertius, Lucretius and, above all,
Horace. His early bi-lingualism matured into a bi-literacy.
Language, sensibility and poetry are the three things that we
notice in his early years.

His evaluation of classical poets is found already in the first
edition of his *Essais* in 1580. Naturally, it was deepened, added
to, and matured in the subsequent editions but, as we shall see,
it is built into the texture of the essays; it is not the product of
a critical intelligence (or rather not only critical) but of a
creative mind. I shall not touch upon his favourite prose
authors – Plutarch and Seneca – partly because they have been

looked closely at by other critics[1] and partly because my attention will be directly focussed on the Classical poets, for it is via Horace, Vergil, Propertius, Ovid, Catullus, Tibullus, Lucretius and Martial that we can see how dynamic was the Roman tradition for Montaigne.

Montaigne evaluates himself in relation to Ancient Rome, and particularly the poets and poetic-prose writers of the first century:

> me reconnoistre, au prix de ces gens là, si foible et si chetif, si poisant et si endormy, je me fay pitié ou desdain à moy mesmes. (1. 26, a 1 passage)

A certain sensitivity to literature, to the things that have been analysed with subtlety by ancient authors, is synonymous with a feeling that Roman writers are beings who are superior to him. Yet the sentence immediately following brings Montaigne close to a certain realisation,

> Si [meaning *ainsi*] me gratifie-je de cecy, que mes opinions ont cet honneur de rencontrer souvent aux leurs...Aussi que j'ay cela, qu'un chacun n'a pas, de connoistre l'extreme difference d'entre eux et moy. Et laisse, ce neant-moins, courir mes inventions ainsi foibles et basses, comme je les ay produites, sans en replastrer et recoudre les defaux que cette comparaison m'y a descouvert. (a 1 passage)

What interests us in these two quotations is Montaigne's awareness of writing from a bi-focal point of view: he is an adult, imbued with Classical literature, aware of all the differences between himself and, say Plutarch, and yet he will not be a plagiarising author. It is not so much what he reads, as the way of looking at things that Montaigne time and again presses home. Judgement and the *moraliste* tradition – which as we have seen entered France via the poets of the Renaissance – are important catalysts to his own writing.

Montaigne lives, breathes and eats with living people, with Plutarch and Livy, Vergil and Horace; he understands that

---

[1] See for example, Robert Aulotte, *Amyot et Plutarque: la tradition des Moralia au XVIe siècle* (Geneva, 1965), and Carol E. Clarke, 'Seneca's Letters to Lucilius as a source of some of Montaigne's imagery', *BHR*, xxx (1968), pp. 249–66.

learning about wise men is the best way of becoming one, that chewing over a word in a passage of Lucan, translating or paraphrasing it in one's own words is part of the training of a writer; that puzzling over virtue, good, evil, conscience and repentance is part of a probationer's life; and that sounding out the depths of psychological laws is an integral form of his writing. For him the creative work of Roman writers becomes re-creation in his hand, because

> Que nous sert-il d'avoir la panse pleine de viande, si elle ne se digere? si elle ne se transforme en nous? si elle ne nous augmente et fortifie?   (I. 25, a I passage)

Montaigne's one affectation is to pretend to have none. In spite of his professed negligence in almost everything, his care for style is quite apparent. A mere glance at the I, II, III passages (the 1580, 1588 and the 'exemplaire de Bordeaux' editions) would convince one of that. Re-creation for him was poetic; it was the poetic tradition of Ancient Rome on which he nourished himself and it was that tradition that he was grafting his writing upon. Montaigne rarely translated or interpreted his quotations: another clue to the fact that bi-lingualism and bi-literacy meant that he was structuring his French around his Latin, that he was trying to make a new language work, and that he was doing this consistently.

We are still not sure how bi-lingualism works. Professor George Steiner in his book, *After Babel. Aspects of Language and Translation* (London, 1975, pp. 115–21), gives a fascinating account of his tri-lingualism – English, French and German – but comes to the conclusion that he has no memory of there being a first language or mother tongue with him. He gives us an anecdote to prove this:

> in the course of a road accident, while my car was being hurled across oncoming traffic, I apparently shouted a phrase or sentence of some length. My wife does not remember in what language.

Thus, in a moment of extreme shock, one language may or may not have taken over. Montaigne's bi-lingualism is rather different: his mother tongue was Latin, but we cannot say, with any degree of certainty, which language Montaigne was thinking in at any precise moment. For example, did he create his 'own' Latin quotations? We shall see later, that perhaps he did. 'Avant le premier desnouement de ma langue' (i. 26) he was taught Latin and in certain moments of shock it was the language that he used. He gives as an example his father fainting:

> Le langage latin m'est comme naturel, je l'entens mieux que le François [which is an extraordinary thing to say when he is creating in French and not in Latin] mais il y a quarante ans que je ne m'en suis du tout poinct servy à parler, ny à escrire; si est-ce que à des extremes et soudaines esmotions ou je suis tombé deux ou trois fois en ma vie, et l'une, voyent mon pere tout sain se renverser sur moy, pasmé, j'ay tousjours eslancé du fond des entrailles les premieres paroles Latines; (III) nature se sourdant et s'exprimant à force, à l'encontre d'un long usage. (II) Et cet exemple se dict d'assez d'autres.
>
> (III. 2)

The last sentence may cover at least two moments of shock where there is nothing specific said about the language he was using. The first one was the loss of La Boëtie. We shall analyse it in the next chapter. The other is an experience which is vital: the loss of consciousness when he was knocked off his horse – II. 6, 'De l'exercitation'. There is no suggestion in the essay that he spoke in Latin rather than French: when he was 'unconscious' he 'respondois quelque mot a ce qu'on me demandoit' and these words must have been in French. But one thing is certain – a mono-lingual French person will 'hear' Montaigne's 'tone' in a very different way from a bi-lingual Latin/French person. This is important.[1]

The generation of Racine already had to have the Latin quotations translated: for instance, the 1659 editon of the *Essais*

---

[1] In his introduction to *Classical Influences on European Culture. A.D. 1500–1700* (Cambridge, 1976), p. 6, Dr Bolgar discusses this bilingualism of the Renaissance and points out that research is badly needed on this topic. And he further offers a statement (p. 11) which is crucial. 'Educated men in the Renaissance – certainly those who were bilingual – lived in two distinct, if overlapping, intellectual worlds; *and the precise effect of this is something we have yet to discover.*' (My italics.) I would corroborate Dr Bolgar's point here: in every writer who is bilingual, research – both linguistic and literary – needs to be done.

has 'les versions des passages grecs, latins et italiens' inserted. The position of Latin had changed in the sixty years since Montaigne's death. One must keep one's mind open about which language was more culturally important for Montaigne when he was actually writing. And the possibility that he was thinking in a combination of the two languages must be borne in mind.

It was through his bi-literacy that he started composing 'prose' in French. He scorned all that Cicero said about style and rhetoric. Montaigne allied himself with Horace, one of his favourite poets:

> Horace ne se contente point d'une superficielle expression, elle le trahiroit. Il voit plus cler et plus outre dans la chose; son esprit crochette et furette tout le magasin des mots et des figures pour se representer.   (III. 5, a II passage)

And Montaigne faced one of the problems that faced Horace in Rome in the first century B.C.: what form or shape to follow, what reader to write for, or what structure his writing would take. Montaigne was writing at a time when self-revelation was in its infancy, and his mixture of fiction and of actual experience was new. It was hard to create some thing new, where there were no existing models.

Let us start at the beginning: on opening the *Essais* we read the preface 'Au lecteur', which is the presentation of his book to the public in 1580.[1] I am going to show that this piece of writing is Montaigne's version of a Horatian *recusatio*: that is, a refusal of grand themes, of epic literature, a refusal of rhetoric on the grand scale, a plea in defence of the 'lowness' of his work, which only deals with himself and with commonplace themes like nature, love and death; and a request that people should not waste their time in reading his *Essais*.[2]

---

[1] I do not think one can accurately do as Villey in his massive volume did, that is work hypothetically towards the stage when individual essays were written from 1572 to 1580. The real beginning, in my opinion, is the first printed edition.

[2] Gordon Williams in his *Tradition and originality in Roman poetry* (Oxford, 1968), pp. 42ff, summarises the poet's use of the *recusatio*: 'They sadly regret that their poor talents will not rise to great subjects and the subjects to which they will not rise are not the old mythological tales but the great affairs of contemporary Roman history and in particular, the deeds of Augustus.' Professor Williams suggests that in using the themes of *recusatio*, poets put themselves before a public world and a wide-ranging audience. This applies to Montaigne's use of *recusatio*, as we shall see.

The preface 'Au lecteur' seems to offer as many difficulties as it contains words. Montaigne wrote it before delivering his manuscript to the printer for the first edition in 1580. He retained it in its pure state (except for dating it accurately, according to which edition it was in) for the 1582, the 1587 and 1588 editions. After his death, most of the 1595 editions are without it, but this is due to the carelessness of his 'fille d'alliance' rather than to any expressed intention of Montaigne's.[1] We can see that in the 'exemplaire de Bordeaux', the copy of the 1588 edition – his own text, the one on which he was working when he died, the preface is still the first piece that Montaigne wants the reader to read.

Now Montaigne is an extremely intellectual writer, and the reader is confronted with the question of assessing the large role played by tradition in the writing of the *Essais*. A whole dimension of his life – his ideals, his moral, intellectual and aesthetic values, his aspirations, his craftsmanship, his emotions and sensations – is tied to Latin authors. The self-consciousness of a poet became a prime factor in Horace's creation of literary work, precisely because Latin literature was derivative and all the modes of communicating were intensely studied in Rome.

As we have seen all the writers of the sixteenth century who themselves had received a humanist education, aimed at imitating the Ancients, at picking one of the literary topoi and re-working it for their own use. The dedication of a book is such a topos, and Montaigne knew what it was that he was offering.

When one is presenting a book to the public there are different ways of doing it. For example, works of modern scholarship have prefaces which specify who has helped in the making of the book, conventionally adding a note that the author is alone responsible for wrong statements, wrong judgement and wrong reason. A creative work such as George Eliot's *Middlemarch* may have a 'Prelude', where the author sets down certain elements in woman's lot throughout history in order to put her feminine novel in some kind of perspective. Into his *Collected Poems*, published in 1952, Dylan Thomas inserted a note from himself to his readers, and printed in addition a poem

---

[1] For a full account of the textual tradition of the *Essais* see R. A. Sayce, *The Essays of Montaigne: a Critical Exploration*, pp. 8–24.

entitled 'Author's Prologue', in which he addresses the strangers
who are his readers:

> At poor peace I sing
> To you strangers (though song
> Is a burning and crested act,
> The fire of birds in
> The world's turning wood,
> For my sawn, splay sounds),
> Out of these seathumbed leaves
> That will fly and fall
> Like leaves of trees and as soon
> Crumble and undie
> Into the dogdayed night...

In Ancient Rome the topos had known several virtuoso
variations. For example, the poets used the journey to Helicon
to call upon the Muses to suggest their own literary uniqueness.
As early as Lucretius, the mountain Parnassus was used as a
device to assert priority in singing themes,

> avia Pieridum peragro loca nullius ante
> trita solo.   (i, lines 926–7)

> I traverse the distant haunts of the Pierides, never trodden
> before by the foot of man.

whereas Vergil in the *Georgics* had said

> primus ego in patriam mecum modo vita supersit
> Aonio rediens deducam vertice Musas;
> primus Idumeas referam tibi, Mantua, palmas.
> (*Georgics*, iii, lines 10–12)

> First will I lead home with me, if life but last, the Muses from
> their Aonian hill, first, my Mantua, bring thee back the palms
> of Idume...

Propertius had said

> sed quod pace legas, opus hoc de monte Sororum
> detulit intacta pagina nostra via.(*Elegies*, iii. 1, lines 17–18)

> but this work of mine, I have brought down from the
> mountain of the Muses by an untrodden way, that you may
> read it in the midst of peace.

Whilst Ovid had proclaimed that his songs had no mother, only a father,

> Palladis exemplo de me sine matre creata
> carmina sunt; stirps haec progeniesque mea est.
>
> (*Tristia*, III. 14, 13)

Many writers address themselves to the book as a father to his son. Horace has a humorous sketch in which he calls the book his slave, wanting to be released from his master's clutch,

> Vertumnum Ianumque, liber, spectare videris,
> scilicet ut prostes Sosiorum pumice mundus.
>
> (*Epistles*, I. 20, lines 1–2)
>
> You seem, my book, to be looking wistfully toward Vertumnus and Janus, in order that you go on sale, neatly polished with the pumice of the Sosii.

Cervantes, when he published the first part of his *Don Quixote* in 1604, used the topos of begetting a child:

> what could my sterile and ill-cultivated genius beget but the story of a lean, shrivelled, whimsical child, full of varied fancies that no-one has ever imagined...

And in the rest of his prologue Cervantes gently satirises the way that a writer starts off his work with innumerable sonnets from colleagues, eulogies and epigrams from friends – all of which deserve a place at the beginning of all books.

Montaigne, writing his preface, is adding himself to the long list of authors who used this topos and could be dismissed with that contemptuous remark of Proust,

> L'écrivain ne dit que par une habitude prise dans le langage insincère des préfaces et des dédicaces: 'Mon lecteur'.
>
> (Pléiade ed., vol. III, p. 911)

But is the convention 'insincere'? According to Proust the writer who uses the preface is insincere because he does not literally mean what he says. But the writer could be using words to suggest something: that is to say, to be allusive again. I now analyse at length Montaigne's *Avis* in an attempt to work out its explicit and implicit meanings.

C'est icy un livre de bonne foy, lecteur.

This can have two implications: good faith towards the reader and good faith towards oneself – sincerity, frankness and authenticity. In all works of art it is the author's view that one gets, and in this is implied a whole experience of life. In this contract between the author and reader the pledge is one of good faith: the author guarantees sincerity towards what he is writing and the reader is asked, in return, for an attentive ear. In the *Essais* the phrase *de bonne foy* will be looked at from many different angles: for instance, from a public and a private point of view. From a public viewpoint one could say, as Gide did, 'on ne peut à la fois être sincère et le paraître'. This is taking the *faux-monnayage* metaphor seriously. Montaigne says elsewhere:

> Nostre verité de maintenant, ce n'est pas ce qui est, mais ce qui se persuade à autruy: comme nous appellons monnaye non celle qui est loyalle seulement mais la fauce aussi qui a mise.   (II. 18, a 1 passage)

He implies that this preoccupation with sincerity, reality, illusion, persuasiveness to other people, and authenticity is at the deep root of his questioning the values that man has attached to things, his stripping down of a man's character, his denouncing of false learning and his wish to see the *condition humaine* as it is without the false illusion of metaphysics. And at this point Gide joins Montaigne, and keeps the metaphor of *faux-monnayage* constantly in his mind.

From a private viewpoint the whole question of sincerity is going to be seen as immensely problematic. A glance at his own copy of the *Essais*, the 'exemplaire de Bordeaux' shows us the extensive marginalia, the crossings out and the additions so that in one way, Montaigne's personal, private portrait is instilled into our minds by his sincerity. But he said in Book II, Ch. 1.

> Je donne à mon ame tantost un visage, tantost un autre selon le costé où je la couche. Si je parle diversement de moy, c'est que je me regarde diversement.   (a II passage)

Thus the first statement in this dedication is allusive, complex and ambiguous. For finally the 'sincerity' of Montaigne, his *bonne foy*, cannot be known except – and perhaps not even understood there – in Montaigne's own thoughts, as articulated to himself.

Il t'advertit dés l'entrée, que je ne m'y suis proposé aucune fin, que domestique et privée.
There is humility in this assertion and yet it seems rather overwrought. When we enter the universe of the *Essais* it seems rather different: the first essay, 'Par divers moyens on arrive à pareille fin' begins,

> La plus commune façon d'amollir les cœurs de ceux qu'on a offensez, lors qu'ayant la vengeance en main, ils nous tiennent à leur mercy, c'est de les esmouvoir par submission à commiseration et à pitié.

It sounds as though Montaigne is going to talk about military affairs, weighing one tactic against another, and the behaviour of man analysed schematically in the manner of Livy. When we read other essays we doubt that they warn the reader *dés l'entrée*; we would be inclined to say that they do not do anything as simple as that. Is the remark mere self-confidence? Not really. At this stage of the life of the *Essais* Montaigne is not certain that anyone will buy and read them. That may be the reason why his first edition was published in Bordeaux rather than in Paris. For after all he had already published in Paris his translation of Sebond's *Theologia Naturalis* or *Liber Creaturarum* in 1569 and the works of his friend La Boëtie in 1571–2. But they are not the *Essais* and in the dedication Montaigne is probably covering himself against criticism.

Je n'y ay eu nulle consideration de ton service, ny de ma gloire.
This rather contradicts the pledge given in the first statement. The reader is now not even superficially considered; Montaigne has no regard for him. The gift of this book to his family and a few friends is all that counts. But obviously he could have done that without having it published at all, so it is equally clear that this statement is not literally true. But one remembers Horace, and one remembers the essay 'Du dementir', II. 18, where Montaigne goes to great lengths in justifying his self-portrait.

Montaigne does not have the excuse that he is a great man like Caesar or Xenophon; he is an *homme de la commune façon*, so has nothing grand or uplifting to reveal. He accepts this,

> Cette remonstrance est très-vraie, mais elle ne me touche que bien peu: (a 1 passage)

After a colon Horace's words come to mind in answer to the public's objections,

> non recito cuiquam, nisi amicis, idque rogatus,
> non ubivis, corámve quibuslibet. In medio qui
> scripta foro recitent, sunt multi, quique lavantes.
>
> *(Satires,* I. 4, 73)[1]

Note that this is a 1 passage – and therefore was inserted in 1580. It reads in English,

> I do not read this to anyone; I read it to my friends only and at their request; I do not read my work just anywhere nor in front of any audience. There are many authors however who read their works in the middle of the forum and in public baths.

Montaigne adds – still in a 1 passage – 'Je ne dresse pas icy une statue à planter au carrefour d'une ville, ou dans une Eglise, ou place publique' which is a way of resituating the Horatian quotation, transferring the forum to the square of a town, the public baths into a Church and making an addition in the form of a statue in front of the listeners. The theme of 'I am writing for a few chosen friends' is a leit-motif throughout Horace's work and Montaigne in the first edition goes on to say,

> C'est pour le coin d'une librairie, et pour en amuser un voisin, un parent, un amy, qui aura plaisir à me racointer et repratiquer en cett'image. Les autres ont pris cœur de parler d'eux pour y avoir trouvé le subject digne et riche; moy, au rebours, pour l'avoir trouvé si sterile et si maigre qu'il n'y peut eschoir soupçon d'ostentation.

The *fin privée* of the dedication statement is asserted in *Du dementir* too,

[1] In the Oxford text of the *Satires* we find the *non* of Montaigne's version has become a *nec* and instead of *rogatus* the word *coactus* is inserted.

ils ne sçauroient faire moins de conte de moy que j'en feray
d'eux en ce temps là. (again a 1 passage)

He could not care less whether his descendants read his work
or not. When he says in the last part of the dedication *ny de ma
gloire* the one word *gloire* works ambiguously: Montaigne does
not want immortality through posterity, as the Pléiade did, who
aimed so eagerly and ardently at immortality via their works.
And yet we shall see that *gloire* is crucially important for
Montaigne as a writer.

Mes forces ne sont pas capables d'un tel dessein.

In one sense this humility and self-abasement are not to be
taken as Montaigne's psychological confession. For this topos
too was in Ancient literature; and Horace, in particular, had
used it time and again.

The element of self-belittlement is a social convention which
arises spontaneously in all civilised societies. With a thousand
other topoi and conventions of Ancient rhetoric, affected
modesty passed into the literature of the Christian culture. For
the mediaeval Latin writers the *captatio benevolentiae* had a
number of stereotyped phrases as leit-motifs: for example,
apologies for style (*sermo*) or for talent (*ingenium*); excuses that
their writing was artless (*rudis, simplex, communis, incompositus,
incomptus, incultus*) or crude (*impolitus*) or paltry (*inopia, paupertas,
exilitas, sterilitas*). Writers are fond of accusing themselves of
rusticitas, that is of a crude and faulty style. The profession of
unworthiness can be seen in Saint Paul in II Cor. 11. 6, where
he answers criticism of his letters thus: 'But though I be rude
in speech, yet not in knowledge.' It is clear that he held that
the matter was superior to mere skill in discourse. Thus he was
to be preferred, according to him, to other people who simply
had the *sermo* but not the *scientia*.

The Renaissance tradition of self-depreciation is a rich one.
We may think of Marguerite de Navarre's *Heptaméron*, where
in the preface she exempts the whole group of story-tellers from
aiming at rhetoric and literature. They are gathered together
to amuse themselves by telling true stories:

> Et prosmirent les dictes dames et monseigneur le Daulphin avecq d'en faire chascun dix et d'assembler jusques à dix personnes qu'ilz pensoient plus dignes de racompter quelque chose, *sauf ceulx qui avoient estudié et estoient gens de lettres*; car monseigneur le Daulphin ne voulloit que *leur art y fut meslé, et aussy de paour que la beaulté de la rhetorique feit tort en quelque partye à la verité de l'histoire.*[1]   (my italics)

Or we may think of More's *Utopia* which was written in his spare moments – 'that time which I steal from sleep and meat' – or Rabelais's claim to compose while eating and drinking, or Erasmus ending the epistle before *The Praise of Folly* with a dateline 'ex rure'.[2] These were all devices to remove the books from the scholarly domain in which they could more easily be attacked.

Even so, the sentence *Mes forces ne sont pas capables d'un tel dessein* reeks of mock-modesty. We remember that whenever Horace deals with his refusal of epic themes – odes on victory, poems on military campaigns, the voyages of Ulysses – he uses the negative technique and follows it with a 'poor little me' kind of phrase. For example, in *Odes* i. 6, all such subjects are too great for me to write on:

> nos, Agrippa, neque haec dicere nec gravem
> Pelidae stomachum cedere nescii,
> nec cursus duplicis per mare Ulixei,
>   nec saevam Pelopis domum
> conamur...

> For us, Agrippa, we are not engaged upon such exploits, we are not singing of the fatal anger of ungovernable Achilles, nor the voyages of crafty Ulysses, nor the crimes of the race of Pelops...

---

[1] *L'Heptaméron*, ed. M. François (Paris, 1943), p. 9.

[2] The style of Erasmus is a reflection of the irony that is the base of the work. For example, in the preface to Thomas More, 'nisi plane me fallit...stultitiam laudavimus, sed non omnino stulte' where there is a play on the words *stultitiam/stulte*. Or take a further example, 'maxime si nugae seria ducant, atque ita tractentur ludicra ut ex his aliquanto plus frugis referat lector...Vt enim nihil nugatius, quam seria nugatorie tractare, ita nihil festiuius, quam ita tractare nugas, ut nihil minus quam nugatus fuisse uidearis...' where a constant use of double or triple negatives, the constant presence of *nugae* (*nugae/nugatius/nugatorie/nugatus*) and the opposition with *seria* establishes it as a masterpiece of a defence of 'light' literature. The edition used was the 1526 one. A MSS. note gives the date and possessor, but not the place published.

and then there comes his humble offering,

> tenues grandia, dum pudor
> imbellisque lyrae Musa potens vetat
> laudes egregii Caesaris et tuos
> culpa deterere ingeni.

We are too small for such subjects; our reserve and the Muse, mistress of our peaceful lyre, forbid us to diminish the glory of the great Caesar and you, our genius is weak...

Some writers can deal with this, others with that, but I'll not write of those things. I am poor and mediocre; I cannot do that but

> nos convivia, nos proelia virginum
> sectis in juvenes unguibus acrium
> cantamus, vacui, sive quid urimur
> non praeter solitum leves.

We are singing of feasts, the struggle between young girls with clipped nails and young men; whether our heart is free or whether, light as usual, we are burned with some passion.

We may remember the sonnet in Du Bellay's *Les Regrets* when he tells us what he is not going to do:

> Je ne veulx fueilleter les exemplaires Grecs,
>   Je ne veulx retracer les beaux traicts d'un Horace,
>   Et moins veulx-je imiter d'un Petrarque la grace,
>   Ou la voix d'un Ronsard, pour chanter mes regrets.
>   [....]
> Je me contenteray de simplement escrire
>   Ce que la passion seulement me fait dire,
>   Sans rechercher ailleurs plus graves argumens.

We 'nose' the false naïveté here since from the very beginning Du Bellay is using Horace's Epistles and Satires as Classical model. This Horatian *recusatio* technique was well known to all sixteenth-century writers, and of course to Montaigne. Thus he incorporates it into his dedication lest he like Horace 'should spread my tiny sails upon the Tyrrhenian sea' (*Odes*, IV. 15, 3–4)

Je l'ay voué à la commodité particuliere de mes parens et amis: à ce que m'ayant perdu (ce qu'ils ont à faire bien tost) ils y puissent retrouver aucuns

traits de mes conditions et humeurs, et que par ce moyen ils nourrissent
plus entiere et plus vifve, la connoissance qu'ils ont eu de moy.

Vergil and Horace, even when supposedly writing for the
public, still meant their work to stand the private scrutiny of
a few chosen friends. Indeed, in one of his Odes, *Odes* II. 16,
Horace, as we have seen (p. 49 above), rejects the *malignum
vulgus* as an audience for his *tenuis spiritus*,

> . . . mihi parva rura et
> spiritum Graiae tenuem Camenae
> Parca non mendax dedit et malignum
> spernere vulgus.

Both Rabelais and Montaigne constantly mock their critics.
When Montaigne talks of the *commodité* of his friends there is as
much irony as when Rabelais says,

> A moy n'est que honneur et gloire d'estre dit et reputé bon
> gaultier et bon compaignon. . . .
> (Prologue to *Gargantua*, ed. Jourda, p. 9)

It is true that Montaigne in a number of *Essais* shows how fine
it is to think about one's ancestors, to caress some of their
possessions, to read about the peculiar traits of their character,
to try and recall concretely the shape of a person's features and
the turn of his mind. Thus again in 'Du dementir', II. 18, we
can see that the shape was already fixed in 1580, but when we
come to the parts added in the 'exemplaire de Bordeaux'
edition the concrete suppleness is added:

> Quel contentement me seroit ce d'ouir ainsi quel – qu'un qui
> me recitast les meurs   (a 1 passage)

Montaigne here baldly states that it is a great joy to him to hear
about ancestors. But a III passage follows hard on this sentence's
heels:

> le visage, la contenance, les parolles communes

after which the 1 passage continues

> et les fortunes de mes ancestres! Combien j'y serois attentif!
> Vrayement cela partiroit d'une mauvaise nature, d'avoir à
> mespris les portraits mesmes de nos amis et predecesseurs,

This is in direct correspondence with the preface 'Au lecteur', and we do not doubt the 'sincerity' of Montaigne in hoping that his immediate circle of friends and relations would know him better if these *Essais* were read. He goes much further, and writes more personally in the III passage following:

> la forme de leurs vestements et de leurs armes. J'en conserve l'escriture, le seing, des heures et un'espée peculiere qui leur a servi, et n'ay point chassé de mon cabinet des longues gaules que mon pere portoit ordinairement en la main.

Yet despite this evidence, we sense that he is thinking of an audience and of posterity. This audience, and Montaigne's views on it, are very important in the *Essais*, but already we have become aware that his self-depiction was meant to go beyond the family's use of such knowledge of him after he is dead. Already, too, he was aware that the social and aesthetic conditions did not favour honest self-portraiture, as indeed the Roman writers were also sure.

Si c'eust esté pour rechercher la faveur du monde, je me fusse mieux paré et me presenterois en une marche estudiée.

The additional phrase *paré de beautez empruntées* in the 1588 version (removed in the final version quoted above) avoids the near cliché of the metaphor which Cervantes uses in 1604 for the first part of his *Don Quixote*:

> naked of that precious adornment of elegance and erudition in which works composed in the houses of the learned usually go clothed...

And Montaigne also altered the *meilleure demarche* of 1588 to the final *marche estudiée*, so that it is clear that he no longer felt that there was a better or worse kind of character that he himself could paint; it was rather that he could do it in a studied, elaborate manner or he could do it in the simple manner and he opted for the latter. There is, incidentally, a certain mock-modesty about the rejection of earthly glory, worldly favour and praise since these were so much part of the society that had dazzled the Pléiade. There is no doubt that Montaigne was deliberately evaluating all writers and himself when he used these phrases about earthly glory.

Je veus qu'on m'y voie en ma façon simple, naturelle et ordinaire, sans contantion et artifice: car c'est moy que je peins.

The 1580 version had *estude*, now altered to *contantion*: the change is merely stylistic – not repeating the *estudiée* of the previous phrase. The idea of a battle, of a physical struggle, is preserved in the word *contantion*. The contrast that Montaigne is making is between the rhetoricians' ideal – working upon nature to produce a more perfect nature, one that could be admired as an artifact – and the simple ideal that he wishes to aim at. This contrast depends on the stylistic positioning of, on the one hand, three adjectives – *simple, naturelle et ordinaire* – and, on the other, the two nouns *contantion et artifice*. This is similar to the contrast in the *recusationes* which Horace, Propertius and Vergil made between *magnus, grandis, tumidus* and *vastis* and the much more humble adjectives like *parvus, mollis, tenuis* and *parcus*. Now the interesting thing is that when Horace writes his Odes, he is consciously working on a grand scale, even though he constantly, ironically, used the *recusatio*. So he drew to the reader's attention that though he said that he was not doing anything grand, he was doing precisely that. Claims like the famous *Odi profanum vulgus et arceo* (*Odes*, III 1. 1) or *Exegi monumentum aere perennius* (III. 30. 1) make one realise that in this smaller genre (as opposed to drama or epic) Horace is aiming at 'high lyric'. On the other hand, when he is writing his satires and epistles the irony of the *recusatio* is even more apparent. When he has nothing else to do, then he just scribbles:

> haec ego mecum
> conpressis agito labris: ubi quid datur oti
> illudo chartis.   (*Satires*, I. 4, 137–9)

These works are not for publication. They are only to be read to friends. He despises the *doctus poeta* of the Augustan age – when he is in a satirical or conversational mood, at any rate. The opposition of the *docte* and the *indocte*, of the *sçavant* and the *insçavant* was to be one of Montaigne's leit-motifs in the *Essais*. The contrast is always with his own simplicity, his ordinary condition, and his natural form. Montaigne presents the reader with a self-portrait which shows little of the affected modesty we saw in the preface 'Au lecteur'. However, we do notice that he has two tones built into his *moi* – the highly self-conscious tone which tells us not to bother with his essays because they are trivial, and a dogmatic tone which underlies the whole piece. Look at the way he puts a logical word like *car* before *c'est moy que je peins*. It is as if he were acutely aware of the singularity, the uniqueness of his project, and aware too that the self-belittling tone was vital to the enterprise. The combination of these two tones is a permanent leit-motif in his work, not merely in the 1580 edition but right up to the 'exemplaire de Bordeaux'. We shall examine these different tones later.

Mes defauts s'y liront au vif, et ma forme naïfve, autant que la reverence publique me l'a permis.

The self-portrait that Montaigne is aiming at will cover all the defects and concrete qualities he is aware of. He has chosen the *I* or *moi* as the witness and protagonist. The angle of vision is a fixed centre. We are to have only the thoughts and perceptions of the *moi* through whom he can convey his information. Similarly Burton starts his *Anatomy of Melancholy* with a poem by 'Democritus Junior' (his quasi-pseudonym), calling the style of the book a 'nutmeg grater': but the life which it is concerned to display is at least *proba*.

Montaigne's commitment to showing the authentic shape of his life seems serious here: so in 1580 he had committed himself to writing solely about himself. And there is a comment in III. 9. 'De la vanité' in the 1588 version – but later crossed out, so that the 'exemplaire de Bordeaux', Montaigne's own copy, has six lines violently erased[1] – which corroborates the point. If we look at it we shall see more clearly what went before the 1580 commitment to writing in this way.

---

[1] The violence is such that marks have come out in the page directly underneath. Furthermore, there is a marginal addition which is crossed out as well. We can see that Montaigne corrects the 1588 version at first but then decides to cut the whole passage out. This is evidence for thinking that it is the real reason for writing, a reason that Montaigne the artist – not Montaigne the man – thought it best to hide. This is another example of the extreme difficulty of proving 'sincerity' in any writer.

Je sçay bien, que je ne lairray après moy aucun respondant si affectionné de bien loing et entendu en mon faict comme j'ay esté au sien. Il n'y a personne à qui je vousisse pleinement compromettre de ma peinture: luy seul jouyssoit de ma vraye image et l'emporta. C'est pourquoy je me deschiffre moy-mesme, si curieusement.

If La Boëtie had lived the *Essais* would have not been written – at least not in the shape they took. There would be no need of 'seeing oneself', for while he was alive La Boëtie was the only man who could enter Montaigne's personality, his mind and his thoughts. This suggests that the most perfect kind of communication is friendship. We shall see in the next chapter when we analyse 'De l'amitié' how much the Roman world and especially the Augustan poets were the link between La Boëtie and Montaigne. But the commitment to giving his *forme* in writing is a totally serious statement. It is the only means of giving some sense to his inner shape.

Now the Pléiade were involved with artifice and preoccupied by the 'heroic' genre and the grand style of writing. The Protestant theologians of Montaigne's age were concerned with expounding what they thought the Word of God was; Erasmus in his *Adagia* had started a fashion in *leçons* that captured Europe for well over a hundred years; Montluc in his *Commentaires* was to take up the taste for biography; Benvenuto Cellini had written his Memoirs. All these writers influenced Montaigne – *sentences* here and there, *exempla* from Ancient history, the lives and deaths of fine men in Amyot's Plutarch – but none of these influences was crucial in the evolution of the *Essais*. The work of fiction plus experience was new: but even in this very newness of self-revelation there was one model on which Montaigne could work: and that was the poetry of Horace. We can see and even hear, below the surface of Montaigne's work, the intimate, confidential tone that Horace adapted in that poetry, particularly in his Epistles, from the framework of conversation. It is even the framework of chattiness, but so perfected by art that the critic can contemplate elements like sincerity, authenticity and frankness because that poetry has entered his experience to become part of his inner form. We shall return to this point.

autant que la reverence publique me l'a permis.

This leit-motif is closely linked with the rest of the dedication. Because society, because the public is what it is, he cannot paint himself wholly. For one thing, sex is a taboo subject. It is not until 1588 that he ventures upon it: towards the end of III. 5, 'Sur des Vers de Virgile' – where sexual fulfilment is the central topic – he asserts that sex is crucial for his total self-portrait:

> Chacune de mes pieces me faict esgalement moy que toute autre. Et nulle autre ne me faict plus proprement homme que cette-cy. Je dois au publiq universellement mon pourtrait.
>
> (a III passage)

And there is a statement in the 'exemplaire de Bordeaux' which harks back to the preface 'Au lecteur' in a vital way, so that the interconnexion between his portrait and the subject matter is made quite clear. There are two versions of the personal statement:

> 1. Ma preface liminere [*liminere* was added later] montre que ie n'esperois pas tant. Les plus sages et sains escris des auteurs m'ont enhardi. Et le recueil qu'on a faict a mon premier proiect [followed by two words which are unintelligible] ie me suis pique a rompre la glace et monstrer a nos [the end of this variant is unintelligible and later Montaigne modified the statement to]...auteurs et le recueil qu'on a faict a ma proposition m'ont enhardi si que ie me suis piqué...
>
> 2. Et les praeceptes de nos maistres et leurs exemples portent que tout esprit ~~dont~~ qui par fois ne se sente agite de quelque allegresse foliante...[1]

Wanting to make his position less ambiguous Montaigne added, crossed out and tried to find the words that would express his personal statement: his beloved ancient authors provided the authority, and a reading public – witness the sale of his first editions – furnished the audience.[2]

It is important to realise that Montaigne is very aware of the

---

[1] References to the edition 'exemplaire de Bordeaux' are from the 'Edition municipale': Montaigne, *Essais*, ed. F. Strowski, F. Gebelin, P. Villey, Bordeaux, 1906–33. They are given under the letter EM. Here it is EM III, p. 132.

[2] For the discussion on sex in this essay see D. Coleman, 'Montaigne's "Sur des Vers de Virgile": taboo subject, taboo author', in R.R. Bolgar (ed.) *Classical influences on European Culture, AD 1500–1700* (Cambridge, 1976), pp. 135–40.

public. But the perspective in which he presents himself, at first and later in his approaches at intimacy, is a totally private one. The sex taboo he will break in the third Book.

Que si j'eusse esté entre ces nations qu'on dict vivre encore sous la douce liberté des premieres loix de nature, je t'asseure que je m'y fusse très-volontiers peint tout entier, et tout nud.

This extra reservation – the inability to paint himself *tout nud* because of the nature of the society he lives in – is interesting for its reference to the New World. This is to be another leit-motif in the *Essais* as a whole, and reaches its climax in the essay ' Des cannibales ', in 1. 31, in the 'exemplaire de Bordeaux'.

Nevertheless Montaigne's professed inability to express the whole truth about himself admits exceptions. For example in 1. 2, 'De la Tristesse ', he is implicitly discussing sexual fulfilment; he is able to do this allusively by quoting Catullus, Vergil and Seneca on strong passions – the physiological analysis of what happens to a lover and a mistress when faced with insurmountable lust. In the 1580 version the Catullan quotation is there, but without the analysis Montaigne made of it in 1588. It is followed in 1580 by a statement on impotence,

> Et de là s'engendre par fois la defaillance fortuite, qui surprent les amoureux si hors de saison, et cette glace qui les saisit par la force d'une ardeur extreme, au giron mesme de la joüyssance.

In the 1588 version Montaigne adds to this statement – *Accident qui ne m'est pas incogneu* – but later cuts it out. Again, in the essay 'Des coustumes anciennes', 1. 49, certain voluptuous customs of Rome are commented on directly: eating, dressing, behaviour in bathing – are all recited with detailed and loving analysis. Interesting too is that here Martial is used for a particularly ambiguous example – a 1580 version:

> Ils se torchoyent le cul (il faut laisser aux femmes cette vaine superstition des parolles) avec une esponge: voylà pourquoy *spongia* est un mot obscœne en Latin...

Montaigne leaves the linguistic taboo to the women and

unhesitatingly uses the word *cul*. A little later – still a I passage
– he says:

> Ils s'essuyoient le catze de laine perfumée, quand ils en
> avoyent faict:
>
> At tibi nil faciam, sed lota mentula lana.

The context in Martial's epigram is homosexuality; and it seems
as if Montaigne wanted his readers to think of that while
explicitly talking about *torche-culs*. Thus, even in the 1580
edition there are a number of complex and allusive ways in
which Montaigne can sever the cord around certain taboo
subjects: and one of the chief is the use of Latin quotations.[1]

*Ainsi, lecteur, je suis moy-mesmes la matiere de mon livre: ce n'est pas
raison que tu employes ton loisir en un subject si frivole et si vain.*

Beneath this statement we can hear Horace's sophisticated
reply to criticism of his own poetry – that what he writes does
not deserve the name of poetry – in much the same way as
Montaigne says he does not deserve to be read. The subject is
so trivial that it is almost a game; Horace's main quality as
defined by Petronius was a *curiosa felicitas*. This is apt: for *felicitas*
means fertility, while *curiosa* means painstaking. The phrase thus
conveys the union of imposed discipline and inborn creativity,
of *ars* and *ingenium*. Montaigne's self-disparaging remarks in this
dedication are as unlikely to convince us as Horace's apparent
refusal to tackle great themes: unlikely because in both cases it
is a *prima facie* case of being aware of doing something new in
literature and thus of having to persuade the readers that both
the subject and the treatment are actually well worth a minute's
attention. Both Horace and Montaigne shared this *curiosa
felicitas*.

---

[1] The use of Martial is crucial here. Not only does practically every quotation have
a homosexual content; but Montaigne uses him very much in the first two books
– in I. 49 – an indecent quotation about Roman women naked in baths; I. 55 – on
smells of the human body; II. 3 and II. 7, II. 10, II. 12 – three quotations from Martial;
II. 15; II. 17; II. 18; II. 25; II. 26; II. 35; II. 37. There is a gap in research here where
the use of Martial might be seen to be important to an understanding of Montaigne's
sexual views, in particular the sensuality of the quotations and the homosexuality.
I shall return to this point.

Implicitly Montaigne takes from Horace and Vergil, whom he calls 'le maistre du cœur' (I. 37), their evaluation of man; and his reading, re-reading and meditating on the *condition humaine* is from the outset a pattern he takes from the Classical poets. Already in the dedication we see Montaigne and the Roman poets in a dialogue the one with the other.

But let us pass to an essay which was a mile-stone of autobiographical writing in order to see precisely how the form of Horace's poetry influenced the form of the *Essais*.

For Montaigne internal autobiography means to try and describe the pluralities of the *moi*. An external autobiography sees the person, encrusted with his own summing up of his character – which is largely intellectual – and this is in itself a daily barrier against seeing him. All the person does is to re-discover his notions about himself, based on his memories of how he acted in what he thinks are the same circumstances; and he then pigeon-holes himself in a certain category. Montaigne sees acutely that in wishing to write faithfully, to offer the authentic coin of himself, he cannot say anything except through words; and even when he is putting them down, he is committed to them, to an aspect of his thought which had been merely stuttering in his mind hitherto. He is really *engagé* by those very words. Picking up the threads means making your writing a part of your personality.

The 'milestone' essay is of course 'De la præsumption', II. 17. It is very dense. Let us begin with a passage near the start:

> Mais je sens bien que par fois je m'y laisse trop aller, et qu'à force de vouloir eviter l'art et l'affectation, j'y retombe d'une autre part:
>
> > brevis esse laboro
> > Obscurus fio.   (a 1 passage)

The context is important: in the quotation Horace turns to the Pisones, and uses the first person singular: is he teaching or practising? Surely the latter. How impossible it is in writing to aim at brevity and avoid obscurity. If it were in a didactic way we would read,

> breves esse laborant
> obscuri fiunt.

But Horace's statement is far from being didactic. The poet/ critic is talking in the first person and we overhear some of his remarks. Montaigne takes the passage over as another writer who is trying to see the problems of writing.[1] Not only is this whole passage of Montaigne very reminiscent of Horace – the tone of conversation, the reader overhearing bits of literary criticism – but there are also Horatian parallels in the humorous wrapping-up of serious gifts on which other people would write solemn treatises but which Montaigne and Horace converse about in the course of their own experience of writing. Montaigne seems to be re-texturing Horace's words to suit his own conditions: these are serious matters for a writer, put in a self-critical, self-deprecating and highly conversational way.[2]

Three or four pages earlier in this essay Montaigne is highly critical of himself in a literary matter, and once again there is a clue from Horace. Montaigne cannot stand his own poems,

> J'ay la veuë assez claire et reglée; mais à l'ouvrer, elle se trouble: comme j'essaye plus evidemment en la poësie. Je l'ayme infiniment; je me congnois assez aux ouvrages d'autruy; mais je fay, à la verité, l'enfant quand j'y veux mettre la main; je ne me puis souffrir. On peut faire le sot par tout ailleurs, mais non en la Poësie,
>
> > mediocribus esse poetis
> > non dii, non homines, non concessere columnae.
>
> (a 1 passage)

Montaigne could not have used the quotation without remem-

---

[1] Interesting statistics on Horace's *Ars poetica* in the *Essais* are worth mentioning here: (*a*) Most of the quotations from the *Ars poetica* are in Book I. There are none in Book III. It is clear that by the third Book Montaigne knows where he is going and does not need the Horace quotations any longer. (*b*) *Where* these quotations occur: I. 8 on his own work; I. 26 on his writing seen in the larger perspective of educational theories; I. 28 an essay which could be called 'imitative' in a very creative, sensitive way; II. 17 the autobiographical landmark.

[2] Montaigne in the essay 'De la Vanite', III. 9, gives exactly the same opinion as Horace and Valéry (*Œuvres* (Pléiade ed., Paris, 1957), vol. I, p. 1626) when he says, 'Et puis il est des humeurs comme cela, à qui l'intelligence porte desdain, qui m'en estimeront mieux de ce qu'ils ne sçauront ce que je dis: ils conclurront la profondeur de mon sens par *l'obscurité, laquelle, à parler en bon escient, je hay bien fort, et l'éviterois si je me sçavois éviter*.' (My italics.)

bering the whole passage around it, and this Horatian passage is implicitly in the reader's mind when he is reading Montaigne. Montaigne has tried writing Latin poetry but he has 'une condition singeresse et imitatrice: quand je me meslois de faire des vers (et n'en fis jamais que des latins)...' (iii. 5). So he had experimented in different styles before he came to write the essays. He had written Latin verse; he had tried translating from Latin to French. In 1569 he translated Sebond's *Theologia Naturalis*, and one example from this work will prove how his style was already what it becomes in the *Essais*: for the phrase

> debet videre et comparare

he renders as

> que chascun se taste et se sonde soy mesme

where the verbs *se taste* and *se sonde* combine sensations, and where one can say that he is already using metaphorical language as the essential way of talking about the interior life. Already he is *intellectuellement sensible* and *sensiblement intellectuel*. But in poetry he had edited La Boëtie's work. Why write in prose? There is one explanation only: he would be a mediocre poet. And the sheer emotional hatred of that – suggested by those lines of Horace – made him shun verse-making in either Latin or French. He puts poetry much higher than anything else, and he has seen the miserable figure that he was cutting in that field. Now if this is not a confession of a defect, nothing is. He would have liked to be a French Horace but he cannot be so. Thus he is forced to follow another path. He chooses a form that is neither wholly poetry nor wholly prose: each essay is, in many senses, a poem in prose.[1]

The problem of mental creative power is crucial, and Montaigne comes back to it again and again: the instruments used to grasp the subjective reality are words; and if words do not seize on it it vapours away. Even in his reading Montaigne says that it is not by conscious memory he reads but through his temperament, through his sense of feeling, and through involuntary memory.

---

[1] This point will be more fully analysed in the next chapter.

> Je feuillette les livres, je ne les estudie pas: ce qui m'en
> demeure, c'est chose que je ne reconnois plus estre d'autruy:
> c'est cela seulement dequoy mon jugement a faict son profict,
> les discours et les imaginations dequoy il s'est imbu; l'autheur,
> le lieu, les mots et autres circonstances, je les oublie
> incontinent.   (II. 17, a 1 passage)

This is not a critical logical mind but a creative imaginative
mind which can remember the colour of the leather binding of
a book but not the title nor the author. This is a poet's mind.

If we remember that the self-deprecation in the 'Au lecteur'
is inherent in the Horatian *recusatio* technique, we can say that
the uniqueness of the *Essais* was already part and parcel of
Montaigne's belief from the beginning in 1580. There is a phrase
in the 'exemplaire de Bordeaux' edition which holds the truth.
In II. 8, 'De l'affection des peres aux enfans', he stresses the
estrangeté and the *nouvelleté* of his project, the solitude 'qui m'a
mis premierement en teste cette resverie de me mesler d'escrire'.
Note the word *resverie*, which is suggestive: it is fantasy, which
at times he belittles but which he sees as a fundamental quality
of poetry. The self-deprecation is similar to that of the dedication: the book is 'd'un dessein farouche et extravagant' with
nothing to commend it but its *bizarrerie*. And suddenly there
comes this III addition – it is *le seul livre au monde de son espece*. In
other words, Montaigne can now in the 1590s say what has been
in his mind all along, though it had to be veiled by the affected
modesty of his tone in the early stages of the *Essais*. Look back
on an essay, 'Du dementir', II. 18, where he quotes Horace on
the audience he is writing for; and see that in the 1588 edition
he had added another classical poet to the whole discussion.
Persius is brought in to say,

> non equidem hoc studeo, bullatis ut mihi nugis
> pagina turgescat...
> secreti loquimur.   (*Saturae*, ed. W. V. Clausen, v. 19–21)

The phrase *secreti loquimur* – *parler tête à tête* – is vital: we must
see that this is not any old quotation that he bundles in; this
precise phrase covers the whole relationship between author
and reader in a literary work. Furthermore, Montaigne links
this concept of writing to his own desire to be known in his

natural, ordinary and simple condition. A III addition later in the same essay has the important phrase *livre consubstantiel à son autheur.* In the whole addition, *resverie, fantaisie, menues pensées* and *renger* are qualities that he approves of,

> J'escoute à mes resveries par ce que j'ay à les enroller.

What is remarkable (particularly in view of the Montaignian critics' concentration on Plutarch, Seneca, letter-writers and rhetoricians like Cicero) is that there seems to be a close correspondence between Horace's way of writing poetry, that close *tête à tête* he developed most surely in his *Epistles* and *Satires*, and Montaigne's choice of form for his *Essais.*

The only way of understanding Montaigne is to see him through ambiguity, plurivalence and allusive suggestion. Proust has characterised the readers of any book in the *Temps Retrouvé* thus,

> Car ils ne seraient pas, selon moi, mes lecteurs, mais les propres lecteurs d'eux-mêmes, mon livre n'étant qu'une sorte de ces verres grossissants comme ceux que tendait à un acheteur l'opticien de Combray; mon livre, grâce auquel je leur fournirais le moyen de lire en eux-mêmes.
>
> (Pléiade ed., vol. III, p. 1033)

And surely that is how one has to read Montaigne. We shall try to read one essay by Montaigne, to see how he writes and what the tones of his writing on friendship will convey.

7

An Essay in re-creation

We have already noted the chattiness of Horace, the extremely subtle *ars et ingenium*, the whole attitude towards his work; and we have said that Horace was a principal force in Montaigne's choice of form. In Montaigne we find two or three levels in the *moi*; also the Janus-faced *nous* – either speaking for all Frenchmen in the sixteenth century or speaking for the whole of mankind – and the *tu* form applied to man from a distant, ironical angle as for example,

> He! pauvre homme, tu as assez d'incommoditez necessaires, sans les augmenter par ton invention...Tu as des laideurs reelles et essentielles à suffisance, sans en forger d'imaginaires... (III. 5, a II passage)

We can also hear voices which enter to ask questions, as for example in I. 14. From the beginning of this essay there is a *nous* who speaks for humanity,

> pour le soulagement de *nostre* miserable condition humaine... (my italics)

There are stories and examples which are lively precisely because they incorporate dialogues between the *on* form, the *vous*, the *je* and the *tu* forms as in

> Bien, me dira l'on...
> mais que direz vous de l'indigence?
> je leur donne...
> Tu ne la sentiras guiere long temps.

Montaigne introduces other voices and relates them in a

conflict of attitudes. We have the impression that he turns to us, his readers; a third person chips in with another view; then he introduces a fourth voice to put a totally different attitude. The voices speak to each other and reply to the questions, so that there are multifarious points of view around the major theme of life and death. This complexity, these layers of Montaigne speaking, give the illusion of a *comédie humaine* where several voices are heard before a vast backcloth of mankind. Montaigne is there to organise the voices and to let them speak artistically. It is remarkable that these are present in the 1580 edition, ready to deepen in the 1588 edition and in the 'exemplaire de Bordeaux'. This multivalence of voices replicates what Horace was doing in his *Epistles*, *Satires* and the *Ars Poetica*. Even in his *Odes* he achieved the same dynamic control. Professor Quinn (*Latin Explorations*, p. 75) studies the shape of a Horatian ode and says,

> The typical Horatian ode is hardly ever a static lyric revolving descriptively round a single idea. It sometimes sets out a logical sequence of ideas; but more often what we have is an organic succession of ideas, one leading out of another and the whole owing its unity to the poet's personality, and not to any logical structure.

Horace can use monologues or a quasi-dialogue to present an experience or several experiences moulded together by the poet. In Montaigne we have a combination of style and thought which are consubstantial. He moulds his reading, his experimenting, his trying out of topics into a poetic prose. Chapter headings may or may not be the major chord in his symphony. Montaigne has a thread, indeed in most cases a framework, and then 'plays' with his thought and language backwards and forwards *as if in a poem*. And what is most remarkable is that it is a poem in two languages at once: Latin and French: with its own density, suggestiveness, allusiveness. And in every case the reader – at least, ideally – has to have both languages before he can begin to hear the tones in which the thought is being sung. Montaigne himself could see how difficult the process of reading his essays was, for did he not say,

C'est l'indiligent lecteur qui pert mon subject, non pas moy;
il s'en trouvera tousjours en un coing quelque mot qui ne
laisse pas d'estre bastant, quoy qu'il soit serré. . .

> (III. 9, 'De la vanité', a III passage)

If we look at the context of this remark we find a dense texture
of literary criticism there. Montaigne, like Valéry, sees poetry
and literary prose as related, the two set against prosaic
discourse,

Mille poëtes trainent et languissent à la prosaïque; mais la
meilleure prose ancienne (III) (*et je la seme ceans indifferemment
pour vers*) (II) reluit par tout de la vigueur et hardiesse
poëtique, et represente l'air de sa fureur.

> (The italics are mine)

This not only makes a sharp distinction between the two but
implicitly we know that this is the kind of prose that Montaigne
loves reading and therefore loves creating. For earlier in this
piece of literary criticism we find

J'ayme l'alleure poetique, à sauts et à gambades. (III) C'est
une art, comme dict Platon, legere, volage, demoniacle.

The prose that Montaigne is composing is a poetic prose. 'Mon
stile et mon esprit vont vagabondant de mesmes' (a III passage)
– fantasy, imagination, impulsive drives, inspiration – these are
all elements he caresses. He has no hesitation in placing himself
as a writer on the same level as Plato. He repeats here an idea
we see also in the last passage of I. 11, 'Des Prognostications',
which was a re-working-through the 1588 edition and the
'exemplaire de Bordeaux'. We can call it *une inspiration divine* and
can see it as a confession on the part of Montaigne that he is
aware of an inspiration which moves him as if he were rushed
by a divine fire or demon.

From the first edition he establishes a role for the reader: a
participating role. In the essay 'Divers Evenemens de mesme
conseil', I. 24 – note the chord from the non-logical title – he
demonstrates this role.

Mais la fortune montre bien encores plus evidemment la part
qu'elle a en tous ces ouvrages, par les graces et beautez qui

> s'y treuvent, non seulement *sans l'intention, mais sans la cognoissance mesme de l'ouvrier.* Un suffisant lecteur descouvre souvant ès escrits d'autruy des perfections autres que celles que l'autheur y a mises et apperceües, et y preste des sens et des visages plus riches.   (a I passage, my italics)

This perceptive critic expects his readers to participate. In the spirit of the *cognois toy* tradition from Antiquity, Montaigne sees quite clearly that all the literature he holds within him is changed by him, re-transformed by him and bodied forth in a new and original manner by him. The reader will be able to read between the lines; opening the *Essais* at random, he will chew over thoughts that are expressed there. He will hear the sounds of the words, the concrete language invading the field of abstraction, the rhythmic flow, the puns, the playing with the look of words, their assonance and alliteration. A reader who is humanist in cultural values will read and masticate the *Essais* in the same way as Montaigne read Seneca, Vergil, Horace and Plutarch; Montaigne, seeing *des visages plus riches* in Vergil or Horace, can hope that the reader will find, without his intention or knowledge, things that were subconsciously in his mind when he wrote. Note how Montaigne is starting a new tradition in France: from the Ancients there will derive in France great men who will be humanists in the true sense of the word. As Eliot wrote in 'Tradition and the Individual Talent', by 1600 the French had already a more mature prose than the English had, and the Greek and Latin classics were read as living works. Montaigne was trying to awake in France an audience with the intellectual and emotional awareness that had existed in Rome in the first century B.C. In II. 17 he had this comment on the audience,

> Et puis, pour qui escrivez vous?

He answers this *vous* voice by dividing people into three categories: the *sçavants*, the *ames communes et populaires* and,

> La tierce, à qui vous tombez en partage, des ames reglées et fortes d'elles-mesmes est si rare, que justement elle n'a ny nom, ny rang entre nous...   (a III passage)

At the present moment the right readers are *si rares*; nonetheless it is worth cultivating the qualities which he finds in Ancient civilisation. This is what Montaigne means by *honnete homme*. And very importantly, he gives La Boëtie as an example of the best soul,

> je di des parties naturelles de l'ame et le mieux né...c'estoit vrayment un'ame pleine et qui montroit un beau visage à tout sens; un'ame à la vieille marque... (II. 17, a 1 passage)

Thus in Montaigne we find a commitment to two things: to writing and to friendship. In III. 9, 'De la Vanité' he makes this perceptive comment,

> Outre ce profit que je tire d'escrire de moy, j'en espere cet autre que, s'il advient que mes humeurs plaisent et accordent à quelque honneste homme avant que je meure, il recerchera de nous joindre. (a II passage)

Let us now analyse the essay on La Boëtie, I. 28, 'De l'amitié'. It has the extraordinary character of being a *poème en prose* in its last three pages, and of demonstrating the emotional value of a friendship which had a metaphysical dimension. In fact the two essays – 'Sur des vers de Virgile', III. 5, and this one – give a double perspective on love. The first is purely sexual, while the essay on friendship renders this metaphysical dimension reached through the 'sealing' of two friends together.

Every essay, and particularly 'De l'amitié', follows a hidden order, tucked away through the folds of disorder. Montaigne is aware of this, saying:

> Je m'esgare, mais plustost par licence que par mesgarde. Mes fantasies se suyvent, mais par fois c'est de loing, et se regardent mais d'une veue oblique. (III. 9, a II passage)

The essay seems at first sight to be following a highly articulated, logical order: with an introduction, a narrative account of the meeting with La Boëtie, a discussion of friendship (sub-divided as friendship between father and son, between brothers, with women, in marriage, homosexual friendship, ordinary friendship, supreme friendship) and finally the character of La Boëtie. We know that Cicero had written a *de amicitia*, and that Seneca in his Epistles had devoted space to this topic. We know too that Montaigne had read these works. We would remind ourselves what true friendship is: friends are attracted to each other by their wisdom and beauty; to give love and be loved; to trust and be trusted; to feel an instinctive confidence in one another; to treat a true friend as a second self. This enlargement of our own sympathies is part of the human condition.

Strict reality, biography, even accuracy of dates are minor matters in this essay. Many critics dismiss it as just another attempt to falsify facts to make them more interesting to the reader, and ultimately as just another exercise in the art of persuasion. They can list inaccuracies in different editions, such as the change Montaigne makes from 18 to 16 years as La Boëtie's age when he composed the discourse *La Servitude Volontaire*; they can point to mosaics which Montaigne 'filched' from Plato's *Symposium*, from Diogenes Laertius' *Life of Aristippus*, Plutarch's *Life of Agesilaus* and from the *de amicitia* of Cicero. But if we do not see that this essay is essentially a literary fiction there is little point in these 'truths', which merely scratch the surface of the densely textured piece of prose. For 'De l'amitié' has a bi-focal attitude to language and a bi-literacy in composition in which Montaigne uses Latin in quotations from Classical authors, and French to re-structure them into a new form of art.

The use of the first person singular supports the fiction that Montaigne is speaking from his personal experience only. He uses it as Horace does in the *Ars poetica*: the reader is over-hearing the poet talking and chatting. Listen to the tone in these first five lines of the *Ars poetica*,

> humano capiti cervicem pictor equinam
> iungere si velit, et varias inducere plumas
> undique collatis membris, ut turpiter atrum
> desinat in piscem mulier formosa superne,
> spectatum admissi risum teneatis, amici?

> If a painter chose to join a human head to the neck of a horse, and to spread feathers of many a colour over limbs picked up here and there, so that what at the top is a lovely woman ends below in a black and ugly fish, could you, my friends, if favoured with a private view, refrain from laughing?

Horace is speaking as a private *persona* here, about a work of art that is monstrous. He takes delight in fitting together preposterous elements from the human species, allies them to bits from the animal and fish world, and expects the reader to laugh. We are asked to participate and to exercise our imagination. We read the first ten lines of Montaigne, note that he uses the fourth line of the passage above –

desinat in piscem mulier formosa superne

– and conclude that he would not have used one line without remembering the whole passage. Horace is saying implicitly that too much unruly imagination has been used and not enough skilled art. This implicit comment is Montaigne's comment also. We realise that this piece on friendship is echoing Horace's counsel: making the distinction between *ars et ingenium* and *ars sine arte*.

This beginning – comparing the painter who fills his painting with *crotesques* or *peintures* and himself, the writer of this essay – is a piece of self-depreciation, similar to the self-belittlement in the preface 'Au Lecteur'. The terms are also very similar to those in the essay 'De l'oisiveté', i. 8 – the first essay in which he showed his true aim: 'et m'enfante tant de chimeres et monstres fantasques'.

Borrowing the central part of his essay from the discourse of La Boëtie lays more weight on fortune, accident, hasard than on any feeling for craftsmanship in writing. But this interpretation is only on one level; if we look at it more closely, we realise that by borrowing a subject from La Boëtie Montaigne can come close to the Graeco-Roman civilisation that both he and La Boëtie loved. If La Boëtie had done what Montaigne is doing, if

> il eut pris un tel desseing que le mien de mettre par escrit ses fantasies, nous verrions plusieurs choses rares et qui nous approcheroient bien près de l'honneur de l'antiquité.

The link is clear here: the *fantasies* are creative writing. The admiration of both men for Ancient Rome is obvious. The death of his friend deprived Montaigne of someone to talk to; the loss of a second self. This becomes the reason for writing. We remember that Horace was also the poet of friendship in

Augustan Rome; and the poet of urbanity, the concept of the gentleman.

Montaigne has as his materials actual raw experience and the Classical expression of friendship. Towards the end of the essay he compares the whole of his life – which is *pleine de tranquillité d'esprit* (a stoic leit-motif in Montaigne) – to the four years of their friendship, and it is but a

> fumée, ce n'est qu'une nuit obscure et ennuyeuse.[1]

The last part of the essay, from these words onwards, is a prose poem with the quotations from Vergil, Terence, Plato, Horace and Catullus so deeply interwoven that we might say it is a French/Latin re-creation through sensibility and intelligence. The experience and the sensibility come first, and the intelligence follows afterwards. As Proust said:

> L'impression est pour l'écrivain ce qu'est l'expérimentation pour le savant, avec cette différence que chez le savant le travail de l'intelligence précède et chez l'écrivain vient après.
> (Pléiade ed., vol. III, p. 880)

The experience makes us discover new sensations or new truths. For an artist the work of intelligence always comes after the experience. Montaigne's essay is both an emotional exploitation of the classical poets and a critical one: the evocation through the quotations is part of the essay and a very fundamental part; to enrich the expression of an idea is already to enrich the idea itself.[2]

This friendship was very close; hence the use of the term of *frères*

[1] Margaret McGowan in her book *Montaigne's Deceits* (London, 1974), p. 144 in discussing this simile says: 'the same man allowed his friendship for La Boëtie so to obscure his senses that he described the latter, four (*sic*) years after his death, in terms similar to those used by the disciples after the death of Christ.' La Boëtie's death was in 1563, thus seventeen years before *De l'Amitié* was published, or nine years before 1572 – if one accepts Villey's hypothesis that Montaigne started writing his *Essais* around that date. Secondly, the meaning is in terms of Montaigne's life after the death of La Boëtie. Thirdly, this seems to me a dipping into the 'wrong' civilisation, for it is very clearly the Graeco-Roman civilisation that Montaigne and La Boëtie admired and not the Christian world.

[2] I think that it is fundamentally wrong to say as Eva Marcu, in *Répertoire des idées de Montaigne* (Geneva, 1965), p. viii, stated 'Les vers et les exemples livresques ont en principe été omis comme ne constituant pas, à proprement parler, la pensée de Montaigne'.

> C'est à la verité, un beau nom et plein de dilection que le nom
> de frère, et à cette cause en fismes nous, luy et moy, nostre
> alliance. (a 1 passage)

Montaigne compares affection for women with affection for a
male friend: both have a physical basis but the heterosexual one
is *un feu temeraire et volage, ondoyant et divers*; the other 'c'est une
chaleur generale et universelle, temperée au demeurant et égale,
une chaleur constante et rassize, toute douceur et polissure, qui
n'a rien d'aspre et de poignant' (a 1 passage). Montaigne refers
to both as *ces deux passions*. It is pointless to try to prove that
Montaigne and La Boëtie were or were not practising homo-
sexuals. We shall never know that. What we can say is that
Montaigne expresses their relationship as something higher
than Greek homosexuality. In his discussion of Greek homosexuality he is at pains to point out that the physical attraction
was greater than the mental one; that the partners in most
relationships were an older man and an adolescent boy; that
it was ephemeral; that it was purely human. In all these respects
such a relationship was unlike his supreme friendship with La
Boëtie. The union was

> ne sçay quelle force inexplicable et fatale,
> mediatrice de cette union. (a 1 passage)

Montaigne uses the same terminology for this male-to-male
friendship as Donne uses for male-to-female love,

> Ce n'est pas une speciale consideration, ny deux, ny trois, ny
> quatre, ny mille: c'est je ne sçay quelle quinte essence de tout
> ce meslange, qui, ayant saisi toute ma volonté, l'amena se
> plonger et se perdre dans la sienne. (a 1 passage)

In 'The Ecstasy' Donne uses the same kind of language when
he says

> When love, with one another so
>   Interinanimates two souls,
> That abler soul, which thence doth flow,
>   Defects of loneliness controls.
> We then, who are this new soul, know,
>   Of what we are compos'd, and made,
> For, th'Atomies of which we grow,
>   Are souls, whom no change can invade.

With one new soul the two bodies are 'ours, though they are not we'. This, in Montaigne's case, was a friendship that had no other idea but of itself and could have no other reference but to itself. Citing Donne again, we could say:

> But as all several souls contain
>   Mixture of things, they know not what,
> Love these mix'd souls doth mix again,
>   And makes both one, each this and that.

There was commitment in this friendship which lifted Montaigne to a higher level, just as two lovers are of one identity as lovers and are two if considered as human beings. This was a unique experience for Montaigne; and whether or not the actual friendship was divine, as he says, is irrelevant. He has used all his art to convince us that it was. That this was sentiment and sensibility on Montaigne's part is evident:

> les discours mesmes que l'antiquité nous a laissé sur ce subject me semblent lâches au pris du sentiment que j'en ay.

> (a 1 passage)

He goes on to characterise this friendship, the latter part of the phrase being a III addition:

> Si on me presse de dire pourquoy je l'aymais, je sens que cela ne se peut exprimer, (III) qu'en respondant: 'Par ce que c'estoit luy; par ce que c'estoit moy'[1]

The alliteration, the combination of *p* and *s* sounds, of the 1580 edition is reinforced by the III addition; the combination of the two clauses gives a simple, lyrical movement and sober quality. The weight of the emotion behind the sentence is colossal and yet Montaigne used the simplest words he could. It is their arrangement, the syntax, and the gift of poetry that makes the sentence rich.

In the last pages the French/Latin re-creation can be studied in detail. Immediately after the phrases

---

[1] In Montaigne's own copy of the 'exemplaire de Bordeaux' this addition is in the right hand margin. It clearly shows two inks – therefore it was not written at the same time: the phrase *par ce que c'estoit luy* had a full stop after it. Then he adds, maybe years later, *par ce que c'estoit moy*.

ce n'est que fumée, ce n'est qu'une nuit obscure et
ennuyeuse... (a 1 passage)

(notice the present tense and the formation of a metaphoric
evocation not through a *comme* clause but through a *c'est*) we
have Montaigne moulding elements from both languages into
a poetic whole.

Depuis le jour que je le perdy,

> *quem semper acerbum,*
> *semper honoratum (sic, Dii, voluistis) habebo...*

The quotation from Vergil is from *Aeneid, V.* 448–9: Aeneas in
Sicily determines to commemorate the death of his father
Anchises by holding a day of games. It comes from a speech that
Aeneas gives to his men, recalling his father's death on this
particular day twelve months ago; and twice he says – such was
the will of the Gods. Montaigne incorporates it, the meaning
and the sounds of the words being perfectly appropriate. Notice
too that the family relationship – of father and son – is deliberately chosen.

je ne fay que trainer languissant...

The present tense of the verb *faire* is absolutely precise; the
actual life he is living now, not his past nor his future life. *Trainer*
means, according to Cotgrave: 'to traile, drag, draw, carrie or
lead after him'. *Languissant* means: 'languishing, drooping,
fainting, hange down the heade'. The combination of both is
a fine concrete phrase suggesting that Montaigne is physically
wasting away.

*et les plaisirs mesmes qui s'offrent à moy, au lieu de me consoler me
redoublent le regret de sa perte.*

Note how he uses the continual present tense. Even the
pleasures of his present life are filled with a hollow sense of loss.

Nous estions à moitié de tout; il me semble que je luy desrobe sa part...

A part of his life, of his thoughts, of his ideas, and even of the
words he is writing are being 'filched' from La Boëtie.

Montaigne finishes this sentence with another quotation, this time from Terence's play *Heautontimoroumenos*:

> *nec fas esse ulla me voluptate hic frui*
> *decrevi, tantisper dum ille abest meus particeps.*

Montaigne uses two lines in a reversed order: line 95 and line 97; he puts 97 first and 95 second. *ille abest meus particeps* is put last, as it provides a transition to the next phrase in French. Furthermore the word *particeps* sums up the leit-motif of life and death, sharing and owning. The phrase *voluptate . . . frui* is doubly concrete and, combined with a negative *nec*, is bold. The Terentian context is comic, but Montaigne uses the two lines to stress again the family relationship – father and son. The Vergilian context has been reversed, so that it is the father here who laments the loss of a son. The two quotations 'play' the relationship to and fro and reinforce the theme of loss of the partner.

J'estois desjà si fait et accoustumé à estre deuxiesme par tout, qu'il me semble n'estre plus qu'à demy.

Instead of being the second person to La Boëtie's first, he is now only half of himself, the other half having died when La Boëtie died. Montaigne expresses the loss of an integral part of his personality. This strikes one as very much like Ficino's concept of the soul which had once been in love and had lost that love, so that it was nothing more than half an existence. The whole terminology is Neo-Platonic and metaphysical. A passage of Ficino's *quatrième discours* runs:[1]

> C'est sûrement depuis qu'est inné dans l'homme cet amour mutuel, qui nous ramène à notre nature première, s'efforçant avec deux êtres d'en faire un seul et de guérir ainsi l'espèce humaine...Chacun cherche donc sa moitié. Aussi chaque fois que le hasard met sur la route de chacun sa moitié, quel que soit le sexe qu'il désire, il se sent violemment attiré, s'unit à elle d'un ardent amour et ne souffre pas d'en être séparé, fût-ce un instant. C'est précisément ce désir et cet effort pour reconstituer l'être total qui a reçu le nom d'Amour.

[1] Marsile Ficin, *Commentaire sur le Banquet de Platon*, ed. Raymond Marcel (Paris, 1956), 4ᵉ discours, Ch. 1, p. 168.

This Ficinian-Platonic metaphysical concept of love provides the context into which this essay on friendship fits. Montaigne makes no concessions to the reader: he never mentions any physical contact betwen him and La Boëtie and he never mentions Love. But one can feel the intense, violent emotion that this friendship was composed of, and the physical incapacity to register the loss of that love.

This loss is then immediately followed by a quotation from Horace, *Odes*, II. 17, lines 5ff.

> *Illam meae si partem animae tulit*
> *Maturior vis, quid moror altera,*
>   *Nec charus aeque, nec superstes*
> *Integer? Ille dies utramque*
> *Duxit ruinam.*

Montaigne has tampered with the Horatian text, deliberately so. Instead of *Ah! te* he puts *illam* and he changes the tense of the last verb which in Horace is future and in Montaigne is past: *duxit* instead of *ducet*. Furthermore he has changed the Horatian *rapit* and substituted *tulit*: the meaning alters from 'snatch, seize' to 'bring, bear, lift up'. The formulation has become more weighty and dignified: where Horace was imagining Maecenas' death and using the future, La Boëtie has died and Montaigne is looking back with nostalgia. As usual, he manipulates ancient authors at will and often changes the value of a Latin statement by introducing an *et* instead of a *sed*, or a different tense, or indeed a different person of a verb. We can watch him re-texturing the context of a quotation and using it for a purpose which is his own.

The Horatian ode is addressed to Maecenas, Horace's great friend and patron. He was a great invalid; he died in 8 B.C., and Horace survived him by only three days. But the poem itself is in the future: if Maecenas should die, then Horace will not live. And all the verb tenses are either future (line 10 *ibimus, ibimus,* in line 32 *feriemus*) or conditional, e.g. line 14, *resurgat* or line 15 *divellet*. The ode is a careful interweaving of self and the other self, the friend. It was not used in the 1580 edition of the *Essais*. Why did Montaigne insert it in the 1588 edition? One reason we can infer – because it carries on the terminology of the

Terentian lines he had used earlier. For example *superstes* echoes *particeps*; without Maecenas Horace would not remain a complete whole; he would be but a fraction of himself; one half of two parts. By changing the tense of *ducere* Montaigne is talking of what La Boëtie and himself were, so that *nec superstes integer* is immediately followed by *ille dies* – the moment of death for one part of himself. Note too the echo in these lines of the Vergilian lines about the day when Anchises died. Again this is 'playing' with the quotations and comments as if they were integral parts of a poem.

After this quotation from Horace Montaigne goes on to give a commentary in French on what he feels like *after* half his soul has died,

Il n'est action ou imagination où je ne le trouve à dire comme si eut-il bien faict à moy.

Montaigne hears La Boëtie's voice at every moment of his life, whether it is in some action he undertakes or some thought that possesses him. This is a haunting memory, so vivid that he knows what his friend would be saying at each precise minute of the day.

Car, de mesme qu'il me surpassoit d'une distance infinie en toute autre suffisance et vertu, aussi faisoit-il au devoir de l'amitié.

In everything he surpassed Montaigne, and there follows a very dense piece of creative imitation: a line and a half from Horace and two interspersed passages from Catullus on the death of his brother,

> *Quis desiderio sit pudor aut modus*
> *Tam chari capitis?*

[First line and a half of *Odes*, 1. 24, addressed to Vergil on the unexpected death of their common friend Quintilius Varus.]

> *O misero frater adempte mihi,* (68. 20)
> *Omnia tecum una perierunt gaudia nostra,* (68. 23–4)
> *Quae tuus in vita dulcis alebat amor.*

> *Tu mea, tu moriens fregisti commoda, frater;* (68. 21–2)
> *Tecum una tota est nostra sepulta anima,*

Cujus ego interitu tota de mente fugavi (68. 25–6)
Haec studia atque omnes delicias animi.

Alloquar? audiero nunquam tua verba loquentem? (65. 9–11)
Nunquam ego te, vita frater amabilior,
Aspiciam posthac? At certe semper amabo.

Seven lines are taken from Catullus 68, and then three from 65. He alters *domus* in line 22 to *anima*, and *facta* in line 9 to *verba*. The context of all three quotations is the death of a human being who mattered very deeply to the poets. Horace is speaking of a dearly beloved friend; Catullus of the death of his brother. They are all strongly emotional poems.

Montaigne starts with Horace; in rather general terms Horace says 'Is there shame, is there measure in the regret for such a loved being?' Montaigne would have the rest of the Horatian ode in his head: the address to Vergil, the phrases *perpetuus sopor, nulli flebilior quam tibi, Virgilii* and *durum*. We may notice that Montaigne is moving from the difficult, metaphysical stage of describing the relationship to another stage, in which Vergil, Terence, Horace and Catullus have nourished his thoughts, and where he can touch on a more intimate note: the family link, and death.

He breaks the beginning of the line in Catullus – *abstulit* is omitted – 'o unhappy that I am in having my brother taken away from me'. The order, the shock of the loss that Catullus felt are now transferred to Montaigne's loss of La Boëtie. Furthermore, the lament and consolation here aptly record both Catullus' and Montaigne's attitude. Catullus has given up writing poetry and having mistresses (for a short time) and Montaigne wishes his readers to believe that he has shunned *haec studia atque omnes delicias animi* too. Note how many times *frater* enters: in the first line in the very emotional lament, in the fourth line where it is isolated by commas at the end, and then the third time where it is given a qualifying clause – of *vita frater amabilior*. Note too the recurrence of *tecum, tuus amor, tu* and *tu, tecum*.

Then Montaigne sounds a more intimate note by bringing in the three lines from Catullus 65: *Alloquar* – the future tense seems to capture a moment in time, isolated from other moments in existence, a momentary action suspended outside time; similarly the future perfect *audiero nunquam*, 'Shall I never for a moment hear thee?' *Vita frater amabilior* brings the intimate loss a shade nearer. The assertion *amabo* means 'I will always love thee' – the future tense being assertive here – so immortalising the brother both through his actual love and through poetry. Montaigne creates the emotional insistence here through his use of poetry. *Domus* – meaning the family name – was dropped as irrelevant, and *anima* substituted. And Montaigne preferred to have *verba* rather than *facta* because in his supreme friendship with La Boëtie it was through communication between two human beings that the value was created.

Instead of quoting the last line of the strophe,

> Semper maesta tua carmina morte tegam,

Montaigne breaks off and the next sentence, in a totally different tone from the preceding paragraph, begins

> Mais oyons un peu parler ce garson de seize ans.

He altered *dix huit* to *seize* in the later editions, which gives the secret of 'sincerity' away completely. It is once more Montaigne the artist who wants to portray La Boëtie as being much younger than he really was. Literal 'sincerity' is not to be sought for here.

If we now re-read the whole of 'De l'amitié', several things become clearer. Montaigne's first paragraph, the simile between the painter and himself, suggests that he wants the reader to think that his *crotesques* are *sans certaine figure, n'ayants ordre, suite, ny proportion que fortuite*. But we know that they are anything but *fortuite*. We have seen the precise order imposed, the dense creativity, the suggestion through allusiveness. Second, La Boëtie 'avoit son esprit moulé au patron d'autres siecles que ceux-cy'. Now, given that Montaigne had 'proved' that their friendship was permanent and indivisible, it was in imitation of the Ancient world that he could best write about his dear friend. Third, given that this friendship was the only intensely felt thing in Montaigne's experience, given that he chose to express it in such metaphysical terms, given that through this theme he chooses to express so many concepts that are relevant throughout the *Essais* – for instance the double self, as commentator and as active man – it would be strange if Montaigne having 'said his piece' about rare friendship forgot it completely in the rest of the *Essais*. He did not forget.

There are of course very many mentions of La Boëtie in the rest of the *Essais*: for instance, talking of medicine in II. 37, he says,

> Cependant qu'ils craignent d'arrester le cours d'un dysenterique pour ne luy causer la fiévre, ils me tuarent un amy qui valoit mieux que tous, tant qu'ils sont... (a III passage)

and we have no doubt as to who this friend was.[1] The extreme affection comes through his hyperbolical language: for instance in III. 3.

> Je suis *très*-capable d'acquerir et maintenir des amitiez *rares* et *exquises*...ma fortune, m'ayant duit et affriandy dès jeunesse à une amitié *seule* et *parfaicte*...
>
> (a II passage) (my italics)

Nowhere is the link between Ancient Rome, La Boëtie's death, Montaigne's writing, his sensitivity and the dual validity – emotional and intellectual – of the *Essais* better seen than in the essay 'De la vanité', III. 9. We have already seen in the previous chapter (p. 129) that the reason which Montaigne gave for composing his essays – La Boëtie's death – was deleted from the 'exemplaire de Bordeaux' edition. There are more such indications.

At the very beginning there is the comparison between decadent Rome and sixteenth-century France – both full of scribblers:

> On banniroit des mains de nostre peuple et moy et cent autres. (a II passage)

This ironical view is typical: it includes himself and his writing and sets them against the worst view of Rome. The radiating

---

Other examples of his view on friendship are: I. 9 'qui ne sçay rien si bien faire qu'estre amy' (a II passage); II. 17 'A l'adventure que le commerce continuel que j'ay avec les humeurs anciennes...'; III. 8 'Je souffrirois estre rudement heurté par mes amis...J'ayme une société et familiarité forte et virile, une amitié qui se flatte en l'aspreté et vigueur de son commerce, comme l'amour, és morsures et esgratigneures sanglantes.'

circles of his foci are: myself and my book; myself and my father; myself and friendship; absence and presence; writing poetic prose; and (the largest circle of all) Ancient Rome. There is a homage to his father – his father to whom his bi-lingualism was due – which is,

> Jà, à Dieu ne plaise que je laisse faillir entre mes mains aucune image de vie que je puisse rendre à un si bon pere!
>
> (a II passage)

We can feel the warmth of the emotion here, and are prepared for the alteration of passages about his work and passages on friends. His first piece on friendship has almost the metaphysical language we found in 'De l'amitié':

> En la vraye amitié, de laquelle je suis expert, je me donne à mon amy plus que je ne le tire à moy.

This leads to a comparison between absence and presence, where the former 'n'est pas proprement absence, quand il y a moyen de s'entr'advertir'. There is a profundity in this thought:

> La separation du lieu rendoit la conjonction de nos volontez plus riche. Cette faim insatiable de la presence corporelle accuse un peu la foiblesse en la jouyssance des ames.
>
> (a II passage)

There is awareness that man is bound to be alone in life, that however closely and lovingly any relationship is built up, nobody can get inside the partner's skin; and behind this thought there is normally in many human beings incipient despair. Montaigne seems to evaluate in a different way their friendship: other human beings are dependent on the physical, and this is a sign that their will-power is weak. But in this supreme friendship between Montaigne and La Boëtie there is a spiritual communion: in life – 'il vivoit, il jouissoit, il voyoit pour moy, et moy pour luy, autant plainement que s'il eust esté' – and in death:

> Ceux qui ont merité de moy de l'amitié et de la reconnoissance ne l'ont jamais perdue pour n'y estre plus: je les ay mieux payez et plus soigneusement, absens et ignorans. Je parle plus affectueusement de mes amis quand il n'y a plus moyen qu'ils le sçachent.   (a II statement towards the end of this essay)

And Montaigne goes on to make the link between his friend and Ancient Rome. This is not explicit, but needs to be 'heard' implicitly: he does not overtly tie together the two things; it is the reader who does it. In the next paragraph Montaigne says:

> Me trouvant inutile à ce siecle, je me rejecte à cet autre, et en suis si *embabouyné* que l'estat de cette vieille Romme, libre, juste et florissante (car je n'en aime ny la naissance, ny la vieillesse) m'interesse et *me passionne*.   (my italics)

The emotive language and the style tell us that this is the primary source of Montaigne's self-sufficiency in the Religious Wars and after the loss of his friend.

One other clear effect of La Boëtie's relationship with Montaigne and a result of his death is that in one of the subtlest essays – 'De la Diversion', III. 4 – the emotional experience leads Montaigne to make psychological discoveries. Here is the passage on the death of the partner:

> Je fus autrefois touché d'un puissant desplaisir, selon ma complexion, et encores plus juste que puissant; je m'y fusse perdu à l'avanture si je m'en fusse simplement fié à mes forces. Ayant besoing d'une vehemente diversion pour m'en distraire, je me fis, par art, amoureux, et par estude, à quoy l'aage m'aidoit. L'amour me soulagea et retira du mal qui m'estoit causé par l'amitié.   (a II passage)

We can see the way his personality, his intelligence and his sensibility organised themselves: *touché* suggests the emotional loss; the repetition of *puissant* makes the charge of emotion higher; 'par art, amoureux et par estude' – these were the substitutions, the variations, the changes he used to counter the dismaying shock. Rather than trying to dominate the pain, one substitutes something not too far away from the pain; for instance love instead of friendship, books instead of conversations, and writing instead of confiding. We can see here that virtue, instead of being a conflict of opposing ideas, has become a harmonious blending of them, almost like a painting. Aesthetic considerations, as we know, play a large role in Montaigne's conception of virtue, and it comes out finely in dealing with grief or pain. It is only a hypothesis – and is bound to remain so – that an emotional experience that he has learned how to deal with underlies this essay; that when he had learnt for himself, he could take the experience as the centre and work out from there. It would be a mistake to over-emphasise La Boëtie's single role in the composition of the *Essais*. But it would not be a mistake to link Montaigne, Ancient Rome and La Boëtie; to say that Montaigne's own personality, the older civilisation, the loss of an *alter ego* were themes which reacted upon each other to produce his art.

8

Roman values in Montaigne

How many Roman values can we find in Montaigne? Can we see, underlying the element of 'modernity' in him, a gamut of associations that stretches back to Ancient Rome? I suggest that the five Roman values identified in Chapter 3 – disdain for the *vulgaire*, concentration on aesthetic questions, the separation of ordinary language and 'poetic' language, the *moraliste* tradition, and the contrast between allusiveness and explicitness – all stand like pillars beneath the dense and complicated structure of the *Essais*.

First, the *moraliste* tradition. We become aware of a leit-motif in the antithesis of *plaire* and *instruire* in Montaigne. In the essay 'Des Livres', II. 10, he makes a distinction between 'les livres simplement plaisans' – among which we find Rabelais and the Latin poets, Vergil, Lucretius, Catullus and Horace – and 'mon autre leçon, qui mesle un peu plus de fruit au plaisir, par où j'apprens à renger mes humeurs et mes conditions'. Among these books are Plutarch and Seneca. Montaigne considers this second category of books because he wants to learn, *instruire*, about self-knowledge and the *art de bien vivre et de bien mourir*.[1] He shows a creative and not a logical intelligence. In reading it may be a thought or it may be the expression of a thought

---

[1] Cf. the same division in I. 39, 'De la Solitude': 'Je n'ayme , pour moy, que des livres ou plaisans et faciles, qui me chatouillent, ou ceux qui me consolent et conseillent à regler ma vie et ma mort. . .' He follows this with two lines of Horace which express perfectly the solitude of a thinking, creative, poetry-reading man:

tacitum sylvas inter reptare salubres,
curentem quidquid dignùm sapiente bonoque est.   (*Epistles*, I. 4. 40)

Montaigne seems implicitly to say that behind this division of books there lies a dual attitude to reading: either involvement with the pattern, the experience and poetry of a work, or learning from books how to live well and how to die well.

that captures his *primsautier* mind; it will not be the whole book, or the logical sequence of ideas. Judgements on certain books have nothing to do with whether he likes them or not. He accepts the judgement of the centuries – for example that of Ancient Rome; but sensibility he has to have. Montaigne's standards of judgement are taken from his Classical reading: for instance, II. 32, 'Defence de Seneque et de Plutarque' he disagrees with Bodin and makes us see how Seneca and Plutarch are judged through their own writings:

> Moy, je considere aucuns hommes fort loing au-dessus de moy, nommément entre les anciens.

For all his admiration for the writings of Caesar, therefore, Montaigne does not hesitate to judge him as a man: his ambition, a passion that dominated all else, ruined him and made him vicious in *la plus puissante et fleurissante chose publique que le monde verra jamais* – note the future tense.

This *moraliste* aspect of Montaigne has been fully analysed, and it would be tedious to list the qualities that make him the father of the seventeenth century.[1] Nonetheless there is a point which is worth insisting upon: Montaigne stands out for his emotional exploitation of Roman poets, his moral analysis of the *condition humaine* by Vergil and Horace, his evocation of them through his quotations. Horace is, in my opinion, the man who helped him to find the right voices, the one who taught him the *tête à tête* note in conversation, the one who by his very choice of 'high' style of his lyrical odes and 'low' style of his Satires and Epistles sowed the seeds of experimentation in Montaigne's mind. But it is clearly Vergil who is his favourite reading. In the masterly analysis he makes, at the end of the essay 'Du jeune Caton', I. 37, of the single lines in praise of Cato by Martial,

---

[1] One must still go back to the seminal book by Pierre Villey, *Les sources et l'évolution des Essais de Montaigne* (2nd ed., 2 vols., Paris, 1933), for the first steps in Montaigne's *moralisme*. Other works include: Alan M. Boase, *The fortunes of Montaigne* (London, 1935); Georges Poulet, *Études sur le temps humain* (Paris, 1950); Erich Auerbach, *Mimesis: the representation of reality in Western literature*, tr. W. Trask (New York, 1953); Albert Thibaudet, *Montaigne*, ed. F. Gray (Paris, 1963); Anthony Levi, *French moralists: the theory of the passions 1585–1649* (Oxford, 1964); F. Friedrich, *Montaigne*, tr. Rovini (Paris, 1968); E. Lablénie, *Montaigne auteur de maximes* (Paris, 1968) and M. Baraz, *L'être et la connaissance selon Montaigne* (Paris, 1968).

Manilius, Lucan, Horace and Vergil, he gives the best praise to Vergil:

> Au dernier, premier de quelque espace, mais la quelle espace il jurera ne pouvoir estre remplie par nul esperit humain, il s'estonnera, il se transira. (a III passage)

Vergil is the 'maistre du cœur' and it would not be unjust to say that Montaigne admired more than any other work the dignity, the majesty of his *Georgics*, 'que j'estime le plus accomply ouvrage de la Poësie', II. 10. Although Montaigne did not use the term it was the *douce gravité* of Vergil that made him his favourite Roman poet.

Finally, the *moraliste* is anti-metaphysical – surely Montaigne is that – and humanist. He is looking at the *condition humaine* with lucidity and perceptiveness; he sees it as at once comic and tragic; is at once witty and tender; at once sensitive and willing to ridicule. In his essay *Comme nous pleurons et rions d'une mesme chose*, I. 38, he suggests that laughing or crying is primarily a change in the onlookers' point of view; we can either laugh or cry because

> il n'y a rien de changé, mais nostre ame regarde la chose d'un autre œil, et se la represente par un autre visage; car chaque chose a plusieurs biais et plusieurs lustres. La parenté, les anciennes accointances et amitiez saisissent nostre imagina- tion et la passionnent pour l'heure, selon leur condition; mais le contour en est si brusque, qu'il nous eschappe.
>
> (a I passage)

It is a tremendous step that Montaigne makes here. Think of the seventeenth-century attitude towards drama and compare the angle of vision of Racine and Molière. They both ask us to look at man's behaviour: the one takes a tragic point of view; the other a comic point of view. But really the moral meditation on the *condition humaine* is fundamentally the same. What is important to recognise is that any subject can be viewed from a comic or tragic viewpoint; the comic – provided that we have the detachment to suspend emotion and moral judgement; the tragic – provided that we have an emotional involvement in the situation.

In another way this paragraph expresses something very close to Proust's idea that our social person is the creation of other people's thought:

> Mais même au point de vue des plus insignifiantes choses de la vie, nous ne sommes pas un tout matériellement constitué, identique pour tout le monde et dont chacun n'a qu'à aller prendre connaissance comme d'un cahier des charges ou d'un testament; notre personnalité sociale est une création de la pensée des autres.   (Pléiade ed, vol., 1, p. 19)

We can see that Montaigne is after that unknown personality, *le mystère de la personnalité* as Valéry would say, that makes everyone different from everyone else. And in this Montaigne is pushing the *moraliste* tradition further than it had reached in Rome – to delve psychologically into the mind and behaviour of man.

Secondly, in the separation of prosaic prose from 'poetic' language we have seen (pp. 140–1) that Montaigne came out clearly in 'De la Vanité' for 'poetic' language. But he does more than merely separate the two. He uses two 'poetic' languages – Latin and French – as his mode of communicating. As a bi-lingual person he can 'feel' the words of two different languages. His Latin is surrounded with the pressure of his French and vice-versa. He can move from one to the other with animation and will-power, and he renders them more expressive and richer in resources than one language used alone. But there are problems that one cannot solve in Montaigne's case. For instance, we could far more easily identify a working-method in creative writing if he had learnt French first and then Latin. He would 'feel' the French words in their 'tentacular associations' if he had known them as a small child, and they would, as it were, form a matrix in his adult brain. Latin, as his second language, would 'feel' like an acquired product; it would have its tentacular associations as merely the product of reading literature or ancient history or metaphysics or ethics. Professor George Steiner[1] deals with parts of this problem when discussing inter-lingual translation in terms of bi- and tri- or

---

[1] *After Babel* (London, 1975), Ch. 3, 'Word against object', is important as a whole but pp. 118–21 contains the main argument on polyglots.

multilinguists. What and how do polyglots work? He says (p. 120)

> Are the mechanisms of self-address, of interior dialogue between syntax and identity, different in a polyglot and in a single-language speaker? It may be – I will argue so – that communication outward is only a secondary, socially stimulated phase in the acquisition of language. Speaking to oneself would be the primary function (considered by L. S. Vygotsky in the early 1930s, this profoundly suggestive hypothesis has received little serious examination since). For a human being possessed of several native tongues and a sense of personal identity arrived at in the course of multilingual interior speech, the turn outward, the encounter of language with others and the world, would of necessity be very different, metaphysically, psychologically different, from that experienced by the user of a single mother-tongue. But can this difference be formulated and measured? Are there degrees of linguistic monism and of multiplicity or unhoused-ness that can be accurately described and tested?
>
> In what language am *I*, suis-*je*, bin *ich*, when I am inmost? What is the tone of the self?
>
> One finds few answers to these questions in the literature.

The words in a language do structure reality: but if you have two languages do you structure two realities? The thing about Montaigne was that Latin felt 'natural' to him and that he understood what it meant better than French. It follows from this that his bi-literacy started from Latin and ended in French. Let us look at one passage – which is a fine piece of literary criticism – and see how it works. The piece is in the middle of 'Sur des Vers de Virgile', III. 5, and it starts by commenting critically on a passage from Lucretius; this leads him into a number of interesting observations about language and what it means for him:

> Ce que Virgile dict de Venus et de Vulcan, Lucrece l'avoit dict plus sortablement d'une jouissance desrobée d'elle et de Mars:

> belli fera moenera Mavors
> Armipotens regit, in gremium qui saepe tuum se
> Rejicit, aeterno devinctus vulnere amoris:
> Pascit amore avidos inhians in te, Dea, visus,

Eque tuo pendet resupini spiritus ore:
Hunc tu, diva, tuo recubantem corpore sancto
Circunfusa super, suaveis ex ore loquelas
Funde.

Quand je rumine ce 'rejicit, pascit, inhians, molli, fovet
medullas, labefacta, pendet, percurrit', et cette noble 'circunfusa', mere du gentil 'infusus', j'ay desdain de ces menues
pointes et allusions verballes qui nasquirent depuis. A ces
bonnes gens, il ne falloit pas d'aigüe et subtile rencontre; leur
langage est tout plein et gros d'une vigueur naturelle et
constante; ils sont tout epigramme, non la queuë seulement,
mais la teste, l'estomac et les pieds. Il n'y a rien d'efforcé, rien
de treinant, tout y marche d'une pareille teneur. (III)
'Contextus totus virilis est; non sunt circa flosculos occupati.'
(II) Ce n'est pas une eloquence molle et seulement sans
offence: elle est nerveuse et solide, qui ne plaict pas tant
comme elle remplit et ravit; et ravit le plus les plus forts espris.
Quand je voy ces braves formes de s'expliquer, si vifves, si
profondes, je ne dicts pas que c'est bien dire, je dicts que c'est
bien penser. C'est la gaillardise de l'imagination qui esleve
et enfle les parolles...

(III) Elles signifient plus qu'elles ne disent. (II) Les imbecilles
sentent encores quelque image de cecy: car, en Italie, je disois
ce qu'il me plaisoit en devis communs; mais, aus propos
roides, je n'eusse osé me fier à un Idiome que je ne pouvois
plier, ny contourner outre son alleure commune. J'y veux
pouvoir quelque chose du mien.

This is a description of Venus, making love to Mars. The
Venus of the passage is not the goddess of religion and
mythology but the creative power of nature, *Venus physica* as she
was known in Latin. The choice of the passage is incisive,
showing Montaigne's taste and critical and creative powers to
the full. The picture of Mars resting in the arms of Venus
combines directness, the imaginative power of conceiving vividly
and expressing a conception in concrete words. For example,
pascit avidos inhians has the simple directness of terms which have
singular force. Montaigne had 'chewed' the previous Vergilian
passage quoted earlier in the essay, and now he re-applies this
to the Lucretian piece – implicitly showing the differences and
resemblances. For immediately after *rejicit, pascit, inhians* we find
fovet medullas – a very typical Vergilian expression – which

Montaigne applies to Lucretius. He does the same thing with *labefacta* and *percurrit*. We feel that this tone of the self is sure, mature, poetic and sensitive. And it is this tone that predominates in the whole passage. Hence, his comparison between the Latin language and the French of the sixteenth century is, in one way, authoritative. His judgement is based on a sure base, so that when he glances at 'ces menues pointes et allusions verballes' in French poetry we can see that it is immature compared to the virility of Latin. In the Latin quotation from Seneca there is one word which is vital – *virilis*. This masculinity underlies all the later comments, and provides a link with our earlier discussion of the Pléiade's theory of style. It is true and proper eloquence or rhetoric because it uses a mixture of imagination and intellect, or emotion and reasoning. Montaigne states that words 'signifient plus qu'elles ne disent' thereby starting a line of allusiveness in literary prose which was to become peculiarly French.

Furthermore, by using both languages he has gone much further than Ronsard and Du Bellay: he has thought more deeply about language. I shall give a few examples to illustrate how deeply he had considered it. He sees the shape and sound of words, 'Le son mesme des noms, qui nous tintouine aux oreilles...me pinsent...c'est une plainte grammairiene et voyelle.' He notices how tone and movement in expression alter the reaction to its contents (III. 13). He realises that the kinds of language that are most important for discussing copulation are unquotable ('Sur des Vers de Virgile', and *passim* in the *Essais*), that language is at its poorest in this area and that though all words are ambiguous, those concerning sex are especially so. He loves words which qualify statements, 'J'ayme ces mots qui amollissent et moderent la temerité de nos propositions: A l'aventure...' (III. 11). And he observed that words have a 'life' and a 'vitality' of their own: 'Il nous faut fortifier l'ouie et la durcir contre cette tendreur du son ceremonieux des parolles' (III. 8).

Montaigne inquires into language; its arbitrariness, its forms, its modes of communication, and its poetic, fantastic and private uses. In this, his own 'invented' language is the same as Rabelais' verbal universe: totally unique and totally different.

Thirdly, the Roman sense of aesthetic value. Thibaudet called the *Essais* 'une esthétique de la vie' and it is this as a phrase we must briefly consider. Let us take the short essay, I. 19, on the theme of death – precisely because life/death and living/dying is one of the larger circles in the *Essais*. The title is 'Qu'il ne faut juger de nostre heur, qu'apres la mort', and the *point de départ* is a quotation from Ovid:

> Scilicet ultima semper
> Expectanda dies homini est, dicique beatus
> Ante obitum nemo, supremaque funera debet.
>
> You must always wait for the last day of a man, there is no-one who can be said to be happy before his death and funeral.
> (Ovid, *Metamorphoses*, III. 135)

This stands at the head, like the text of a sermon, which gives a quotation from the Bible which contains the conclusion in it and is used by the sermonist as the way in to his thoughts and meditations. Montaigne brings in *exempla* of attitudes towards death before he switches to a personal digression framed by a relative clause,

> ce mesme bon-heur de nostre vie, qui dépend de la tranquillité et contentement d'un esprit bien né, et de la resolution et asseurance d'un' ame reglée.   (a 1 passage)

The attitude here is purely Stoic, but a couple of sentences later we find Montaigne's own transformation of the Stoic ideal of death into something which we can call aesthetic. For he sees death as a kind of tableau, which is for everyone to compose as he wills, or like the last act of a drama:

> Mais à ce dernier rolle de la mort et de nous, il n'y a plus que faindre, il faut parler François, il faut montrer ce qu'il y a de bon et de net dans le fond du pot,
>
> Nam verae voces tum demum pectore ab imo
> Ejiciuntur, et eripitur persona, manet res.
>
> It is then at last that sincere words are thrown upward by the heart; the mask falls, reality remains.   (a 1 passage)

Montaigne channels his thought inward: the whole essay gives thoughts on the way of dying, of remaining sincere, of making your last act the act you do well; but these thoughts are not considered humanistically – as Erasmus does in his *Adagia* – but psychologically and artistically. Life is regarded as a work of art. Montaigne judges this not as a piece of knowledge: how many ways of dying there are, what are the concepts underlying each one, what the Ancients have to say about it. Rather it is something which every individual *composes* for himself:

> Je remets à la mort l'essay du fruict de mes etudes. Nous verrons là si mes discours me partent de la bouche ou du cœur. (a 1 passage)

There are two styles of preparing for death: the brave, daring one and the quiet and calm one. Montaigne chooses the latter; in comparing himself with others this is how he wishes to die, and the essay ends with this private assertion:

> Au Jugement de la vie d'autruy, je regarde tousjours comment s'en est porté le bout; et des principaux estudes de la mienne, c'est qu'il se porte bien, c'est à dire quietement et sourdement. (a 11 passage)

In the whole essay what is important is the association of ideas. In formal composition there is logic; points are treated one by one. In this creative writing one thing lies behind or is implicit in the other; one topic triggers off another, and one thought can 'play' between different *Essais*, so holding a light to itself and to the other examples of 'playing chess' with death.

Fourth, Montaigne like Horace and like the Pléiade disdained the *vulgaire*. But he turns this attitude into an emotional exploitation of Stoical values. This is a 'playing' with the term *bien né*. The Christian Humanists (here, as throughout the book, we mean Humanists in the sixteenth-century sense of Classicists) – for example Erasmus – reject entirely the purely aristocratic view of nobility as resting on ancestry or wealth. They prefer to fix it in a mobile state, an inner piety, virtue and learning which is close to Seneca's statements in *Ad Lucilium epistulae morales*,

Then who is well born? [*bene natus*] He who is by nature fitted for virtue...A hall full of smoke-begrimed busts does not make the nobleman. The soul alone renders us noble, and it may rise superior to Fortune out of any earlier condition.[1]

Perfectibility seems to be a basic assumption of Montaigne's, as indeed it was for others in the first half of the sixteenth century.[2] For instance, in the essay on education, 'Du pedantisme', I. 25, one of his essential concerns is the bringing together of the moral and the intellectual, the *boni* and the *docti* in education. Or again in II. 8, 'De l'affection des peres aux enfans', which is addressed to Madame d'Estissac, he speaks of a *nature bien née*, contrasting it with *bestes furieuses*:

> J'essayeroy, par une douce conversation, de nourrir en mes enfans une vive amitié et bienveillance non feincte en mon endroit, ce qu'on gaigne aiséement en une nature bien née; car si ce sont bestes furieuses comme nostre siecle en produit à foison, il les faut hayr et fuyr pour telles.

Then there is the famous *boutade* in 'De l'institution des enfans', I. 26 – if one cannot do anything with a child, let the child be strangled – as Montaigne says rather slyly –

> *s'il est sans tesmoins*, ou qu'on le mette patissier dans quelque bonne ville, fust-il fils d'un duc, suivant le precepte de Platon qu'il faut colloquer les enfans non selon les facultez de leur pere, mais selon les facultez de leur ame.   (my italics)

Finally, the greatest compliment he could pay La Boëtie was to call him *le mieux né* – not in aristocratic sense but in a moral, intellectual and Stoic sense.[3] The people Montaigne admires are 'ames reglées d'elles mesmes et bien nées' and he defines *un honneste homme* (I. 26) as an intellectual or moral gentleman

---

[1] Seneca, XLIV. 5: 'Quis est generosus? ad virtutem bene a natura compositus...Non facit nobilem atrium plenum fumosis imaginibus...animus facit nobilem, cui ex quacumque condicione supra fortunam licet surgere.'

[2] For a fuller analysis see D. G. Coleman, *Rabelais. A critical study in prose fiction*, (Cambridge, 1971), Ch. 2. 'Orientations: "Artful Rab'lais".' And for a fine analysis of the role of Stoicism in Ancient Rome see E. Vernon Arnold, *Roman Stoicism* (London, 1911, re-issued in 1958).

[3] For a far fuller treatment on education see Paul Porteau, *Montaigne et la vie pédagogique de son temps* (Paris, 1935), and Jean Chateau, *Montaigne psychologue et pédagogue* (Paris, 1964).

who has in him the civilised values of the Ancient world. If I could walk neck and neck with the Ancient writers, he says,

> je serois honneste homme, car je ne les entreprens que par où ils sont les plus roides.

Fifthly, allusiveness as opposed to explicitness in the whole way of writing the *Essais*. In many ways this canon entails the whole of Montaigne's artistic position. Many critics have been concerned with style.[1] And so I merely focus light on less well-known elements, the light itself being that of Ancient Rome.

Sayce has said that Montaigne has 'the allusive style which relies on the complicity of an intelligent reader'.[2] I propose to view this allusiveness through one essay and one model – Horace; considering also the use of quotations from Martial – 'Sur des vers de Virgile' – and one element of the suggestiveness of words. This allusiveness is Montaigne's greatest faculty, and certainly he knows it: for he is aware that *no* reader will ever get to the furthest reaches of what he wrote. Every commentary is a way of *nous entregloser* (III. 13); every human being has a

> esprit [qui] ne trouve pas le champ moins spatieux à contreroller le sens d'autruy qu'à representer le sien, et comme s'il y avoit moins d'animosité et d'aspreté à gloser qu'à inventer. (III. 13)

But Montaigne clearly says in III. 9,

> sans me gloser moymesme. Qui est celuy qui n'aime mieux n'estre pas leu que de l'estre en dormant ou en fuyant?

As we know that 'tout abbregé sur un bon livre est un sot abbregé' (III. 8) emotional resonance and critical, intelligent reading are essential to our interpretation of him.

Some of the Martial quotations in 'Sur des vers de Virgile', III. 5 can be used to illustrate this. We remember what

---

[1] See for example, R. A. Sayce, 'L'ordre des *Essais* de Montaigne', *BHR*, XVIII 1956, pp. 7–22, and his book on *Montaigne* (London, 1972); Floyd Gray, *Le style de Montaigne* (Paris, 1958); Michaël Baraz, 'Les images dans les *Essais* de Montaigne', *BHR*, XXVII (1965), pp. 361–94; Morris W. Croll, '*Attic*' *and baroque prose style: the anti-Ciceronian movement*, ed. Patrick, Evans and Wallace (Princeton, N.J., 1969) and Zoë Samaras, *The comic element of Montaigne's style* (Paris, 1970).

[2] *Montaigne*, p. 283.

Montaigne said about a Martial epigram in II. 35 – 'Il est bien plus vif en son naturel et d'un sens plus riche. . .' – commenting on the richness, directness, simplicity of the Latin tongue; and we note that he does not translate it for people who do not understand Latin. We cannot know the *sens plus riche* as he did, but a few words do point to the greater vigour or powerfulness of Latin. Of the first two words[1] one relates to Arria, the other to her husband – an immediate juxtaposition. *De visceribus strinxerat* denotes a concrete, rather horrible action and the sounds *sc* and *x* reinforce the sense. Note too the verbs in the next line *feci. . .dolet, inquit*, placed close together and almost – but not wholly – repeated in the last line *facies. . .dolet*. We can perhaps imagine Montaigne's appreciation. We remember too how in the *Apologie de Raimond Sebon* he addresses, presumably, Marguerite de Valois rather apologetically for having quoted an epigram of Martial,[2]

> (J'use en liberté de conscience de mon Latin, avecq le congé que vous m'en avez donné.)

This is crucial; the epigram is very coarse: it contains four uses of *futuo* (to copulate), one of *paedicem* (make love between two males) and one of *mentula* (penis). The lasciviousness is made stronger by the taut style – like the two options the male is given – to copulate or make war,

> Aut futue, aut pugnemus, ait. . .

The terms for sexuality are here given in the Latin and not in French, and, in Martial particularly, are used again and again. Montaigne uses the words freely in 'Sur des vers de Virgile' but never translates them. The emotional point is made through the

---

[1] I. 13, Loeb edition:
>   Casta suo gladium cum traderet Arria Paeto,
>   quem de visceribus strinxerat ipsa suis,
>   "Si qua fides, vulnus quod feci non dolet;" inquit
>   "sed tu quod facies, hoc mihi, Paete, dolet."

[2] XI. 20. Montaigne takes lines 3–8:
>   "Quod futuit Glaphyran Antonius, hanc mihi poenam
>   Fulvia constituit, se quoque uti futuam.
>   Fulviam ego ut futuam? quod si me Manius oret
>   pedicem, faciam? non puto, si sapiam.
>   'Aut futue, aut pugnemus' ait. quid quod mihi vita
>   carior est ipsa mentula? signa canant."

Latin, and there is often a deliberate ambiguity. I shall take
three quotations and show what they add to the texture of the
essay.

In the first quotation Montaigne is talking of women: the
effects of lust can seem worse when they are hidden. Into this
context comes a line from Martial, epigram VII. 62,[1]

Illud saepe facit, quod sine teste facit.

Martial's context concerns Amillus, who indulges in various
forms of unnatural lewdness including, of course, buggery. The
last line given by Montaigne has a concise point; it comes after

non pedicari se qui testatur, Amille...

he who protests that he is not making love protests too much.
There is in the Latin a play on words between *testatur* and *teste*:
the testicle and the witness. Now it is not possible that Montaigne
used the last line without knowing that the whole context was
homosexual, without enjoying the *jeu de mot* and without
deliberately calling up for his readers the other poem. He goes
on to say,

Et ceux que nous craignons le moins sont à l'avanture les plus
à craindre; leurs pechez muets sont les pires.

and then quotes another line by Martial – this time the last line
of VI. 7.

offendor moecha simpliciore minus.[2]

This epigram concerns the Julian law – *Lex Iulia de maritandis
ordinibus* of 18 B.C. – against adultery, which was revived by

[1] VII. 62:

Reclusis foribus grandes percidis, Amille,
    et te deprendi, cum facis ista, cupis,
ne quid liberti narrent servique paterni
    et niger obliqua garrulitate cliens.
non pedicari se qui testatur, Amille,
    illud saepe facit quod sine teste facit.

[2] VI. 7:

Iulia lex populis ex quo, Faustine, renata est
    atque intrare domos iussa Pudicitia est,
aut minus aut certe non plus tricesima lux est,
    et nubit decimo iam Telesilla viro.
quae nubit totiens, non nubit: adultera lege est.
    offendor moecha simpliciore minus.

Domitian. It is concerned with those who act against chastity but within the Julian law: Telesilla is now marrying her tenth husband in just thirty days – an adulteress by form of law. In the 'exemplaire de Bordeaux' the following variant comes after *minus*: 'Il 1°: en est; 2° est des effaictz qui offancĕt (non) sciammĕt la pureté corporelle Obstetrix...' which shows that Montaigne has in mind the whole epigram. These two examples of last lines placed very close together in the essay might be just a reminiscence, but it seems to be much more likely that Montaigne was 'playing' on the two complete epigrams – in which case he is really going much further than appears. For he is including sodomy and buggery with heterosexual love, and thus delving more deeply into the whole question of sex and its role in life.[1]

In my last example Montaigne talks of sexual fulfilment in life. Again he takes lines from two different epigrams of Martial,

> tanquam thura merumque parent:
> Absentem marmoreamve putes.

The first line from epigram XI. 104, line 12,[2] originally read *pares* which is in perfect congruence with this quasi-dialogue that Martial creates between the man and woman. Montaigne has altered it to *parent* to suit his context where women are the subject. But he recalls to the reader the Martial context. The second line is from epigram XI. 60, line 8[3] where the first word

---

[1] See also D. Coleman, 'Sur des vers de Virgile' in R. R. Bolgar (ed.), *Classical Influences in European Culture* (Cambridge, 1976), pp. 135–40. In a French translation of the seventeenth century, *Les epigrammes de Martial traduites en vers par M.* – i.e. Michel de Marolles – (Paris, 1671), both VII. 62 – the buggery one – and VI. 7 – the prostitution one – are omitted altogether. In the *Collection des auteurs latins avec la traduction en français*, ed. M. Nisard, Paris, 1842, *paedicari* in VII. 62 is not translated at all nor is the play on words at the end attempted. The line from VI. 7 is translated as 'Une franche catin me scandaliserait moins'.

[2] This epigram is fairly long. It is the husband's complaint that his wife will not make love to him; the kisses she gives are like those she exchanges with her grandmother in the morning; her body is concealed by opaque robes and a tunic; she gets incense ready as though she was purifying herself for the rites of Ceres or Isis. Immediately after the phrase that Montaigne quotes comes,
> masturbabantur Phrygii post ostia servi,
> Hectoreo quotiens sederat uxor equo...
which is a picture that I think Montaigne means his readers to have in mind.

[3] XI. 60:
> Sit Phlogis an Chione Veneri magis apta requiris?
> pulchrior est Chione; sed Phlogis ulcus habet,

of Martial's line is omitted since it would carry with it a totally different context: the word is *adiuvat* – Chione is impassive and she does not encourage one, whilst Phlogis is sexually more fun. The whole context in Montaigne is the way that women do not give in/give in too quickly/give in too furiously. Montaigne once again dares to tell a great deal about the enjoyment of sexual fulfilment, yet by way of hints and allusions.¹ Martial lends Montaigne a wealth of sexual vocabulary; he gives him the coarser ranges of the language of sex. But Montaigne says in this essay, that Vergil and Lucretius treat lust/love *reservéement et discrettement*, and a line from Ovid like

> Et nudum pressi corpus adúsque meum   (*Amores*, I. 5. 24)

is more effective than Martial:

> Que Martial retrousse Venus à sa poste, il n'arrive pas à la faire paroistre si entiere. Celuy qui dict tout, il nous saoule et nous desgouste.

The evaluation is made on literary terms: choice of vocabulary, unwillingness to go too far and a firm nuance in saying things. The emotional resonance is brought into this essay by the exploitation of Roman poets through quotation. We must have the context in mind; we must read carefully; then perhaps we are ready to 'hear' Montaigne aright.²

> ulcus habet Priami quod tendere possit alutam
>   quodque senem Pelian non sinat esse senem;
> ulcus habet quod habere suam vult quisque puellam,
>   quod sanare Criton, non quod Hygia potest.
> at Chione non sentit opus nec vocibus ullis
>   adiuvat, absentem marmoreamve putes.
> exorare, dei, si vos tam magna liceret
>   et bona velletis tam pretiosa dare,
> hoc quod habet Chione corpus faceretis haberet
>   ut Phlogis, et Chione quod Phlogis ulcus habet.

¹ Other examples of quotations from Martial are: early in the essay epigram x. 23: here the whole epigram is very congruous; Montaigne talks of old age and Martial makes the point that one can doubly enjoy the pleasures one has in youth by remembering them in old age. Some more lines from vii. 58 – an epigram he has used before – are very free and Montaigne has found it useful to render them in the original rather than in the vernacular.

² The emotional range of quotations from Roman poets throughout the *Essais* is a topic too vast for this book, but it seems to me crucial in our evaluation of Montaigne's emotions. Most critics seem to agree that in spite of his sensitivity there is a fairly small charge of emotion or passion in the *Essais*. But, as far as I know, there is very little work on the bi-lingualism and the bi-literacy of Montaigne using French/Latin

The second method of 'hearing' him is to see how one quotation can be made to provide themes and poetic structure for a whole essay. An example is in I. 11, 'Des Prognostications' – extensive quotation from two of Horace's odes. It is given in the 1580 version, and the subsequent editions thicken the texture greatly, but precisely from the themes that Horace proposes. It is a rhetorical attempt at re-texturing Horace's poem. The context from which these stanzas are lifted will tell us something about the way in which Montaigne uses Ancient literature. The first nine lines are from an ode of heroic proportions – III. 29. The imagery is allusive, and the content shows Maecenas what life is really about. It is a call to acceptance of the human condition: no future, no past, merely a present – a far more burdensome responsibility than it sounds. Human life is placed in a framework of nature: capricious, ever unstable yet constant in its variability. The last verse presents the image of the tiny skiff, free from Fortune's changes, sailing on the sea, with a private tranquillity which is not touched by questions of wealth or poverty, of private and public, of the whole social and intellectual scene in which the ode is set. This ode is a private dramatisation of Horace's inner tranquillity of mind and peace of heart in which he always uses as leit-motifs the humbleness of the poet's craft, the shunning of the world's glory, the exploitation of the sensuous which he spurns at the same time.

Montaigne uses the ode as proof that the external world, time past and time future are really meaningless. The important thing is to *be*. There are two words in Horace's ode – *Dixisse*, *vixi* – which have caught Montaigne's imagination and which become a leit-motif in the *Essais*. For example, *J'ay vescu* is one of the themes in 'De l'experience'. It is a dominating theme in organising that essay, having correspondence with, and re-texturing, all the essays in all three books. It links back with a French statement in I. 11:

modes of communication. A sampling of Martial quotations in 'Sur des vers de Virgile' and of Catullus and Vergil in I. 2. 'De la Tristesse', suggests to me that a whole dimension of emotion comes through, precisely because of the Latin quotations.

> la forcenée curiosité de nostre nature, s'amusant à preoccuper
> les choses futures, comme si elle n'avoit pas assez affaire à
> digerer les presentes...

first made in the 1580 edition.

Montaigne deprecates excessive anxiety about a future which
we cannot control. The two words *Dixisse, vixi* link with much
of Lucretius' philosophical meditations about life, time and
death. And Montaigne had read Lucretius. Professor Margaret
McGowan (*Montaigne's Deceits*, p. 92) draws our attention to
Marcus Aurelius, saying: 'It is, I believe, possible that Marcus
Aurelius's handbook provided Montaigne with a much richer
source of inspiration than is usually realised.' And I think that
in this essay, 'Des Prognostications', the whole dimension of
time and life is enriched by the emotional exploitation of Stoic
philosophy. The Stoics regarded the concept of time past and
future as indifferent, as something outside man's control.
Present time is the only thing that can be regarded as being
under one's control,

> For the present is equal for all, and what is passing is therefore
> equal: thus what is being lost is proved to be barely a moment.
> For a man could lose neither past nor future; how can one
> rob him of what he has not got? Always remember, then, these
> two things: one, that all things from everlasting are of the
> same kind, and are in rotation; and it matters nothing
> whether it be for a hundred years or for two hundred or for
> an infinite time that a man shall behold the same spectacle;
> the other, that the longest-lived and the soonest to die have
> an equal loss; for it is the present alone of which either will
> be deprived, since (as we saw) this is all he has and a man
> does not lose what he has not got.[1]

Montaigne exploits themes of Stoic philosophy in the same
spirit as he explores Roman poets. The last paragraph (in the
'exemplaire de Bordeaux') explores the demon of Socrates, and
Montaigne links a sudden impulsion of his will with his own
experience,

---

[1] A. S. L. Farquharson, *The Meditations of the Emperor Marcus Aurelius Antonius* (Oxford,
1944), Book. II. 14.

> Et en ay eu, ausquelles je me laissay emporter si utilement
> et heureusement qu'elles pourrayent estre jugées tenir
> quelque chose d'inspiration divine.

This is divine inspiration and in Montaigne's case it is there from
the impulse to set down his essays, from his reading of Horace
and his peers. We can compare the end of this essay to a
statement in the *Apologie*,

> Et   certes   la   philosophie   n'est   qu'une   poesie
> sophistiquée...Platon n'est qu'un poete descousu...

The emotional value of his realisation that the universe has
a doubleness in everything is that it is equally dramatic,
whether tragic or comic. He turned the emotional into the
aesthetic and so makes the reader accept the correspondences
between one part of an essay and another, between statements
from different essays considered as variations on a theme, the
same words in different essays set in different contexts but
converging obliquely on a topic. The statement he makes in
1580, from II. 16, *De la gloire,*

> Mais nous sommes, je ne sçay comment, doubles en nous
> mesmes, qui faict que ce que nous croyons nous ne le croyons
> pas, et ne nous pouvons deffaire de ce que nous condamnons.

this is something that we must bear in mind whatever topic
Montaigne is talking about and wherever we are trying to
interpret the *Essais*.

The remaining aspect of allusiveness is the power of single
words: 'Elles signifient plus qu'elles ne disent' (III. 5). I shall
take a few examples from one essay, II. 37, 'De la ressemblance
des enfans aux peres' to demonstrate how complex, imaginative
and allusive they are. Montaigne is discussing his gall-stones
– a subject that forces him to allude to life and death – and says:
'J'entre des-jà en composition de ce vivre coliqueux.' Instead
of using *la vie*, for life – we find *ce vivre*: 'this going on living'
– the verb turned into a noun makes that noun as active as a
verb; then it is qualified by *coliqueux* – 'with stones in my
gall-bladder'. All this is measured, ruled, ordered by *composition*:
Montaigne giving shape to his internal pain; Montaigne analysing the mixture his life has become; Montaigne using his

gall-stones to see what he can bring out to the matter of living. The whole phrase is part of a leit-motif: it looks back on the 'composition' of death in I. 19; it looks forward to the 'composition' of life in III. 13 – 'composer nos meurs' or 'Nostre grand et glorieux chef-d'oeuvre, c'est vivre à propos'. The juxtaposition of *vivre coliqueux* is the allusive counter, linking it into a long chain of associations which is the leit-motif of life and death. The adjective is from Montaigne's feeling, the verb from commonplace spheres. He makes it dynamic by using his personal experience within a net of philosophical and religious ideas. Then, later in the essay this adjective becomes tied to a type of man who has gall-stones – 'pour nous autres coliqueux' – which makes it a slightly humorous notion, as if we were to think of them all queuing up to have remedies from doctors. It is easy to pass from *vivre coliqueux* to *ma subjection graveleuse* and to link this with *santé*, which is the largest circle in the essay.[1]

Another phrase will demonstrate even more clearly how words are the hinges in such correspondences in the whole of the *Essais*.

> Mais les souffrances vrayment essentielles et corporelles, je les gouste bien vifvement.

The word *gouste* here could mean any of the senses that Cotgrave gives: 'To tast, or take an essay of; to tast, savor; touch upon; feele or conceive a little; also, to admit of, disgest indifferently, take a liking to, to begin to affect, or fancie; also, to have some experience, a little insight, meane knowledge in'. With the adverbial phrase *bien vifvement* it means to 'feel' – so it is the sharpness of the pain, the way it makes itself felt that is conveyed. *Corporelles* is this time in opposition to the *merveilleusement corporel* that man is; tied to *essentielles* the adjective casts a physical taint on the essential parts of the body. The adverb *vrayment* has real force. The whole phrase is dynamic. The adjective *corporelle* recurs again and again in this essay – always throwing a dim light on his suffering. The word *gouste* gives way to *desgouste* further on, when Montaigne is talking about

---

[1] Later on in the essay there is the phrase 'Les choses aperitives sont utiles à un homme coliqueus' where the adjective is used without any hint of a metaphor.

nature's laws as opposed to a medical régime: 'C'est un ordre superbe et impiteux. Nostre crainte, nostre desespoir le desgoute. . .' with the meaning of 'not touch upon, take a liking to'.

My last example has the opposite effect to the words on his gall-stones. It is in the letter to Madame de Duras with which this essay ends:

> Certes, je n'ay point le coeur si enflé, ne si venteux, qu'un plaisir solide, charnu et moëleus comme la santé, je l'alasse eschanger pour un plaisir imaginaire, spirituel et aërée.[1]

The heart image is bold, characterised by two adjectives of concrete physical nature: *enflé* – 'swollen, risen, puffed up, strouted out' (Cotgrave); *venteux* – 'windie, full of wind'. *Santé* is characterised by *plaisir* which is qualified by two sets of triple adjectives; *solide* and *charnu* – 'fleshie, grosse'; *moëleus* – 'marrowie, pithie, full of strength, or strong sap'; health is seen on a physical level, on a mental level and on an intellectual level. This theme is a leit-motif in this essay and throughout the *Essais*. Health is crucial to Montaigne's values: it is muscular, sinewy and earthy. And we may add that he gives it the highest place in the quality of life. In 'Sur des vers de Virgile', III. 5, he places it above divine fury: all writers are at fault:

> Noz maistres ont tort dequoy, cherchant les causes des eslancements extraordinaires de nostre esprit, outre ce qu'ils en attribuent à un ravissement divin, à l'amour, à l'aspreté guerriere, à la poësie, au vin, ils n'en ont donné sa part à la santé; une santé bouillante, vigoureuse, pleine, oisifve. . .

Like Rabelais, Montaigne regards health as a poetic *saillie* without which all other elements in life wilt and die. This is a pagan rather than a Christian value, and should be set alongside the five Roman values that we have seen are embedded in Montaigne: this sixth value is the most important.

Montaigne's *paysage intérieur* is strongly Roman. It derives its features from his mother tongue having been Latin, from the early 'divine' reading of Classical poets, from the friendship

---

[1] Florio's translation of this sentence is rather delightful; 'Surely my heart is not so pufft up, nor so windy, that a solide fleshy and marrowy pleasure as health is, I should change it for an imaginary spirituall and airy delight.'

with La Boëtie – a relationship in which their culture was absolutely Roman – and from the creation of a 'poetic' prose which is at times bi-lingual. Through all this he is able to reach the very bases of literary creation, and to ensure that French prose was infinitely more mature than English prose of the same period. Montaigne's view of the *condition humaine* is tinged with a smiling irony, which is pagan rather than Christian, and which permeates the texture of his prose as though it were the health of the intelligence and the reason.

Conclusion

The points which emerge in conclusion are all points of departure for French literature of the Renaissance and post-Renaissance periods. Certain fundamental features of the sixteenth century make it impossible to say either that:

> The tradition of logic and rhetoric is dead today, so dead that we tend to forget that it ever existed. This is unfortunate, because we cannot begin to understand the sixteenth century until we have realized how much most of its literature owes to this tradition.[1]

Or to make the disarmingly 'true'/'false' comment of these closing remarks of Donald Stone:

> In the humanist aesthetic, it is extremely difficult to distinguish between teaching and pleasing. When we sense, therefore, with what insistence the Classicists spoke of *plaire*, how richly they endowed the inner world of their characters, and how discreet, hidden even, is the "message" of their great works, we have recognized again that French humanism and French Classicism are very distinct aesthetics.[2]

Rhetoric governed the ways of communication in Ancient Rome and Renaissance France. But we have seen it for what it is: merely a mode of communication, a tool of the trade. We have seen that it does not govern our evaluation, and that every writer has to have his own personal mode of communication. From the standpoint of Roman literary criticism we started by analysing a poem by Catullus and one by Propertius, and came

[1] Barbara C. Bowen, *The Age of Bluff. Paradox and Ambiguity in Rabelais and Montaigne* (Urbana, Ill., 1972), pp. 14–15.
[2] Concluding sentences to *From tales to truths. Essays on French Fiction in the sixteenth century, Analecta Romanica*, Heft 34 (Frankfurt am Main, 1973), p. 54.

to the conclusion that they worked by intellectual and aesthetic and imaginative means. For instance, the Propertius elegy expected the reader himself to do the work of experiencing: for example the phrase *admota manu* refers to the action of the hand, whether it is mobile, static, dynamically hovering or even roving – it called for an active interpretation by every reader. But the important point was that the poem contained enough controlling hints to make us visualise the action. We might say that those who read the poem without having had a comparable experience – of seeing a desired one asleep – would have a somewhat different reaction from one whose preoccupation it had been at some time to watch a sleeping desired one. And there might be a significantly different reaction from a reader who had both had the experience and had read Proust's passage on Marcel watching Albertine sleep, or had read Théophile de Viau's exquisite poem on the same theme:

> Quand tu me vois baiser tes bras,
> Que tu poses nuds sur tes draps,
> Bien plus blancs que le linge mesme:
> Quand tu sens ma bruslante main
> Se pourmener dessus ton sein,
> Tu sens bien Cloris que je t'aime.
>
> Comme un devot devers les cieux
> Mes yeux tournez devers tes yeux,
> A genous aupres de ta couche,
> Pressé de mille ardans desirs,
> Je laisse sans ouvrir ma bouche
> Avec toy dormir mes plaisirs.
>
> Le sommeil aise de t'avoir
> Empesche tes yeux de me voir,
> Et te retient dans son Empire
> Avec si peu de liberté,
> Que ton esprit tout arresté
> Ne murmure ny ne respire.
>
> La rose en rendant son odeur,
> Le Soleil donnant son ardeur,
> Diane et le char qui la traine,
> Une Naiade dedans l'eau
> Et les Graces dans un tableau,
> Font plus de bruict que ton haleine.

> La je souspire aupres de toy,
> Et considerant comme quoy
> Ton oeil si doucement repose,
> Je m'escrie: ô Ciel! peux tu bien
> Tirer d'une si belle chose
> Un si cruel mal que le mien?[1]

But all three sets of readers would be experiencing the same poem: one at the level of the single experience of the poem, the second on a plane of shared experience of life – he/she might in theory want to take the poem to the room and compare notes between the real actions he/she saw and the *admota manu*. The third group would be in a position to receive the poem at a level which combined experience of this poem, experience of life, and experience of other related literature – perhaps on more than one language.

The fact that Roman literary tradition took hold of the French climate in the sixteenth century but did not evoke exactly the same values as in England is significant for the whole development of literature in both countries. Part of this disparity comes through the intellectuality of French and Roman writing, part through the different view of aesthetics, and part through the aristocratic view of writing. Odette de Mourgues' conclusion in *Metaphysical, Baroque and Précieux Poetry* (Oxford, 1953, p. 174) offers another reason for the differences in the poetry – a difference that this book has not dealt with, but in a sense one of the most crucial features – and that is the fundamental nature of the two languages:

> The English language, with its variety of stresses, its syncopated rhythm of utterance, its freedom of syntax, its mixture of Latin and Saxon words, its great wealth of synonyms, is more spontaneously poetic, so that poetry can afford to be colloquial and deal with everyday reality, whereas the regular unemphatic flow of the French language needs, in order to become poetic, an artificial system not only of scansion but of themes and even of atmosphere.

This is certainly valid; one would like to search more deeply even than Rosemund Tuve has done in her splendid book on

---

[1] Théophile de Viau, *Œuvres poétiques*, ed. Jeanne Streicher, Geneva, 1951, vol. 1, pp. 150–1.

Elizabethan and Metaphysical Imagery (Chicago, 1947) to see how
Roman Literary theory – not the rhetorical handbooks of the
Renaissance – was interpreted in England. For example, she
does not touch on the whole antithesis of *mollis/gravis* – which
we have found to be crucial in France. She analyses the
relationship between decorum and the three styles but merely
puts in a footnote (p. 232): 'In the grand style one looks to find
dignitas, sonus and on occasion *gravitas, vehementia*; in the base
style, always *tenuitas*, occasionally *simplicitas, securitas* in the
moderate style, *rotunditas, volubilitas.*' It would be interesting to
analyse what Shakespeare or Donne made of the theory of
'strong' lines, of masculinity and muscularity of images – which
were inherent in Roman poetry and which passed over to
France as we have seen during the course of this book.[1]

In France bi-literacy is crucial in the sixteenth century even
if it does not imply full bilingualism.[2] It meant that French
writers had a mature literature for use as a standard comparison.
It meant that they had a set of evaluative terms – all borrowed
from Rome – which they could use in their practical criticism.
This practical criticism – for example in Belleau's commentary
on Ronsard's sonnets – was not as yet very sophisticated, but
it did contain evaluative terms. For example Belleau's commentary on the adjective *simple* (*2e Livre des Amours*, sonnet 22, line
14)[3] says,

> sotte, facile à deceuoir, aisée & facile à se laisser tromper
> comme fut Venus par Junon. C'est vn epithete non oisif, mais
> propre & seruant à la cause. Car souuent selon les argumens
> on donne d'autres epithetes à Venus, comme belle, ieune

[1] J.-J. Denonain, *Thèmes et Formes de la Poésie 'Metaphysique'* (Algiers, 1956), pp. 22–7,
has a discussion of masculinity and 'strong' lines in English metaphysical poetry but
he does not go further. I suspect that the *mollis/gravis* juxtaposition would be
interesting to trace in English Renaissance and post-Renaissance poetry.

[2] Montaigne is not unique in his bilingualism. One might mention Agrippa d'Aubigné
who claims that he knew Latin, Greek and Hebrew when he was only six years old.
How much that is a boast or truth one does not know. One remembers too that Du
Perron in his funeral oration on Ronsard said that when the poet was in diplomatic
service in Scotland – roughly for two and a half years – he was read to by 'le seigneur
Paul, tres-bon Poete Latin, [qui] se plaisoit à luy lire tous les jours quelque chose
de Virgile ou d'Horace...', and then Ronsard would try and write verse in Latin.
Thus the progression from bilingualism to bi-literacy was obvious in Ronsard too.

[3] *Œuvres de Pierre de Ronsard Gentilhomme Vandosmois Prince des Poetes François. Reveues et
augmentées* (Paris, 1617), *2e Livre des Amours/commentée par Remy Belleau.*

> trompeuse, pariure, menteuse, puissante, germeuse: mais la
> maniere de bien apposer & appliquer tels adiectifs, ne sert
> que par l'artifice d'vn excellent Poëte, & bien rusé.

And on Ronsard's forging words that did not exist and have
not 'taken' in the French language Belleau makes this
lengthy comment – which is exactly congruent for a critic at
this point –

> en-rocher, en-eauër, en-foüer, en glacer./Tourner en roche,
> en eau, en glace, en feu. Mots nouveaux & necessaires, pour
> enrichir la pauureté de nostre langue laquelle ne manqueroit
> auiourdh'huy d'vne infinité de beaux mots bien inuentez &
> bien recherchez, si du commencement les enuieux de la vertu
> de l'Autheur ne l'eussent, par leurs iapemens, destourné
> d'vne si loüable entreprise. Car de ce mot de feu tournant le
> e en o, vient foüyer, & foüace, qui est vne certaine galette
> ou tourteau cuit au feu. Puis foüe, qui signifie vne grande
> flamme de feu, telle que nous faisons en nos villages la Vigile
> de la S. Iean. En-eauë/Il est certain que nos peres disoient
> eauë pour eau: tesmoins en sont les vieux Romans. Or d'eauë
> le Poëte a fait le verbe En-eauer, comme de glace, en glacer.
> Les François le deuroient suiure en telles compositions,
> pourueu qu'elles fussent bien reiglées & proprement faites.
> At-elle/En lieu de dire A-elle, pour euiter la cacophonie, c'est
> à dire, le mauuais son des voyelles.[1]

If any radical reform is to be effected in poetry, the poet must
start by revitalizing the language itself. We have seen the
Roman poets grappling with the problem in practice, and
certainly theoreticians like Cicero and Quintilian were vitally
concerned with language. This was the first task of the poets in
France during the Renaissance. They were intelligently aware
of it, though they were not always aware of the possible, still
less the best solutions. Thus Ronsard made his coinages, and
deliberately enlarged his vocabulary to make poetry more
expressive – 'chercher les mots les plus expressifs ou les plus
sonores' was his motto. He even boasts:

> Adoncques pour hausser ma langue maternelle,
> Indouté du labeur, je travaillay pour elle,

---

[1] Belleau's commentary, *Œuvres de Pierre Ronsard* (Paris, 1617), on number 55, pp.
369–70.

Je fis des mots nouveaux, je r'appelay les vieux
Si bien que son renom je poussay jusqu'aux cieux.

But this boast is modest compared to Hugo's words in *Réponse à un Acte d'Accusation*,

J'ai mis un bonnet rouge au vieux dictionnaire.

Many critics condemn the Pléiade for instituting poetic diction in French poetry and getting away from the 'natural'. But this move is tied to a perfectly rational theory – inherited from Rome – that poetry is more expressive than prose; it is a more delicate and suggestive instrument. Furthermore the whole concept of the 'natural' is problematic. To whom is it 'natural'? Why should it be 'natural'? To what perspective does the term refer? What is 'natural' in poetry? In writing poetry at all – in whatever language – is one not attempting to channel subjective things into a different kind of form?[1] The Pléiade insist that poetry is not a degraded form of prose but a special form of language with its own unique function to perform; therefore purge poetry of its prosaic elements. For instance, the use of periphrasis is an attempt to get away from prose communication, and it is more evocative and more suggestive. This is clearly the attitude of Mallarmé, who in his poem 'Tombeau d'Edgar Poe' talks of Poe's detractors who accused him of finding inspiration in drink; he puts it in this way: they

Proclamèrent très haut le sortilège bu
Dans le flot sans honneur de quelque noir mélange.

Similarly his use of synecdoche to avoid direct reference – for instance 'le marbre' for marble tomb, or 'un immortel pubis' for a prostitute.

The positive work done and suggestions made by Du Bellay

---

[1] It is interesting to hear Quintilian answering accusations of unnaturalness of rhetoric: 'Neque ignoro quosdam esse, qui curam omnem compositionis excludant, atque illum horridum sermonem, ut forte fluxerit, modo magis naturalem, modo etiam magis virilem esse contendant. Qui se id demum naturale esse dicunt quod natura primum ortum est et quale ante cultum fuit, tota hic ars orandi subvertitur...quorum si fieri nihil melius liceret, ne domibus quidem casas aut vestibus pellium tegmina aut urbibus montes ac silvas mutari oportuit...Verum id est maxime naturale quod fieri natura optime patitur' (IX. 4. 3–6).

and Ronsard correspond to a good deal that came after them in French literature. The combination of *copia* with the need for *un plus hault style* gave birth to the new concept of aesthetics during the Renaissance. The concept of *copia* runs through French literature for four centuries; for instance, it is at the heart of Baudelaire's article on Gautier. The qualities Baudelaire praises are the vast vocabulary and command of the technical devices of poetry so that the poet can capture every fleeting impression:

> Cette prestesse à résoudre tout problème de style et de composition ne fait-elle pas rêver à la sévère maxime qu'il avait une fois laissé tomber devant moi dans la conversation, et dont il s'est fait sans doute un constant devoir: "Tout homme qu'une idée, si subtile et si imprévue qu'on la suppose, prend en défaut, n'est pas un écrivain. L'inexprimable n'existe pas."[1]

The emphasis on transferring an effect to the reader rather than merely apprehending personal experiences may be found both in literary Rome and later poets. According to Valéry, a poem is 'une sorte de machine à produire l'état poétique au moyen des mots...Un poète...n'a pas pour fonction de ressentir l'état poétique: ceci est une affaire privée. Il a pour fonction de la créer chez les autres.' And this is what Ronsard recommended above all:

> Tu seras industrieux à esmouvoir les passions et affections de l'ame, car c'est la meilleure partie de ton mestier, par des carmes qui t'esmouveront le premier, soit à rire ou à pleurer, afin que les lecteurs en facent après toy.
> Ronsard, *Œuvres complètes* (Pléiade edition, Paris, 1950, vol. II, p. 1024)

Here the grand style, the heroic stance, poetic diction and *douce gravité* and finally the vitality of poetic theory itself enter the stage of French literature, to remain in active possession of it for centuries to come. The muscular terms in Roman poetic

---

[1] Baudelaire, *Œuvres complètes* (Pléiade edition, Paris 1954), pp. 1035–6. The whole article is splendidly illuminating on the concepts of both poets, on language, discipline of poetry, artificial and natural elements in the composing of a poem.

theory destroy the false opposition of so-called 'functional' and 'decorative' elements in French Renaissance criticism.

The break with the past conditions French writing as a whole. The sixteenth-century writers – poets and prose-writers – look back to a Golden Age which is not their own; it is situated in Greece and Rome. It marks the beginning of the separation between Christian/religious and pagan literature: also the ability as a man to be devoutly religious and at the same time to be pagan in literary works. It is simply a question of masks: the public and the private mask. Montaigne can be seen as the best example here (though one may already be thinking of people like La Rochefoucauld and Racine in the next century). There is no doubt that he was a practising Christian: in 'Des prieres', I. 56, he disavows anything which goes against 'les sainctes prescriptions de l'Eglise catholique, apostolique et Romeine, en la quelle je meurs et en la quelle je suis né'. His constant mention of divine as opposed to human reason (not only in the *Apologie* but throughout the *Essais*) and his receiving the Host on his death-bed convince us that he was a Christian. But every value that we have found in him was deeply pagan, deeply Roman. For instance, his views on sex. Not only does he talk openly and deeply of its role in life; he follows a non-Christian morality. Part of Christian 'civilisation' is a violent reprobation of sex. But sex is allowed into the heart of the *Essais* because Montaigne recognised that it was an essential part of every human being.

Perhaps the French Renaissance did lack historical sense. Perhaps its writers were wrong to think that they lived in something like *ce bienheureux siècle d'Auguste*. But they did have a historical and aesthetic perspective: they were writing the same kind of creative literature as the Romans were; they were exploiting the same kind of feelings and they held the same kind of values. Horace and Vergil were their dominant poets and they were *moralistes*. Will the same be true in the seventeenth century? We wonder.

Select Bibliography

BOOKS BEFORE 1800

Boccaccio, Giovanni, *De Genealogia Deorum Gentilium*, Basel, 1532
Cotgrave, Randle, *A Dictionarie of the French and English Tongues*, London, 1611
Erasmus, Desiderius, *Adagia*, Basel, 1519
Fontaine, Charles, *La Fontaine d'amour, contenant Elegies, Epistres & Epigrammes*, Paris, 1545
Medici, Lorenzo de, *Commento sopra alcuni de' suoi sonetti*, Venice, 1554
Ronsard, *Œuvres de Pierre De Ronsard Gentilhomme Vandosmois. Prince des Poetes François. Revues et augmentées*, Paris, 1617
Tory, Geoffrey, *Champfleury*, Paris, 1529

ROMAN LITERATURE

Brink, C. O., *Horace on Poetry. Prolegomena to the Literary Epistles*, Cambridge, 1963
Catullus, *Opera*, ed. R. A. B. Mynors, Oxford Classical Texts, Oxford, 1958
Cicero, *Rhetorica, II*, ed. A. S. Wilkins, Oxford Classical Texts, Oxford, 1903, reprinted 1950
De oratore, ed. A. S. Wilkins, Oxford Classical Texts, Oxford, 1924
Ad Atticum, ed. L. C. Purser, Oxford Classical Texts, Oxford, 1903
Epistulae ad familiares, ed. L. C. Purser, Oxford Classical Texts, Oxford, 1901
De senectute, ed. F. G. Moore, Oxford Classical Texts, Oxford, 1903
Farquharson, A. S. L., *The Meditations of the Emperor Marcus Aurelius Antonius*, Oxford, 1944
Horace, *Opera*, ed. H. W. Garrod, Oxford Classical Texts, Oxford, 1901, reprinted 1947
Lyne, R. O. A. M., 'Propertius and Cynthia: Elegy 1.3.', in *Proceedings of the Cambridge Philological Society*, No. 196 (New Series, No. 16), 1970, pp. 60–78

188

Ovid, *Metamorphoses*, tr. Frank Justus Miller, Loeb Classical Library, London, 1916, reprinted 1966
Tristia, ed. S. G. Owen, Oxford Classical Texts, Oxford, 1915, reprinted 1963
Martial, *Epigrams*, ed. Walter C. A. Ker, Loeb Classical Library, London, 1961
Persius, *Saturae*, ed. W. V. Clausen, Oxford, 1956
Propertius, *Opera*, ed. M. Schuster, Bibliotheca Teubneriana, Leipzig, 1954
Quintilian, *The Institutio Oratoria of Quintilian*, ed. H. E. Butler, Loeb Classical Library, London 1921–2
Quinn, Kenneth, *The Catullan Revolution*, Melbourne, 1959
Latin Explorations. Critical Studies in Roman Literature, London, 1963
Rudd, Niall, *The Satires of Horace*, Cambridge, 1966
Seneca, *Ad Lucilium Epistulae morales*, ed. A. Beltrami, Rome, 1949
Tacitus, *Dialogus de oratoribus*, ed. W. Peterson, Oxford, 1893
Tibullus, *The Elegies of Albius Tibullus*, ed. K. F. Smith, New York, 1913, reprinted Darmstadt, 1964
Vergil, *Opera*, ed. R. A. B. Mynors, Oxford Classical Texts, Oxford, 1969
Williams, Gordon, *Tradition and Originality in Roman Poetry*, Oxford, 1968
The Nature of Roman Poetry, Oxford, 1970

GENERAL BOOKS AND ARTICLES AFTER 1800

Allen, W. S., *Vox Latina. A Guide to the Pronunciation of Classical Latin*, Cambridge, 1965
Arnold, E. Vernon, *Roman Stoicism*, London, 1911, reissued 1958
Auerbach, Erich, *Mimesis: the Representation of Reality in Western Literature*, tr. W. R. Trask, New York, 1953
Aulotte, Robert, *Amyot et Plutarque: la tradition des 'Moralia' au XVIe siècle*, Geneva, 1965
Baraz, M., *L'être et la connaissance selon Montaigne*, Paris, 1968
'Les images dans les *Essais* de Montaigne', in *BHR*, vol. XXVII (1965)
Baudelaire, C. *Œuvres complètes*, Pléiade edition, Paris, 1954
Boase, Alan, *The Fortunes of Michel de Montaigne*, London, 1935
'Then Malherbe came', *The Criterion*, vol. X (1930–1)
The Poetry of France, vol. I, *1400–1600*, London, 1964
Bolgar, R. R., *The Classical Heritage and its Beneficiaries*, Cambridge, 1954
Bolgar, R. R. (ed.), *Classical Influences in European Culture*, A.D. *1500–1700*, Cambridge, 1976
Bowen, Barbara, C., *The Age of Bluff. Paradox and Ambiguity in Rabelais and Montaigne*, Urbana, Ill., 1972

Bowman, F. P., *Montaigne: Essays*, London, 1965
Castor, Grahame, *Pléiade Poetics. A Study in Sixteenth-Century Thought and Terminology*, Cambridge, 1964
Chateau, Jean, *Montaigne psychologue et pédagogue*, Paris, 1964
Clarke, Carol E., 'Seneca's Letters to Lucilius as a source of some of Montaigne's Imagery', in *BHR*, vol. xxx (1968)
Clements, Robert J., *Critical Theory and Practice of the Pléiade*, Cambridge, Mass., 1942
Close, A. J., 'Art and Nature in Antiquity and the Renaissance', in *Journal of the History of Ideas*, vol. xxx, No. 4 (1969)
Cocking, J. M., 'Imagination as Order and as Adventure' in *Essays Presented to C. A. Hackett*, ed. E. M. Beaumont, J. M. Cocking and J. Cruikshank, Oxford, 1973
Coleman, D. G., *Maurice Scève, Poet of Love: Tradition and Originality*, Cambridge, 1975
    Rabelais. A Critical Study in Prose Fiction, Cambridge, 1971
Croll, Morris W., '*Attic' and Baroque Prose Style: the Anti-Ciceronian Movement*, ed. J. M. Patrick *et al.*, Princeton, N.J., 1969
Curtius, E. R., *European Literature and the Latin Middle Ages*, tr. W. R. Trask, London, 1953
Denonain, J.-J., *Thèmes et formes de la poésie 'Métaphysique'*, Algiers, 1956
Du Bellay, J., *Deffence et Illustration de la Langue Françoise*, S.T.F.M. edition, ed. H. Chamard, Paris, 1961
    Les Regrets et Autres Œuvres Poëtiques, Textes littéraires français, Geneva, 1966
    L'Olive, Textes littéraires français, Geneva, 1974
Eliot, T. S., *Selected Essays*, London, 1953
Ficino, Marsilio, *Commentaire sur le Banquet de Platon*, ed. Raymond Marcel, Paris, 1956
Friedrich, F., *Montaigne*, tr. R. Rovini, Paris, 1968
Gordon, Alexander L., *Ronsard et la rhétorique*, Geneva, 1970
Gray, Floyd, *Le style de Montaigne*, Paris, 1958
Jones, David, *Epoch and Artist*, London, 1959
Knights, L. C., *Explorations. Essays in Criticism, Mainly on the Literature of the Seventeenth Century*, London, 1963
Lablénie, E., *Montaigne auteur de maximes*, Paris, 1968
La Taille, Jean de, *Dramatic Works of Jean de La Taille*, ed. Kathleen M. Hall and C. N. Smith, London, 1972
Le Hir, Yves, *Rhétorique et stylistique de la Pléiade au Parnasse*, Paris, 1960
Levi, Anthony, *French Moralists: the Theory of the Passions, 1585–1649*, Oxford, 1964
McGowan, Margaret, *Montaigne's Deceits*, London, 1974
Marcu, Eva, *Répertoire des idées de Montaigne*, Geneva, 1965
Marot, Clément, *Œuvres complètes*, ed. C. A. Mayer, London, 1958–73

Maude, Ralph and Davies, Aneirin Talfan, *The Colour of Saying: an Anthology of Verse Spoken by Dylan Thomas*, London, 1963

Montaigne, *Essais*, Les Textes français, ed. J. Plattard, Paris, 1959

Essais, ed. F. Strowski, F. Gebelin and P. Villey, Bordeaux, 1906–33

Mourgues, Odette de, *Metaphysical, Baroque and Précieux Poetry*, Oxford, 1953

Naïs, H., Dresden, S. and Screech, M. A., *Invention et imitation. Études sur la littérature du seizième siècle*, The Hague and Brussels, 1968

Navarre, Marguerite de, *L'Heptaméron*, ed. M. François, Paris, 1943

Nowottny, Winifred, *The Language Poets Use*, London, 1972

Peletier du Mans, Jacques, *L'Art poétique*, ed. A. Boulanger, Paris, 1930

Porteau, Paul, *Montaigne et la vie pédagogique de son temps*, Paris, 1935

Poulet, Georges, *Études sur le temps humain*, Paris, 1950

Proust, Marcel, *A la recherche du temps perdu*, Pléiade edition, 3 vols., Paris, 1954

Rabelais, François, *Œuvres complètes*, ed. P. Jourda, 2 vols, Paris, 1962

Raymond, Marcel, *La poésie française et le Maniérisme*, London, 1971

Ronsard, *Œuvres complètes*, ed. P. Laumonier, I. Silver and R. Lebègue, 20 vols, Paris, 1914–75

Samaras, Zoë, *The Comic Element of Montaigne's Style*, Paris, 1970

Sayce, R. A., *The Essays of Montaigne: a Critical Exploration*, London, 1972

'L'Ordre des *Essais* de Montaigne', in *BHR*, vol. xviii (1956)

Scève, Maurice, *The 'Délie' of Maurice Scève*, ed. I. D. McFarlane, Cambridge, 1966

Smith, P. M., *Clément Marot: Poet of the Renaissance*, London, 1970

Sonnino, Lee Ann, *Handbook of Sixteenth-Century Rhetoric*, London, 1968

Steiner, George, *After Babel. Aspects of Language and Translation*, London, 1975

Stone, Donald, *French Humanist Tragedy*, Manchester, 1974

From Tales to Truths, Essays on French Fiction in the Sixteenth Century, Analecta Romanica, Heft 34, Frankfurt a. M., 1973

Ronsard's Sonnet Cycles. A Study in Tone and Vision, New Haven, Conn., 1966

Thibaudet, Albert, *Montaigne*, ed. F. Gray, Paris, 1963

Thomas, Dylan, *Collected Poems*, London, 1952

Trinquet, R. *La jeunesse de Montaigne*, Paris, 1972

Tuve, Rosemund, *Elizabethan and Metaphysical Imagery*, Chicago, 1947

Valéry, Paul, *Œuvres*, Pléiade edition, 2 vols, Paris, 1957

Villey, Pierre, *Les sources et l'évolution des Essais de Montaigne*, 2nd edition, 2 vols, Paris, 1933

Weber, Henri, *La création poétique au XVIe siècle en France*, Paris, 1956

Index